W9-CLS-008

Cañones

Cañones

Values, Crisis, and Survival in a Northern New Mexico Village

Paul Kutsche and
John R. Van Ness

University of New Mexico Press
Albuquerque

Library of Congress Cataloging in Publication Data

Kutsche, Paul, 1927–
Cañones, values, crisis, and survival in a northern New Mexico village.

Bibliography: p.
Includes index.
1. Cañones (N.M.)—Social life and customs.
2. Hispanic Americans—New Mexico—Cañones—Social life and customs. I. Van Ness, John R. II. Title.
F804.C36K87 978.9′52 80-54562
ISBN 0-8263-0570-9 AACR2

Partial funding for the composition of this book was provided by the Mellon Foundation through a grant to the American Association of University Presses.

Library of Congress Catalog Card Number 80-54562
International Standard Book Number 0-8263-0570-9
Manufactured in the United States of America.
First Edition

Contents

Illustrations

Maps

Figures

Tables

Preface

Contemporary American anthropologists feel obligated to tell their readers who they are and why they write as they do, since all ethnographic studies are enormously influenced by the personalities, training, preconceptions or theoretical biases, previous experience, and goals of those conducting the study. Of equal importance is the methodology employed or manner in which a study is conducted. The types of data as well as their principal sources and methods of collection, and the duration and intensity of the study are crucial to an understanding of ethnography, because field research, involving one's participation as well as observation, is above all a human endeavor. While the ethnographer strives to be objective —a recording and analyzing instrument applying sound methods of data collection and analysis—he is also aware that the experience of conducting field work inevitably alters him and those he is studying.

We think that the reader's appreciation of these assertions will grow from chapter to chapter, for the ethnographers at work in Cañones—participating, observing, questioning, and evaluating the information gathered—are much more visible in this book than in most ethnographies. As we describe ourselves and our field team colleagues, we hope to show how we have been changed and the ways in which this account of life in Cañones is to us more personal than a conventional ethnography. We in turn have probably altered Cañones by unwittingly making it more conscious of itself as representing the Hispanic cultural tradition, and possibly more hopeful for the survival of that tradition.

The Field Team

We were four altogether, although we were never all in residence at the same time.

Paul Kutsche, associate professor of anthropology at Colorado College and thirty-nine years old when the work began in 1966. Born and raised in Grand Rapids, Michigan, of German Universalist parentage on his father's side, New England Congregationalist on his mother's. Educated in public schools, Harvard College (B.A. in history, 1949), University of Michigan (M.A. in anthropology, 1955), University of Pennsylvania (Ph.D in anthropology, 1961). He had done ethnographic field work with the Eastern Cherokee in North Carolina and Southern Appalachian whites in Kentucky as a student of A. Irving Hallowell in psychological anthropology (then called "culture and personality"). His principal motivation in initiating this study in New Mexico was to fill a gap in ethnographic literature while doing field work convenient to his new job in Colorado Springs. He aimed to collect and publish basic ethnographic material on Hispanic land grant community culture in northern New Mexico. It never occurred to him either that he would get emotionally hooked or that this community study would turn into a long-term one. Both happened. After adult Cañoneros began to accept him in their homes, after the teenagers began to take delight in teaching him dirty words and how to drink Cañones style, and the children found him a source of amusement on demand, he began to discover that Cañones did not have a culture of "rural poverty," but one of powerful grace, style, beauty, richness, and amazingly open and warm human relations. He was seduced by these qualities, which are largely absent from Germanic and New England patterns.

It took him several years after the end of intensive field work in 1968 to accept the fact that he could never be a Hispano, that he would forever be an outsider, however friendly. Those years were fallow, however, for scholarly publication requires emotional detachment, and that distance came only later. This is one reason for the length of time it has taken to complete this monograph, and the unexpected growth of the research into a longitudinal study.

Kutsche's field work in Cañones started in October, 1966, when he moved into the house he had rented from Isabel Salazar (see map 3), and continued there until the end of August, 1967, interrupted by a month for back surgery in the summer of 1967. All of the summer of 1968 and for two months in 1969 he lived in the *casita* behind the house of Simón Vigil and his mother-in-law Fidencia Vialpando, who became almost foster parents. He made short but fairly frequent visits thereafter, staying with Simón and Fidencia until ill health forced them to move to Albuquerque. In 1971, 1976, 1977, and 1978 he spent long periods at the Ghost Ranch or in Abiquiu and made many trips to Cañones to check data.

John R. Van Ness was a graduate student in anthropology at the University of Pennsylvania when he came to Cañones in 1967. At Pennsylvania he studied with Ruben Reina, Anthony Wallace, and Robert Netting. His interests and formal training were in Latin America and its Iberian background, community studies, and cultural ecology. Raised in Ohio, B.A. Colorado College 1965, a Navy veteran before he finished his undergraduate education, he had been one of Kutsche's first students in the anthropology major.

Early in Cañones, they fell into a tacit agreement about the division of labor: Van Ness would concentrate on history, prehistory, and cultural ecology, Kutsche on ethnography. Van Ness approached his task in a chronological fashion, writing his master's thesis (1969) on the prehistory of the Chama Valley Drainage, and his doctoral dissertation (1979) on the Hispanic settlement of the same region, concentrating on the Cañones microbasin. His data were drawn from the Spanish and Mexican archives of New Mexico, from the U.S. archives, and from Cañones informants.

Van Ness spent the summer of 1967 in Cañones, and afterwards worked with archives in Santa Fe and elsewhere. He has visited the area and the village periodically ever since. During his arduous research on the history of the Cañones region's land grants, his interest in the Hispanic land grant problem grew, and he became one of the founders of the Center for Land Grant Studies, of which he is now a director. His publications document some of the ways that outsiders have used to despoil grant residents of their holdings.

Kathy Krusnik completed her sophomore year at Colorado College in 1966, and continued at Berkeley after two seasons of fieldwork. Born and raised in Denver, she was the daughter of Near Eastern parents whose families have been storekeepers in northeastern New Mexico. She spoke Spanish fluently in the local dialect and was at home at once with Serafín and Luz Valdez, who acted as foster parents to her in Cañones, where she lived from October to mid-December 1966, and for the summer of 1967.

Kathy Krusnik was a perceptive idealist. After receiving her B.A., she worked in various social service agencies and in the office of Mayor John Lindsay of New York City.

Alice Higman Reich (B.A. Pomona 1966), was a candidate for the M.A. in anthropology at the University of Chicago when she joined the team for the summer of 1968. Raised in Boulder, she first became interested in Hispanic language and culture as a supervisor in a VISTA training program in Monte Vista, Colorado. Although she also lived with Serafín and Luz Valdez, since she was older and more mature than Kathy Krusnik had been, her relation to Luz was less like a daughter and more like a younger sister. She moved confidently through women's spheres in Cañones, and her emotional identification with New Mexican Hispanos was intense.

Alice Reich had studied with Julian Pitt-Rivers and with Clifford Geertz at Chicago, and brought Geertz's fluid and inventive point of view toward the potential of village culture to change and survive (see her dissertation, 1977). With her provocative remark about "the rituals of hello and good-bye," it was she who first proposed cycles as a model for the ceremonial nature of Cañones life (chapter 6).

In 1969 she received her M.A. from the University of Chicago and in 1977 her Ph.D. from the University of Colorado. She is now associate professor of anthropology at Regis College.

From Field Notes to Manuscript

During our field work, information became communal property among the four of us: everyone was entitled to a copy of all field notes. We divided labor only according to interest and ability, as indicated above. Consistent with that division, Van Ness provided the information on history and environment in chapters 2 and 3.

Kutsche collected the data on cycles and values in chapters 6 and 7 with assistance from Krusnik and Reich, on the chronology of the lawsuit about the school in chapter 8, and most of the information on change in Cañones during the past fifteen years (chapter 9). Kutsche and Van Ness share data about subsistence and institutions more or less equally in chapters 4 and 5.

Since we have quite different writing and working styles, we employed a scheme that we had used productively before: Kutsche drafted the entire manuscript from the team's field notes, Van Ness's doctoral dissertation, and other sources. Van Ness then went over the draft with "a fine-tooth eye," and Kutsche rephrased the Van Ness corrections and additions into the Kutsche style.

An unsuccessful effort was made to involve Cañones in revision. Copies of chapters were circulated to various Cañoneros as they were drafted, with a request for critical comment as to accuracy, interpretations, etc. Criticism almost never came, and any comments whatever were rare.

Labels

An unavoidable question is what to call the inhabitants of Hispanic villages in northern New Mexico. If this book were in Spanish there would be no question, for northern New Mexicans call themselves and their language *mejicano*. ("*Usted habla bien mejicano*" is proper local usage.)

But this book is in English, and there is no good term. The choices are *Mexican*, *Mexican American*, *Chicano*, *Spanish American*, *Spaniard*, and *Hispano*. Although *Mexican* seems like an obvious translation of mejicano, it is not. The New Mexican Spanish equivalent is *mejicano de México*. Natives of New Mexico find *Mexican* derogatory. *Mexican American* refers to all people of Hispanic culture in the Southwest; we do not use it because it is too inclusive. *Chicano* will not do. It is an urban term, born in the Mexican-American political movement with its myth of the three faces of Aztlan. New Mexican villagers are insulted by *Chicano* for it was once a term of condescension used by Mexican nationals to refer to their little brothers to the north. *Spanish American* is not ideal because it is an Anglo term and carries the incorrect historical assumption that New Mexican natives are of pure Castilian blood, unmixed with American Indian. *Spaniard* is simply inaccurate. To

New Mexicans both the English word and its Spanish equivalent *español* denote Europeans of the Iberian Peninsula.

This leaves us with *Hispano*—not ideal, but in our opinion preferable to the alternatives because it is a short, single word of Spanish origin. At least one Spaniard agrees with this usage: Alfredo Jiménez Núñez of the University of Seville entitled his study of Española in the 1960s *Los Hispanos de Nuevo México* (Jiménez Núñez 1974). An ideal term will probably not emerge until or unless Hispanos themselves agree, as African Americans did when they decided to be called *blacks*.

The parallel question is what to call non-Hispanos. If this book were in Spanish that question, too, would be easy. They are *americanos*, whether they happen to have white or black skin (although in Spanish one can specify that a person is *blanco* or *negro* if need be), unless they are *indios*, in which case they can be further specified by tribe. Navajos (*los navajoses*) usually are.

But again, the simple translation *American* will not work, because in English *American* denotes legal nationality more often than ethnic group. *Gringo*, *gavacho*, *bolillo*, are all equivalent to *americano*, but they are insults as nasty as their counterparts *greaser*, *spic*, or *dago*. The term that most authors use when writing English is *Anglo*, and that is the term we shall employ here. Readers who are not familiar with the U.S. Southwest might wonder what the fuss is all about, since Americans who are neither black nor Hispanic nor Indian nor oriental are not generally thought to have any ethnic identity, but to be "just plain American." In the social mosaic of the Southwest an Anglo is not a plain American but an ethnic type, as quaint as any other, as legitimate a butt of ethnic humor. He is also subject to cross-ethnic misunderstanding, just like everybody else.

Translations of Terms

We try to use either the Spanish or the English term for things and concepts according to whether one or the other is used locally when speaking English. Words in Spanish like *acequia* (irrigation ditch), *placita* (small settlement; small square), *biscochito* (a pastry about halfway from a biscuit to a cookie) are almost always used in English sentences by Anglos and Hispanos alike, and will be used here. But Spanish terms for stages of life (see chapter 6) are not, and our rule is to introduce each such term in Spanish and then switch to English. We do not follow our own rule consistently, for among bilingual people usage is dependent upon intellectual and social context, not merely on whether there is an equivalent in the cross language.

Readers who are not fluent in the Anglo-Hispanic idiom may find it strange that Eliud Salazar's map legends are partly in Spanish, partly in English. That is the way it is in the Southwest, an accurate reflection of a culture drawn from both. The glossary at the end of the book contains brief translations into English of Spanish terms; so with a bit of patience the reader should be able to find his way through the two languages.

The Ethnographic Present

When ethnographic investigation in a single location goes on for a long time and/or is published long after it began, ethnographers customarily fix on one slice of time for their static description. This is necessary because societies are dynamic and constantly changing, although in some instances change is extremely slow by contemporary American standards.

For the Cañones field team, the ethnographic present is 1967, when Krusnik, Van Ness, and Kutsche virtually completed the household census, and the largest quantity of general information was collected. Whenever possible, we pitched back to that year information that was collected later—e.g., public records pertaining to 1967 were collected later; some genealogies and census data were collected later, but the data were recorded for the status of the household in 1967. In chapters 2, and 4 through 7, the present tense refers to 1967. The events of chapter 8 occurred during 1966 and 1967, but the past tense is used since this account is largely narrative rather than descriptive. The changes in society and culture presented in chapter 9 are changes *from* 1967.

Acknowledgments

The authors have been helped by far too many people in far too many ways to acknowledge more than a small minority of them. Scholarship in general is a social task, a good example of the social and cumulative nature of culture itself. Ethnographic field work is perhaps more social than other kinds of research.

The people of Cañones come first, of course. They have been extraordinarily patient as well as open. They put up with our ignorance and bungling; they taught us as much as we had the wit to learn of their community and culture. They trusted us with information too private to include in this book, and we hope we have violated none of that trust through our eagerness to make this record as complete as possible. Those Cañoneros who have been particularly helpful in providing information to us, and in checking our interpretations of their life, will understand that we cannot single out individuals in print for special thanks. The only tangible thanks we can offer Cañoneros is to share the book's royalties with them through the community organization, El Proyecto.

Whatever insights into women's lives this book contains derive from the field notes and conversations of Kathy Krusnik and Alice Higman Reich. They have shared their insights without restriction. Their sensitivity to women's culture (an area that previous male scholars have left blank) has enriched our understanding of what we could never have gained on our own. Alice Reich further aided us by reading the entire manuscript before it went to press.

Facundo Valdez's influence on Kutsche's thinking about values is so great that he seems almost a member of the field team. He is the first to have written about *verguënza* as a New Mexican value (Valdez 1979). He also provided a great deal of information about the context of the school battle.

Outside of the field team, Chuck Briggs, Tom Hill, and Marc Simmons were invaluable as friends and colleagues to Van Ness during his research. Their knowledge and support was of great benefit.

Eliud Salazar drew the maps and compiled the key for the house locations, 1967 and 1980.

Lorenzo Valdez and Wilfredo Vigil filled gaps in our knowledge of La Academia Real and El Proyecto respectively.

Janet Jordan read an early version of the school fight narrative and made suggestions about theory.

Many employees of the state of New Mexico, officials of the state department of education, and Harry Wugalter, helped us in 1967 to understand their point of view on the legal battle between them and Cañones, despite knowing that we were predisposed against them. To Leonard DeLayo, our thanks for receiving Colorado College students and Kutsche for half a working day in 1972 and enlightening us considerably on how state education bureaucrats perceive their responsibility. John Jasper, when director of the state welfare department, was most helpful, as were various members of his staff. Myra Ellen Jenkins and J. Richard Salazar in the state archives gave freely of their time and knowledge during the archival research. Stephany Eger, librarian in the history library of the Museum of New Mexico was very helpful. The Hydrological Survey Office of the New Mexico state engineer department provided hydrological survey data for the Cañones drainage.

Among federal employees, Edward A. Romero of the Soil Conservation Service office in Española shared his zeal for accuracy with us. The Santa Fe National Forest offices in Española and Santa Fe opened their files to us and assisted us with mapping.

Among politicians, governors David Cargo and Jack Campbell were particularly helpful. Their policies in office were almost diametrically opposed, but each tried thoughtfully to explain his action, and gave credit to the other for correctly interpreting the politics of his day.

The Ghost Ranch Conference Center has been a constant hostel for us since the 1960s, especially for short visits on short notice, when we did not wish to impose on friends in Cañones. The entire staff has been warmly encouraging. During the summer of 1971 director James Hall set aside a study for Kutsche's use, where the first draft of what became chapters 8 and 9 were written. Hall also arranged for Kutsche to be Georgia O'Keeffe's house guest that summer. To her Kutsche owes peace, quiet, and the example of aesthetic economy.

In Abiquiu, where most of the text was written, Benjamín and Susanna Archuleta were landlords and faithful friends. Susanna is a native Cañonera and filled in many informational gaps during the writing. Gilbert Benito Córdova and his wife Juanita gave occasional critical advice after they moved back to Abiquiu. Frances Swadesh (now Mrs. Miguel Quintana) gave the same kind of advice, mostly on visits to Abiquiu. Karl Bode was helpful in our efforts to understand the context of events in Cañones and in Abiquiu; a great regret is that we failed to ask his father Martin to talk about his experience as an immigrant merchant in Hispanic territory before paved highways changed the relations between villagers and storekeepers.

Three friends photographed Cañones at our request and have shared their prints generously with us. They are George McCue, professor emeritus of English at Colorado College (1969), Natalie Owings, a neighbor in Abiquiu now resident in Santa Fe (mid-1970s), and Moana Kutsche, Paul's daughter (1981).

At the University of New Mexico Press, senior editor Beth Hadas encouraged us at a stage in the development of the manuscript when a less supportive press would have said "Don't bother us until it's better." Copy editor Joanna Cattonar was our Maxwell Perkins, saving us from earnest malaprops and turning awkwardness into connected prose.

In Colorado Springs, Carol Erickson typed various drafts of this manuscript as well as others we have worked on, giving us not only technical competence but sensitivity to style and choice of apt expressions.

Financial support to both of us came from the National Science

Foundation (GS-1313 and GS-2155), and to Kutsche from Colorado College (various faculty research grants). Van Ness received support from the Ford Foundation (710-0255), fellowship aid from the University of Pennsylvania, and faculty release time from Knox College. Reich was supported by a National Science Foundation training grant.

Map 1. New Mexico and the Abiquiu Area

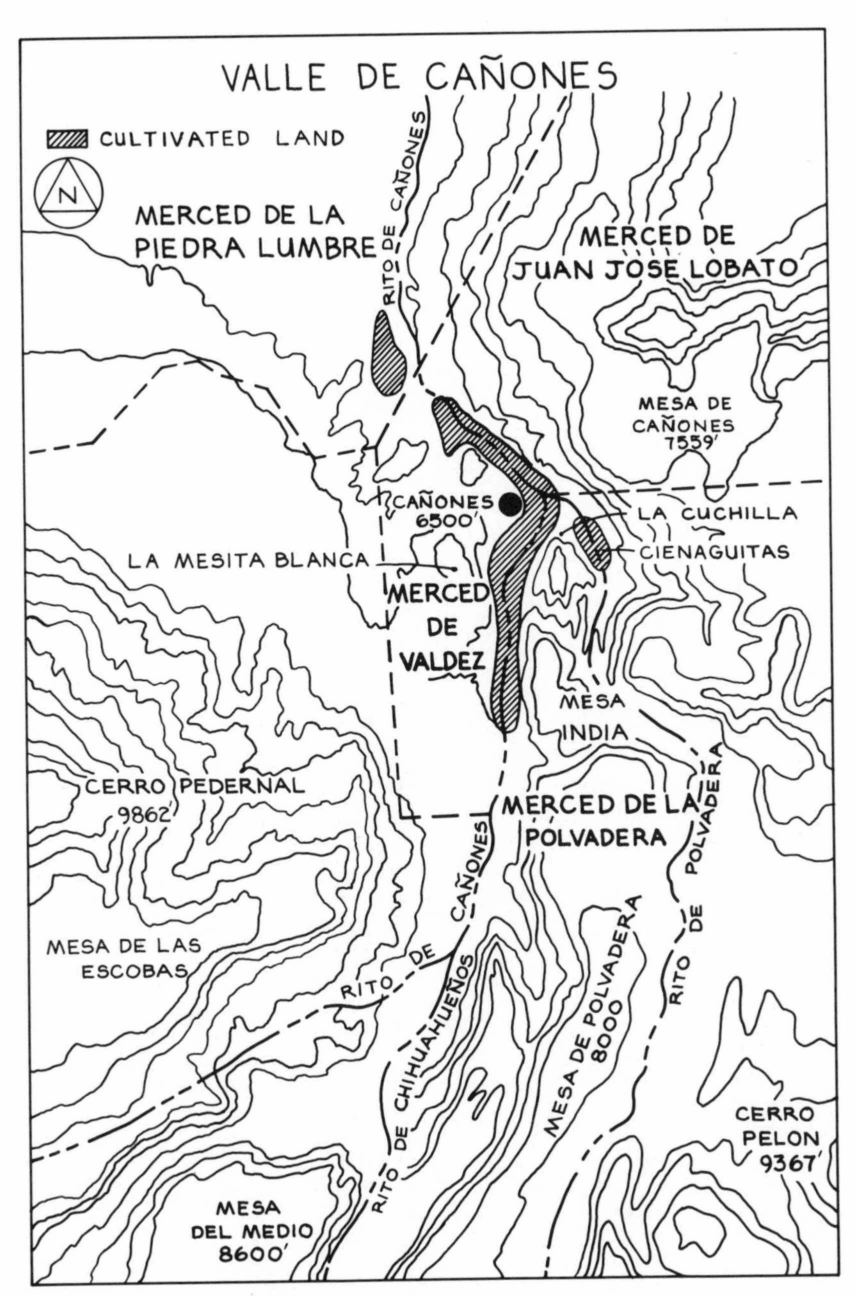

Map 2. Topography of Cañones Valley

CANONES 1967: a key to residences in the placita

1. Jacobo Salazar
2. vacant (Jacobo Salazar)
3. Bernardita Salazar, Guillermo Salazar (summer)
4. vacant
5. Preciliana Salazar
6. vacant
7. vacant
8. José Madrid
9. Serafín Valdez
10. Juan Madrid
11. Eduvigen Lovato
12. Adelaida Lucero
13. Sevedeo Salazar
14. Marcelino Sandoval
15. vacant (cantina)
16. campo santo
17. Genaro Velásquez
18. Antonio Serrano
19. vacant
20. Pacomio Salazar
21. Guillermo Salazar (winter)
22. Teófila Serrano
23. Benita Serrano
24. Emiliano Aragón
25. Aquilino Serrano
26. vacant
27. José Dolores Vialpando
28. Medardo Lovato
29. Delfinia Salazar
30. Asamblea de Dios church
31. Tranquilino Herrera
32. Manuelita Velásquez
33. community water tank
34. Isabel (Joe I.) Salazar (Paul Kutsche)
35. San Miguel church (Catholic)
36. Norman Lovato
38. vacant (Ricardo Madrid)
39. Benjamín Velásquez
40. Isaaque Lovato
41. Dalio Gallegos
42. Francisco Lovato, Sabiñano Lovato
43. schoolhouse
44. Leonardo Velásquez
45. José Vialpando
46. Fidencia Vialpando and Simón Vigil
47. Saquello Salazar
48. vacant (Francisco Lovato)
49. Elipio García
50. Isabel García

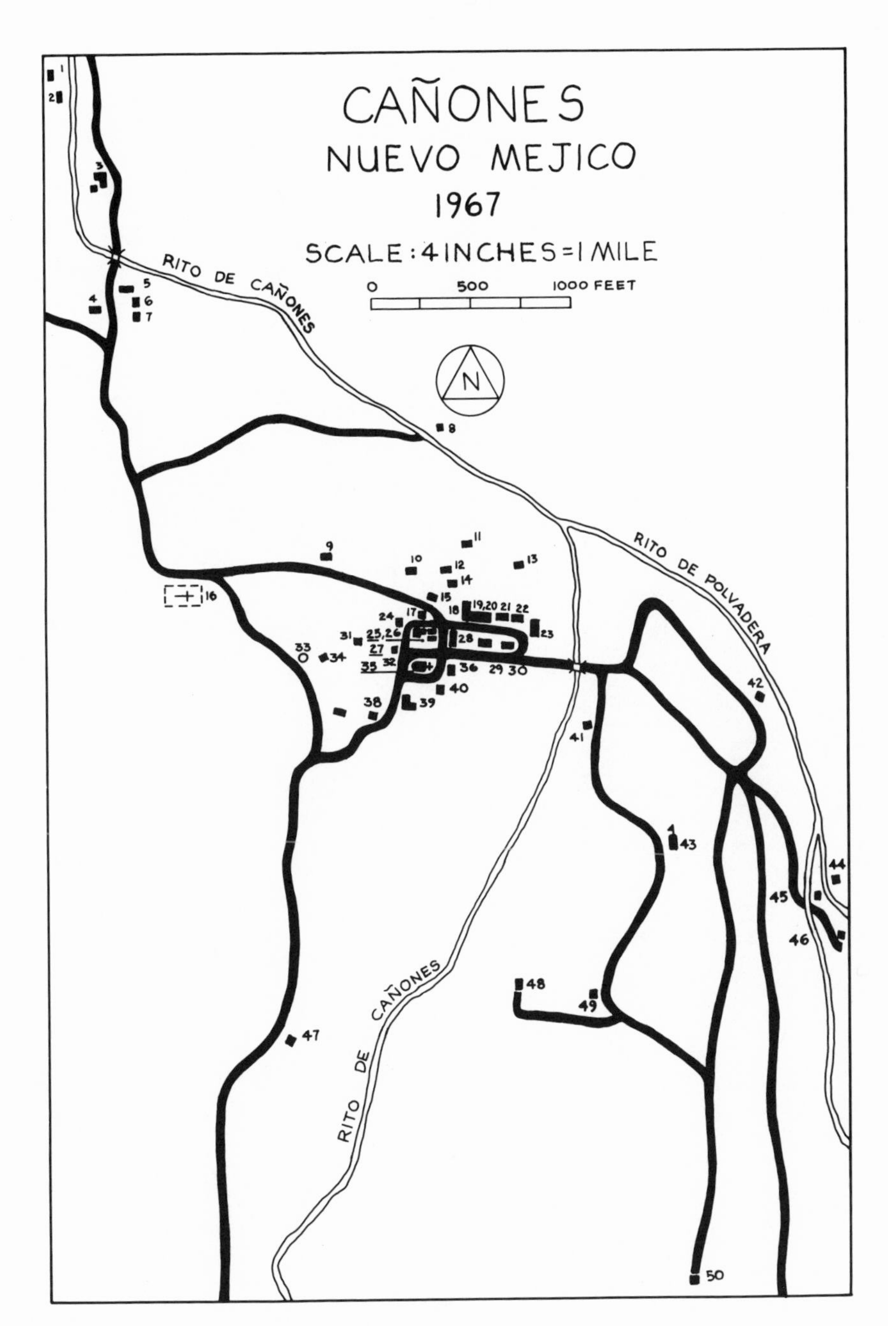

Map 3. Cañones Placita, 1967

1 Introduction

Hispanic culture of the American Southwest is marvelously rich and varied. The five million "people of Spanish Origin" out of a total of thirty-six million in 1970 (U.S. Bureau of the Census 1973, 1975) include residents of the second largest "Mexican city" in the world (Los Angeles) and of hamlets containing less than one hundred people. [For census purposes, Arizona, California, Colorado, New Mexico, and Texas are the Southwest.] They include "Hijos de los Conquistadores" of the sixteenth and seventeenth centuries (Marc Simmons 1979) and some still wet from crossing the Rio Grande. Racially they range from entirely European, save for whatever Moorish genes their ancestors may have brought from Spain, to almost pure American Indian. Their education, their wealth, their political orientation, their sophistication regarding their own and other cultural worlds, cover all logical possibilities.

American anthropology, infatuated for a century with the equally rich and varied cultures of American Indians of the Southwest, is only now beginning to pay Hispanos the attention they deserve. Historians and sociologists have done infinitely better than we have, and Nancie Solien de González's general review of *The Spanish-Americans of New Mexico* (1969)—the best anthropological source now available—is largely drawn from historical and sociological scholarship. A few anthropologists have written doctoral dissertations on rural Hispanic society and culture, but there is no ethnography generally available.

Kutsche's aim in starting this research project in 1966 was to fill that gap. He wanted to find a small, isolated, subsistence village at the end of a dirt road, without telephone or television, totally Roman Catholic, totally Hispanic, monolingual in Spanish—a baseline to serve as a measure for change elsewhere. Cañones appeared at first glance to fill the bill. It was small, it was indeed at the end of a perfectly awful road, it had no telephones, and it had very poor television reception at Jacobo Salazar's house, none at all in the placita (see map 3). It was totally Hispanic but for two summer people—Webster Waide of El Paso and his son David of Santa Fe—who lived far up Cañones Canyon and did not interfere with the life of the placita. It was by no means monolingual in Spanish, although some of its inhabitants were. It was only about two-thirds Roman Catholic: six families were Pentecostal and one belonged to the United Brethren church. Although everyone called himself a rancher or a farmer, it was not really a localized self-sufficient subsistence unit, for every family received cash from wages, welfare, or remittances from family members elsewhere. It was isolated and it was not, depending upon the criteria one used. In terms of formal mechanisms of communication, it certainly was. But by political standards it was already becoming a precinct to be reckoned with, as we explain in chapter 8.

Chapters 2 through 7 of this book are devoted to an ethnography of Cañones, describing it as it is, not as we wanted it to be.

Because of the diversity of rural Hispanic villages in the region, we also try to show that Spanish-Mexican land tenure, law and custom, as well as systems of land utilization, fit the microbasins of northern New Mexico particularly well. In fact, we distinguish between three major geographical environmental zones of Hispanic New Mexico, for in each of them Hispanic settlers have made a different ecological adjustment: the *Rio Arriba* (including Cañones), characterized by community land grants, small economic enterprises, a high degree of *campanilismo* (best defined in this context as community spirit), and relative social equality; the *Rio Abajo* (from the hill called La Bajada just north of Cochiti Pueblo, downstream to the Mexican border), with individual land grants, large *ranchos*, enormous herds of sheep, a distinction between *patrón* and *peón;* and the *Plateau* (east of the Sangre de Cristo Mountains, and west of the Rio Grande and its tributary valleys), which was not settled until U.S. conquest in 1848, and where commercial cattle operations and individual spreads employing cowboys predominate. (These three ecologies are discussed theoretically and schematically in a number of papers: Van Ness 1976, 1979a, 1979b, 1980; Kutsche 1979.) The reader is thus cautioned to be careful in generalizing from this study to all rural Hispanic settlements in New Mexico and southern Colorado.

The third task we set ourselves is the result of what was going on in Cañones when Krusnik and Kutsche arrived in October, 1966, innocently unaware. The state department of education had decided to close the one-room Cañones elementary school and to bus the children to Coyote over some seven miles of indescribably bad and dangerous road (see map 4), and the parents were opposing that decision with every peaceful means at their disposal, including civil disobedience. This "school fight" has become a major focus of the book and the topic of chapter 8, and one of our goals is to present our description of Cañones in such a way that the strengths of Hispanic culture under stress are as clear as the tensed muscles

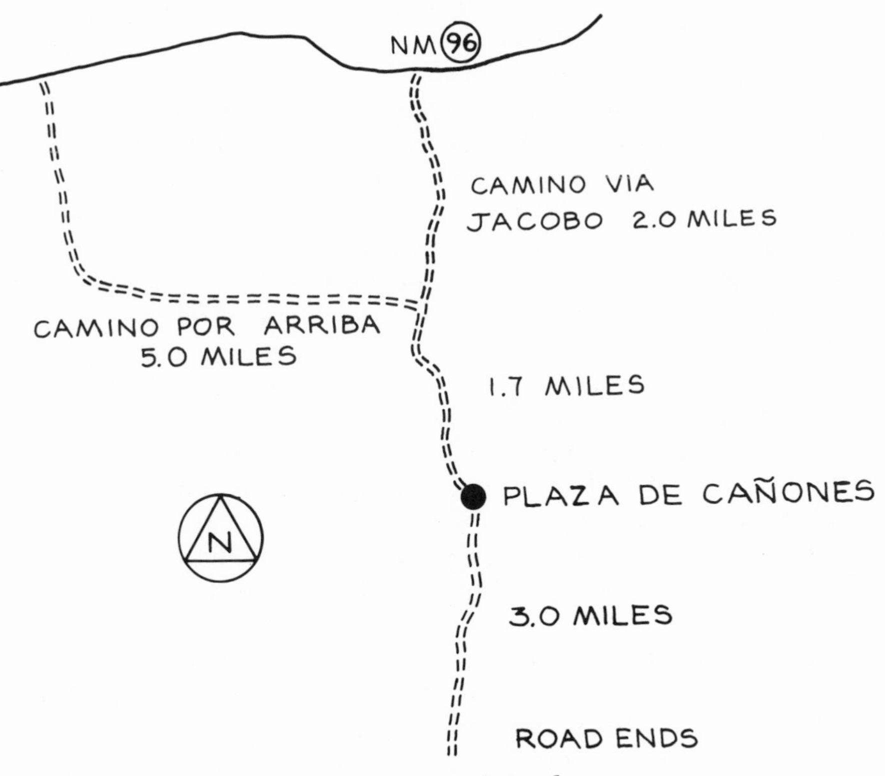

Map 4. Local Roads

of a boxer. Those "muscles" include the traditional rural values, which we describe as fully as we can in chapter 7.

The final aim in writing this book is personal—to communicate a love affair. Both authors fell in love with Hispanic village culture through the people of Cañones, in our different ways. Van Ness's way of expressing it is through his work as a founder and director of the Center for Land Grant Studies, an organization with the goal of redressing the balance of land use and ownership through the courts and remedial legislation. Kutsche's is through words. We try to show Cañones to the reader through the lens of our love for it, while staying loyal to fact and avoiding sentimentality.

Kutsche has tried and abandoned a number of metaphors and descriptive adjectives in this attempt. The word that he gives up most reluctantly is "aristocratic." There are only two places that he knows firsthand in North America where people are so totally at ease with their position in the world that they can say with neither envy nor false pride, "This is the only place in the world where I want to be." They are Brahmin Boston and Cañones. A joke popular when Kutsche was an undergraduate would fit either town equally well: an elderly Cambridge lady is asked at tea where she has traveled. She replies with surprise, "Travel? Why, sir, I *live* in Cambridge." Contentment with one's position is the most prominent of those Cañones qualities that might be called aristocratic, but not the only one. Physical grace and the emphasis on ceremony and style are also essential. Life is an art form to New Mexican Hispanos, and they reserve their highest esteem for the best artists. We have tried to communicate some sense of that attitude, especially in chapter 6 on cycles and rituals and in the section on *picarismo* in chapter 7.

Although we describe all of the major categories of Cañones culture, there are some things we have not attempted. There is little of Hispanic folklore in this book. We feel that others have already covered that topic better than we could. Likewise with *curanderismo* (the lore of curing): we have studied neither the list of healing herbs nor curing practices. Nor do we tell by any means all that we know of the village. Cañones is a real place and in general we name Cañoneros by name. We are not about to return their extraordinary hospitality and generosity with an exposé. Whoever is looking for the private life of the sexy Mexicans of Rio Arriba county, or the sensational religious cults of Lent, can save a few dollars by stopping right here. But those readers who want to share insights into the unexpected persistence and vitality of Hispanic villages, whose death has been predicted many times, we invite to stay with us.

This work is a departure for Kutsche in two ways, although in no way for Van Ness, who was trained in a later generation. First, we have made an earnest attempt to reconstruct the history of the area, but none to reconstruct an idealized memory culture. (In the 1950s, when Kutsche did his Cherokee field work, it was still the practice in American ethnology to abstract what we thought were pure or uncorrupted social and cultural traits out of the welter of Indian reservation life. Our unspoken model of society and culture was static, and our model of change was a one-way continuum toward assimilation into the larger modern American society—which was assumed to be culturally uniform itself.)

The second departure for Kutsche was the realization that we could not understand Cañones until we also understood certain aspects of the state and federal governments, and paid some attention to the conditions that people from Cañones faced when they left home to find work. In retrospect we realized, as countless other American anthropologists are realizing, that we have unconsciously used the relatively isolated Pacific island or the desert oasis as a working model for the study of societies, and that such a model fits very few of them. When this lesson sank in thoroughly, Kutsche faced field work all over again—among those outsiders who have to do with Cañones, and to whom Cañoneros must adjust. One of the causes for delay in finishing this book was the necessity to work systematically through this way of looking at a society and a cultural system in relation to the societies and cultures impinging upon it.

Some Theoretical Considerations

The relation of ethnographic description to ethnological theory is less obvious than one might think. It is not undistilled fact, and it is certainly not pure theory. Ward H. Goodenough, himself both a distinguished ethnographer and a leading ethnological theorist, argues a hierarchy of selection and abstraction (personal communication): 1. At the bottom is raw field experience. 2. Experience is reflected selectively in the ethnographer's field notes. 3. Next is the field report, which is the ethnographer's model of the cultural system. 4. Finally comes ethnological theory, which is built upon a comparison of as many ethnographic models as the theorist cares to use. This book is stage 3—an ethnographic model.

As much as we should like to be mere vessels through whom Cañones speaks its piece to the world, we are not and cannot be. What we are we have tried to explain in the preface. Wenceslao Salazar of Cañones commented aptly when he said to Kutsche after reading a draft of one chapter, "Well, Pablito, you seem to understand Cañones pretty well . . . for an outsider." A book about Cañones written by a Cañonero would make an interesting contrast to this one, and we hope some day to read it.

We have kept theory out of this ethnography as much as we could, but have found the task more difficult with each revision. Nevertheless, a few remarks about our theoretical positions will help clarify the following chapters.

Van Ness's training in cultural ecology led him to inquire into how the Spanish and Mexican legal systems fit the New Mexican landscape, and how Hispanic culture in general fit the microbasins of the Rio Arriba. This view dominates chapters 2 and 3, and strongly influences other chapters. Kutsche's training in culture and personality is evident in his preoccupation with cycles and values in chapters 6 and 7. We have tried to provide the reader with enough information so that he may decide for himself whether the values of Cañones suit the environment. To put it another way, the question is whether the moral code inclines a Cañonero to want to do what for environmental reasons he ought to do. In chapter 9 the question is whether changes in the world Cañones lives in have been accompanied by changes in values which enhance the village's chance of survival.

Both authors feel that for our purposes we must at times distinguish conceptually between *society* and *culture*. Anthropologists in general do so when we find it useful, but lump them as *sociocultural systems* when we do not. (We lump in chapters 2 through 5 and in chapter 8, and distinguish in chapters 7 and 9.) For us, as for Clifford Geertz in *The Interpretation of Cultures* (1973), man is an animal bound by the rules of the animal kingdom. Each society is a group of human animals organized to survive, to reproduce, to enjoy itself; its culture is the complete set of learned techniques it uses to achieve those ends. We can think of culture as a book of recipes arranged in categories (like soup, meats, salad, dessert), with alternatives to be chosen in appropriate categories, but seldom imposing absolute answers on the cook. An experienced cook does not slavishly follow recipes and may even invent a new dish, using the general outlines of the style of cuisine and his own accumulated knowledge. The test of success is in the eating; one can only guess how well a new dish will be received.

Geertz argues that separating society from culture is particularly useful when dealing with historical process (1973:144):

> Though separable only conceptually, culture and social structure will then be seen to be capable of a wide range of modes of integration with one another, of which the simple isomorphic mode is but a limiting case—a case common only in societies which have been stable over such an extended time as to make possible a close adjustment between social and cultural aspects. In most societies, where change is a characteristic rather than an abnormal occurrence, we shall expect to find more or less radical discontinuities between the two. I would argue that it is in these very discontinuities that we shall find some of the primary driving forces in change.

Hispanic northern New Mexico, like Central Java where Geertz worked, is a single area containing several societies with distinct cultures. Change is characteristic, society and culture are discontinuous; society is tough and persistent, but social cooks must constantly revise their cultural recipes. So it was in Cañones in 1965, 1966, and 1967, when its people felt they must face a threat creatively or let their beloved community die. We have tried, especially in chapters 7 and 9, to give an inventory of the cultural recipes that Cañones possessed to face the threat, what they borrowed from outside, and the history of changing events that produced certain changes in culture.

Probably in most cases—certainly in the case of Cañones—the useful recipes for meeting challenges by outsiders are cultural values. Long-held traditional values are particularly useful, just as a host faced with a great and important feast is likely to fall back on recipes he has mastered, saving experiments for low-risk occasions.

These two emphases, on the distinction between society and culture, and on the role of values, help to clarify our understanding of what Cañones did to ensure its survival as a community of thought and action when outsiders threatened to destroy it. They also help clarify our comprehension of what has happened to Cañones in the years between the end of the school fight and publication of this book. Long-term research in ethnography to date has suffered from an excess of narrative and a scarcity of systematic analysis. The consensus of George Foster and his colleagues, in a recent symposium discussing long-term research, seems to be that depth of insight into underlying cultural patterns is the chief benefit of staying in the same place over a long period of time (Foster et al. 1979). We agree on the importance of insight, but feel that anthropology can do better than that. The task is to record carefully the overt changes and their patterns, and then to inquire into the resulting changes of cultural meaning and values.

2 The Settlement and Its Setting

Cañones probably looks very much as it has for a century or so. The pasture land on the hillsides and up in the mountains is almost totally unirrigated and varies from summer to winter only from greenish brown to a gray rust brown. On the other hand, the bottomland abundantly watered by acequias is emerald green. You need only a little imagination to see it as a jewel in a dun-colored setting. Cañoneros themselves think their village pretty in the summer, but ugly in the winter.

Cañones is typical of Hispanic northern New Mexico, situated in one of the microbasins that form natural ecological, economic and social units, as Peter van Dresser points out in his provocative book *Landscape for Humans* (1972). The Cañones microbasin is even more clearly bounded than most: mountain ranges ring it to the east, south, and west, leaving only a narrow exit from Cañones Creek to the north, after it joins Polvadera Creek just below the placita. The entire drainage flows approximately twenty miles from source to outlet in the Chama River in the impoundment for Abiquiu Dam, and is about eight miles wide at its headwaters, as narrow as a quarter of a mile downstream. The area within the Cañones basin is approximately 70,000 acres (110 square miles), 89 percent of which now lies within the Santa Fe National Forest. Of that large area, only 312 acres are touched by the magic fingers of the acequias; the rest is too high and too steep. If the land were flatter, there would be ample water for irrigation, for the streams yield an average of thirty-three acre feet per year—one of the most dependable systems in the region. Downstream from the Cañones microbasin there is no more irrigable land for approximately six miles, a gap that further defines Cañones as a logical natural unit.

Elevations range from 6,058 feet on the north to 11,232 feet atop Polvadera Peak to the south. Cerro Pedernal ("Flint Peak") to the west rises to 9,862 feet—a flat-topped landmark visible from as far away as the mesa south of Taos, and a prominent feature in paintings by Georgia O'Keeffe of Abiquiu. The Cañones placita itself lies at 6,500 feet. The topography is so broken that, although the placitas of Abiquiu and Cañones are only seven miles apart, the land traveler must either hike up and over Cañones Mesa or go twenty miles around by road, via Abiquiu Dam.

Three life zones are found in the range of elevations in the Cañones microbasin. In the Upper Sonoran (to c. 7,000 feet) grow piñon, juniper, cottonwood, grama, western wheat, and other grasses, as well as rabbit brush, mountain mahogany, Gambel oak, and assorted weeds. To be found here are mule deer, bunny and jack rabbit, quail, mourning dove, turkey, prairie dog, coyote, bobcat, and smaller animals. This zone includes the Cañones placita. Rising to the tops of the nearer mesas in Cañones is the Transitional (c. 7,000 to c. 9,000 feet) where yellow and Ponderosa pines, Douglas spruce, a variety of oaks, willows, birches, berries, wild roses, and grasses are to be found, in addition to mule deer, squirrel, chipmunk, beaver, badger, bobcat, porcupine, mountain lion, and (formerly) bear. The heaviest rain falls in the Canadian (c. 9,000 feet, to the top of Polvadera Peak), and provides the source of the perennial streams of the whole region. Spruce, balsam, fir, and aspen proliferate in dense forest with an understory of grasses and flowers. This elevation is populated by elk, mule deer, snowshoe rabbit, lynx, fox, and black bear.

Rain and snowfall vary from about ten to twenty inches per year, depending on elevation, land slope, winds, and other specific local conditions. Rain is usually destructive, for much of it falls in cloudbursts in July and August. Some falls as hail. (One does not grow tomatoes out of doors in Cañones.) Snow, on the other hand, is infrequent, and melts off quickly.

The carrying capacity for cattle varies according to rainfall and other circumstances: an average of one cow to 136 acres in most of the Upper Sonoran, one cow to twelve acres in most of the Transitional (but one cow to seventy-five acres on El Alto Mesa between Abiquiu and Cañones), and one cow to forty-eight acres in the Canadian. *Rancheros* (ranchers) of Cañones and Abiquiu enhance the carrying capacity of their pastures by sheet irrigation, both close to the placita and at the head of Polvadera Canyon.

The soil is gravelly everywhere except in the bottoms. In most places the parent rock is not very far under the gravel, and that rock holds water well. Drainage off the parent rock feeds the streams of the Cañones microbasin year round. The alluvium in the bottoms is sandy or clay loam, loose and rich when irrigated.

The climate in Cañones is better for animals and grasses than for cultivated plants, for the average frost-free period runs only from May 24 to September 26. It is hazardous to grow fruit trees, but almost everyone does, obtaining about one good crop every three years. Since we have no record of average temperatures here, we must rely on impressions: as in all arid and semiarid climes, the daily temperature range is dramatic and the seasonal range somewhat less so. Summer temperatures may rise to 100°F, but seldom do. Freezing temperatures at midday in winter are also unusual except during snowstorms or when the sun is overcast. The thermometer often reaches 50°F on sunny winter afternoons. Only on a very few nights in August does the temperature fail to fall to a comfortable level, and breezes are frequent. Nevertheless, in a few pockets protected from wind and poorly drained, summer mosquitos and other insects are a nuisance.

Because of the elevation, the short growing season, the hail, and the remoteness of Cañones from markets, nothing is grown to sell. The chile, corn, and fruit that brim from the cornucopias of roadside stands in the Española and Santa Cruz Valleys in late summer and early fall are absent in the upper Chama Valley.

The placita of Cañones follows the Mediterranean pattern of houses, as closely bunched together in places as the row houses of large European or eastern seaboard American cities. But Cañones declined to follow the Spanish colonial rule for defensive squares: church on one side, houses on the others. (In fact, Chimayó is virtually the only placita in northern New Mexico that does.) Map 3 shows a dense concentration of buildings, but no explicit plan.

The Roman Catholic church occupies a conspicuous location. More than twenty houses cluster around it and run down the hill from it. In the lower placita is a smaller structure built for the grade school about 1890. It stood vacant for several years after the present schoolhouse was constructed in 1948 on La Cuchilla (from *cuchillo*, knife, because this ridge is so sharp), and now houses the Asamblea de Dios (Pentecostal) church. The Catholic layman's *morada* sits above and to the south of the placita. Two front rooms—one each in the houses of Emiliano Aragón and Benita Serrano—are *tienditas* (small stores). The *campo santo* ("holy field," a term used for Catholic cemeteries, but not for others) is up the hill west of the placita, and the community water tank is close by.

Dwellings outside the placita are dispersed. Hidden by La Cuchilla is *Cienaguitas* (Little Marshes) where four houses sit northern European fashion, each in its own fields. In the same pattern stand two houses on the broader upper portion of the Cuchilla itself, and six houses (two of them unoccupied) two to three miles downstream from the placita. The house of one Cañonero is about a mile up Cañones Canyon from the placita, and the summer residences of two Anglos lie yet farther up that canyon.

Every household with the requisite few square yards of open space is an oasis of garden and orchard. Housewives prize their flowers and trade seeds and lore, while their husbands take pride in their apple and apricot trees that shelter their houses from wind and sun, and provide a pleasure for the eye.

3 History

The Cañones microbasin has been inhabited since before Pueblo Indian times—very likely since before the Christian era. Chert from Cerro Pedernal was used by hunters and gatherers, to make spear and arrow points, at least as far as the eastern slope of the Sangre de Cristos, and continued to be an important trade item into the historic period. Chert quarries are mentioned in mid-eighteenth-century Spanish archives. Indians of the Anasazi tradition, whose descendants include present-day Pueblo Indians, built a succession of villages in the region. One of them, with the Tewa name Tsiping, was constructed about A.D. 1300 on the mesa (Mesa India) which sits like a ship's prow commanding the confluence of Polvadera and Cañones Creeks, and its ruins are well known to Cañoneros. It is a magnificent defensive site that probably formed the gateway to the Rio Grande Tewa pueblos to the east, protecting them against western nomads. The pueblo was abandoned by about A.D. 1500, and for two centuries the microbasin was probably occupied only intermittently by bands of Utes on hunting, trading, raiding, or mining expeditions. Chihuahueños Creek on some early maps is called "Chaguaguas" or "Sabuaganas," the name of a local band of Utes (Swadesh 1974:47).

This is but an indication of the rich prehistory of the area. It is surveyed thoroughly in Van Ness's master's thesis (1969).

The first European record in the region is a grazing grant in the Piedra Lumbre Valley in the 1730s to a wealthy *peninsular*, a native of Santander, Spain, named José de Riaño, who lived in Santa Fe and may or may not have visited the land. Riaño's widow, María Roybal, eventually sold the rights to the Piedra Lumbre grazing land to Captain Antonio Montoya, the eldest of three brothers. The three Montoya brothers also received an adjacent grant to the south in 1740, and ran their livestock on it, but in their turn abandoned their grants about 1745 after Ute raids.

The actual settlement of Cañones came in a more logical and less dramatic fashion as Abiquiu and its sierra filled up. Abiquiu was founded in the early 1730s, confirmed by a grant to Bartolomé Trujillo and others in 1734. The first *plaza*, downstream from present Abiquiu, was Santa Rosa de Lima de Abiquiu (Salazar 1976), whose chapel is now being reconstructed. It was abandoned because of Ute attacks, and resettled at the present site of Santo Tomás de Abiquiu in the early 1750s, with the help of Hispanicized Indians called *genízaros*. The genízaros were awarded a community *merced* and were placed under the supervision of the Franciscan mission which was established at Abiquiu for this purpose. The population and the number of livestock grew, prospered, and pushed up the Chama Valley and over the Mesa de Abiquiu, spilling eventually into the Cañones drainage basin. In 1766 Pedro Martín Serrano, who already owned land at Abiquiu and at Ojo Caliente, requested and received a new grant in the Piedra Lumbre Valley after purchasing the Montoyas' interests, and, more or less simultaneously, his cousin Juan Pablo Martín (Serrano), son of Miguel Martín Serrano, one of the original Abiquiu grantees, was given what became known as the Polvadera grant. The Piedra Lumbre starts at the bottom end of the Cañones Valley, and extends north and west across the Chama River to mountain barriers. It consists of an enormous amount of grazing land between elevations of about 6,500 and 7,000 feet, and very little land that can be irrigated. The Polvadera is within the Cañones drainage and embraces Polvadera Creek and the sierras on both sides. It is ideal for small-scale cultivation of crops.

The Martín Serranos, like José de Riaño and the Montoyas, were wealthy and prominent; they were also veterans of militia service. All of these grants were made primarily to provide land for cattle grazing and for defense against nomads, but the Martín Serranos, each of whom had many children and other relatives, began to develop seasonal ranchos in the Cañones basin. They made their living from sheep, goats, and cattle, as well as from farm plots probably developed close to the present placita. Quite possibly, they also traded with Utes and Navajo (cf. Swadesh 1974:47). Fray Domínguez tells us that by 1776 the annual October fair at Abiquiu between Hispanos and Utes was already well established—horses, grain, hunting knives, for skins and meat, with captives traded both ways (Adams and Chávez 1956:252–53).

The record is blank for the Cañones basin itself for the rest of the eighteenth century. Presumably its inhabitants shared in the gradual increase in numbers and wealth of the mother village of Abiquiu, and in the terror of Comanche, Ute, and Navajo raids. We infer that the descendants of the Martín Serranos lived in scattered ranchos, retreating to Abiquiu for the winter. A "*plaza de San Miguel*" in the census of 1789, with forty-seven households, sounds like Cañones placita, but was more likely where Barranco (a settlement in the Chama Valley west of Abiquiu) now stands. Everyone was a generalist—rancher, farmer, trader, fighter, builder, blacksmith, and whatever else it was necessary to be—changing as the needs of survival changed.

We pick up shortly after 1800 when, according to oral lore, Juan Bautista Valdez bought a piece of land in the narrows of the Cañones Valley from Pedro Martín Serrano (grandson of the grantee) in return for several horses. It seems that Martín Serrano was planting in the valley when a Navajo raiding party ran off with his animals. He was not only inconvenienced but shamed, and did not want to return home on foot. To make this transaction official, Valdez requested a grant for himself, his family, and seven companions, and it was made in 1807. The boundaries of that grant, on which the present Cañones placita sits, were listed as follows:

> . . . on the east the river of the same cañon [then sometimes called Cañon de los Pedernales, Cañon de Riaño, and sometimes Cañon de San Miguel], which reached the boundary of the Polvadera, on the west the mesa blanca, on the north the boundary of the Martíns, and on the south the source of said river (quoted in Van Ness 1979:238).

This grant included that portion of Cañones now called Cañones Canyon, above its confluence with Polvadera Creek. We believe that because Valdez and his cograntees already had rights on the Polvadera Grant that had been acquired through kinship ties and marriage, the two valleys continued to function as a unified microbasin for subsistence purposes. Juan Bautista Valdez was sixty years old in 1807, and settled the grant with nine companions and his numerous children and grandchildren. By 1814 he had outgrown the microbasin, and was allotted an adjacent tract within the grant but on the Rito Encino to the west, where Youngsville now lies. He is reported to have been the largest stock owner, possessing over 50 horses, 200 cattle, over 1,000 sheep, some goats and some burros.

The Navajo drove settlers out of Cañones at least once between 1819 and 1824, and perhaps several times. In the latter year sixteen more families led by Francisco García—surplus population from El Rito—were settled on unoccupied land at the head of the canyon. With this addition, landowners totaled thirty-five, and the population reached 150, close to the 1967 figure.

With each generation, and due to partible inheritance, plots of farm land were bought, sold, and traded among relatives to keep them of viable size. The number of households with rights to common grazing land increased sharply, and by the time a few decades had passed, the farm plot holdings of each household had already become roughly equal. Although the descent of heirship is unbroken at least from Juan Bautista Valdez to the present, families migrated out to new settlements upstream along the Chama and farther, other families migrated in, parcels were bought and sold, and the list of land holders was and is fairly fluid. The Mexican period (1821–46) seems to have produced no change in Cañones, although elsewhere the pattern tended to be new grants for whole communities of relatively poor settlers, rather than the larger grazing grants of the Spanish period.

During the nineteenth century the ways of surviving were communal, involving a mixed village economy: irrigation farming, stock raising, hunting, gathering, and trading were pursued cooperatively. Common work to build and maintain the irrigation system was the single most important communal activity, and is treated separately in chapter 4. Hunting parties for elk and buffalo were made up of men of the whole placita, and the meat was shared when the party returned. (Hunting rabbits, mule deer, and birds was usually only a household matter.)

Parties to trade with Indian nomads might come from various

portions of the parish of Santo Tomás, and would have to be large enough to defend themselves. Hunting and trading might take place on the same journey. While some able-bodied men were gone on such expeditions, others stayed home both for safety and for economic survival, and the assignment of people to one group or the other was a community concern. Some of the more prosaic tasks were also carried out in common—maintenance of the roads and trails, and *la era* (the threshing floor) and the corral. The threshing floor was sometimes composed of earth mixed with ox blood, and was hard enough to use as a dance floor when threshing was finished. And, of course, the church, the campo santo, and the morada were common property to be maintained communally—and still are among those who remain Catholic.

Many events of the nineteenth century in Cañones are lost because no new grants were made, and because Cañones never has had formal political organization, hence no government records. Even parish records of births, marriages, and deaths are largely lost, because of fires in the churches and rectories. From what we know of village organization in general, we may infer that leadership in Cañones was held by the heads of the largest extended families, so long as these individuals had *vergüenza* and their households were held in respect (chapter 7). They married within Cañones or into Abiquiu more than into other placitas. Mass was said in Cañones once a month or less often. For marriages and baptisms they went to Abiquiu, but their graves were dug and their funeral services were conducted by the Cañones penitential *cofradía*, of which a majority of the grown men were members.

The days, the years, the lives of these people ran deeply in cycles not much different from those of the present day (chapter 6), and their diversions were homely. Dancing was perhaps the most visible of these pleasures—either on the era, in a large home, or in a *sala de baile* (dance hall) especially constructed for the purpose. The music was fiddles and guitars played by Cañoneros or by men from nearby villages. The Fiesta de San Miguel in late September was the occasion of the biggest of these dance celebrations, but after weddings of the principal families large dances were also held, and prospective suitors from other villages would ride over to compete with local youths for the affections of the unmarried Cañoneras. Liquor flowed rather freely at these affairs, and fights broke out once in a while.

The diet of Cañones was limited, the staples being wheat or corn flour for tortillas, and pinto beans spiced with chile. The people tightened their belts toward the end of winter and all spring. To deny oneself food or other indulgence during Lent came naturally, because everything was scarce at that season. Everyone rejoiced and suffered together without distinction between patrón and peón (which were not separate classes on the frontier, but temporary statuses), and either through blood, marriage, or *compadrazgo* (co-parenthood) almost every adult man and woman had close formal ties to each other. In many respects life in Cañones is still the same, although automobiles, wage labor, and the conversion of families to non-Catholic sects have complicated the picture.

In the nineteenth century Cañoneros did not, so far as we know, take part in the wars which the United States fought, nor did they in appreciable numbers go off to cities for jobs. They probably did go to Abiquiu occasionally for jobs with the U.S. army post and the Indian agency, and perhaps served some of the private Anglo trading expeditions as muleteers. "Because of these expeditions, Ceran St. Vrain, the well known New Mexican merchant, established a mercantile outlet in Abiquiu under the management of Jacob Leese [in the mid-nineteenth century]" (Van Ness 1979:305). Cañoneros marketed their annual increment of sheep and perhaps small surpluses of crops through this outlet and others established in Abiquiu until recent decades. The present establishment is called "Bode's Mercantile Store," owned from the early 1900s by Martin Bode, an immigrant from Germany, inherited by his son Karl on Martin's death in 1976.

Native Hispanos seldom become merchants in northern New Mexico except on a very small scale, partly because of lack of knowledge and connections, partly because that occupation carried overtones of exploitation and usury which were thought to be *sin vergüenza* (chapter 7). [A well-known exception was Julián Martínez of Arroyo Hondo, a large-scale merchant and sheep owner made famous by his daughter's book *Shadows of the Past* (Jaramillo 1941).]

Toward the end of the century, after the railroad opened up New Mexico to Anglo settlement and capital, outsiders became interested in Rio Arriba county land, and Cañones lost heavily along with the rest of the Hispanic north. The record is exceedingly complicated, so instead of recounting the details (which are contained in Van

Ness 1979), we shall summarize the difference between Spanish-Mexican and Anglo assumptions about land tenure, and then touch the highlights of what happened to the grants that make up the Cañones microbasin.

In Spanish custom, land is not a commodity but a source of livelihood. *Mercedes* (grants), particularly community as opposed to private ones, were made to those who settled, worked, and defended them, and reverted to the government if the conditions were not met. Thus, the mercedes of José Riaño and the Montoyas were succeeded by those of the Martín Serranos and the Valdezes, who did settle and defend. Absentee ownership was not a legal category for Spanish grantees.

Within a community merced, three categories of land were reckoned based upon differing forms of use and tenure.

House plots in the placita or elsewhere ranged from just enough land for the house itself up to perhaps a quarter-acre, or enough for a house and a small kitchen garden.

Irrigable plots in the bottoms consisted of a few acres each—actually measured not as squares of land, but as *varas* (a linear measure of thirty-three inches) fronting a stream, each extending down from irrigation ditch to stream. These two categories of land were private and inherited, partible, and could be traded, bought, and sold.

The common land made up the vast bulk of every New Mexican merced. It was impartible and could not be inherited in fee. Rather, grantholders inherited usufruct (use rights) for grazing livestock, gathering firewood, and gathering food and medicines from wild plants. The common land consisted of all the land above the line of irrigation, to the crest of the mountain ridges (where the next merced began) or the mesas between settlements.

The boundaries were imprecise by Anglo standards for surveying and registration of tracts of land, but this imprecision created little problem given Hispanic subsistence. If a Cañones family moved on to new territory, upstream on the Chama for instance, or to the west along the Rio Puerco, it might sell its house and its farm plot to a new family moving in. With that allotment went the family's private and community rights to the merced. Metaphorically, it sold out of the corporation and the new family bought in. What was bought and what was sold was not so much parcels of land as the right to live and make a living in a particular microbasin.

In Anglo law, land is a marketable good, exchangeable wherever a market can be found; rights to land are separate from residence. With the exception of legally special cases like the Homestead Act of 1862 and certain tax protections for one's principal residence, Anglo law treats real estate like any other capital, and in Anglo economics capital can be hypothecated in the hope of creating more capital. Land is sometimes bought by people who have never set foot on it, and sold again without a visit (Van Ness 1976). New Mexico in the late nineteenth century, from the Anglo capitalist point of view, spread itself open as virgin and almost unoccupied territory ripe for capitalizing.

The Piedra Lumbre Grant was divided, the south two-thirds going to a combine consisting of Thomas Catron, attorney of Santa Fe, General José María Chávez, and Ramón Salazar of Abiquiu; and the northern third to a combine headed by George Hill Howard. The scenario was written in English common law, but the actors in this as in many other cases included local Hispanos who saw the way the wind was blowing and trimmed their sails to it. Chávez and Salazar had already accumulated large quantities of livestock and land in and around Abiquiu, and, in the classic style of successful marginal individuals, played their roles alternately as Hispanos and as Anglos, depending upon the advantage of the moment. When the Piedra Lumbre Grant was finally patented in 1902 to the Chama Improvement Company (an investment company owned by Catron, Chávez, and Salazar), it included a big tract of farmland in Cañones watered by the Salazar and Madrid Ditch and the Lower Cañones Community Ditch, and those living on it were labelled squatters and threatened with being run off.

Early in the twentieth century Manuel Salazar of Cañones acquired about 50,000 acres of the Piedra Lumbre Grant. How he rose from obscurity to such wealth and its attendant power is not clear, but elderly Cañoneros who knew him well speak of him with respect and liking. In the mid-1930s, faced with a slump in the sheep market and needing cash for taxes, he sold 30,000 acres to Arthur Pack, a Presbyterian from Philadelphia who opened a dude ranch on it (Pack 1966:68–70). In 1955 Pack gave the ranch to the Presbyterian Church for a conference center. At Manuel's death his remaining approximately 20,000 acres were divided among his children, with his son Jacobo and his daughter Preciliana receiving most of his land in the Cañones basin. At the present time, Preciliana has sold her land to a cousin and Jacobo remains the largest landowner in Cañones.

The Polvadera Grant was claimed by a few nonresident descendants of the original grantees without regard to the rights of those who had moved there subsequently. Litigation dragged on for a quarter of a century until it was finally patented in 1900 to Alice Perew, widow of a man from Buffalo, New York, who bought rights to it from the descendants. That patent failed to establish undisputed ownership, however, and more litigation followed until 1918 when the grant was sold to Felix García and Emmet Wirt, storekeepers of Lumberton, New Mexico. Those who were grantholders from the Spanish point of view continued as squatters from the Anglo point of view.

The Juan Bautista Valdez Grant, like the others, was treated as a private grant by U.S. authorities, and the litigation concerning it lasted from 1871 to 1899. It was finally patented in 1913 to heirs, but only the farmland in the Cañon de los Pedernales was included. Both the Rito Encinas (Youngsville) and the sierra commons were excluded, and slightly less than 1,500 acres came to the community.

The unity of the microbasin was destroyed. The confirmed boundary between the Valdez and Polvadera Grants ran down the middle of Cañones Creek, and the downstream bottoms fell to Catron and the Abiquiu landlords as Piedra Lumbre. The very placita was cut in two. Fortunately for the villagers, numerous attempts to rent grazing land to large ranchers from outsiders failed because of rapid depletion of grasses, and the rents apparently never even covered the taxes. The Polvadera grant was sold to the U.S. government in 1937. The common lands claimed, but not patented, became public domain in the Valdez Grant. These lands are all now Santa Fe National Forest. Until after our ethnographic present of 1967, the households in Cienaguitas, as the irrigable bottomland of the Polvadera Valley is called, were squatting on federal land. (See chapter 9 for the legal transfer of land to these "squatters.")

One important consequence of these drawn-out lawsuits over ownership of mercedes is that Cañones, like most northern New Mexico villages, now owns the first two categories of its land, but not the third—the vast majority of the total acreage. So its citizens continue to own their houses and grow their crops, but in order to pasture their livestock they must petition *La Floresta* (the National Forest Service) for permits (see chapter 4) and submit to a bureaucracy which is not even responsible to pressure at the state level, but only to Washington. Professional forest service personnel are itinerant, almost totally Anglo, have little patience for the small livestock owner, and move on before they have a chance to learn much about him. Some of these individuals express scorn for the "ignorant Mexicans" of the villages.

The large gaps in the documentary record of nineteenth-century Cañones are partially filled by the memory of people now living there. They speak of greater self-sufficiency, much more cooperative labor than at present—in clearing fields, harvesting, and house building, especially—but these are not "the golden days of yore" sort of tales. Food was less varied and less plentiful. During years when late frosts killed spring blossoms, people didn't eat fruit. During years when insects or other causes diminished the crops or decimated the herds, people didn't eat much of anything. Work was satisfying but tedious, for many of the tools as well as all of the products were made at home, and iron was scarce.

Cañones was too far away from markets to develop crafts like the weaving that for many decades has brought a steady trickle of income to households in the general region of Chimayó. Home weaving lasted until the young womanhood of Bernardita Salazar, now in her seventies, who has some family rugs on her floors. There were no *santeros* (carvers of religious statues) or painters of record in Cañones. The comfort of the Church came seldom to Cañones, and sometimes even Abiquiu lacked a priest.

The tales that the Cañoneros remember often have to do with predatory Indians. Francesquita Salazar, age sixty-five, points out the site of a semisubterranean house up Cañones Canyon a mile from the placita where her grandmother raised her family. One day, says Francesquita, her grandmother was tending her baby while cooking tortillas atop a *comal* that was perched on the *tinamaste* in the middle of the *fogón*. (A tinamaste is an iron tripod that raises the flat stone comal off the fire so the fire can heat it evenly. A fogón is a fireplace). She put on one tortilla, turned around to change the baby, turned back and the tortilla was gone. Thinking her memory bad, she put on another tortilla, and turned again to the baby. This tortilla also disappeared. She still had most of her mind on the chore with the baby, so she grunted and put a third tortilla on the comal, but kept watch out of the corner of her eye. Presently a thin brown arm reached down the short chimney and drew back quickly with the tortilla. It was an Indian, probably a Navajo, stealing lunch for himself. Francesquita chuckles when she tells this story.

Benjamín Archuleta of Abiquiu, a man in his eighties, tells the childhood story his grandfather told him about returning down the *rito* (stream) with a herd of sheep, in the company of another boy, and being chased by Navajo. His grandfather made it but the other was caught and spent a couple of years with his captors before a soldier traded for him and returned him to his family. Since capture went the other way also, northern New Mexico is well populated with men and women who have one or more Navajo or Ute grandparents, and there are people in Vallecitos, above La Madera, who remember knowing two Navajo "slaves" who chose to remain with Hispanos after the U.S. army gave them the chance to return home.

What contemporary Cañoneros appear to think of their own history is that they have always had a hard life. They are descended from poor people, with no memories of ancestral glory. But they are descended from people who made their own livings and their own destinies. The Spanish colonial government was interested in them only to the extent that they could secure the western frontier against nomads. The government could offer no reinforcements if attacks were too severe to be withstood. The Mexican government does not stand out as a separate entity, and the most significant fact about Mexico is that it lost to the United States in the war of 1846. The American government consistently supported the land speculator, and has never stood up for Hispanic small farmers and ranchers. Hispanic politicans at the state and local levels were, with very few exceptions, in league with larger commercial interests, both Anglo and Hispano, and were not much better than the Anglos themselves. The Roman Catholic faith has always been a pillar of the lives of Cañoneros, but the Roman Catholic church during the eighteenth and nineteenth centuries was so poor that it supported the village little better than the various governments. The cofradía, by and large, has been a more important part of Cañones religious life than the church hierarchy has (chapter 5).

The twentieth century has not been kind to village New Mexico, especially since about 1930. People who left to find jobs during the national economic booms of World War I and of the 1920s came back during the depression to discover that there were too many of them for the land to support (González 1969:123). They switched almost en masse from the Republican to the Democratic party, because the New Deal came to the rescue with relief programs. They also, once World War II saved the national economy, began to leave again and to stay away. Weber (1979:87) notes a loss of population from 1940 to 1970 in four of the six northern counties (Mora, San Miguel, Taos, and Rio Arriba), with a gain in two (Sandoval and Santa Fe), at the same time that New Mexico as a whole nearly doubled in population.

One sad consequence of the increase in wage labor is that cooperative farm and ranching work is harder to maintain. The acequias are still cleaned out every spring, the cattle are still rounded up for branding and for the annual consultation with Floresta officials about where the village must pasture this year. But fields are no longer cleared communally, the harvest is no longer brought in communally, cattle no longer graze on the stubble of all fields in common, and house building is no longer the occasion for joint work groups.

Hispanic villages, including Cañones, are no longer economically self-sufficient. Weber argues that they are no longer economically or socially viable. We disagree. In 1967, which is "present time" for our ethnographic description, Cañones was very much intact socially and, to a surprising extent, economically. But it was in transition, regretting the loss of the closeness of past generations, and inventing new cultural solutions to new social problems.

4
Material and Economic Life

The economic unit—the group of people that makes a living together and consumes its income together—is the household. A century ago, in certain respects—clearing fields, building acequias, harvesting, herding, hunting—that unit was the entire village. Now only clearing acequias unites the labor of more than one household. For Cañones, perhaps for northern New Mexico in general, a household should be defined with some care. It is, as everywhere, those who live under a single roof, pool their incomes, and eat together. As everywhere, it usually consists of spouses and their children plus other relatives (parents, unmarried siblings, et al.) who share bed and board. But also, the New Mexican Hispanic household should be defined as including those temporarily living away at work. These include both the male head, who may spend months at a time working as a sheepherder in Utah or as a wage earner in a city, and also the unmarried sons working for wages away from home but returning periodically until they marry and establish separate households in the city or in Cañones.

The initial sections of this chapter treat demographic and material culture; later ones describe the ways a household deploys itself to produce and consume.

The Population

There are thirty households in Cañones, a total population of 173. The following have been excluded: Isabel García (father of Elipio), who is living primarily in Abiquiu; Preciliana Salazar, whose principal residence is in Santa Fe; Isabel (Joe I.) Salazar, whose principal residence is in Youngsville; José Madrid, whose principal residence is in Cuba; and Webster and David Waide, Anglos whose summer places are several miles up Cañones Canyon from the placita (they winter in El Paso and Santa Fe respectively). They all own land in Cañones, and several of them considerable acreage. Isabel Salazar farms his land, is a working member of the largest acequia system, and often figures in local decisions. José Madrid ranches his property. Although they reside elsewhere, all four Hispanos consider themselves Cañoneros.

On the other hand, Manuel Salazar, twenty-six-year-old son of Jacobo and Severiana, is counted in because he is young and unmarried, and considers his parents' home his principal abode although he teaches elsewhere. He spends summers and vacations in Cañones. (He was not the only Cañonero with education beyond high school in 1967, although he is the only one who shows up on the census. Wenceslao Salazar, son of Saquello and Francesquita, had a master's degree, and taught Spanish in Española where he lived with his wife and children.)

The breakdown of Cañones population shows few surprises. The population pyramid (table 1) is heavy in children and old people, scanty in young adults and in children under the age of four. A few more men than women appear to be away from home, but the difference may not be significant. Because of the chance skew toward female infants, population is recalculated without regard to sex in table 2, which shows the age distribution more clearly. It would appear from this table that to some extent people come back to Cañones when their families grow large, perhaps because they feel it is a more healthy and less expensive place to bring up children.

Household size (table 3) is quite evenly distributed, with a mean of 5.76 people per household, and weak modes at two and at seven. There are numerous small households of elderly people whose children have established their own families.

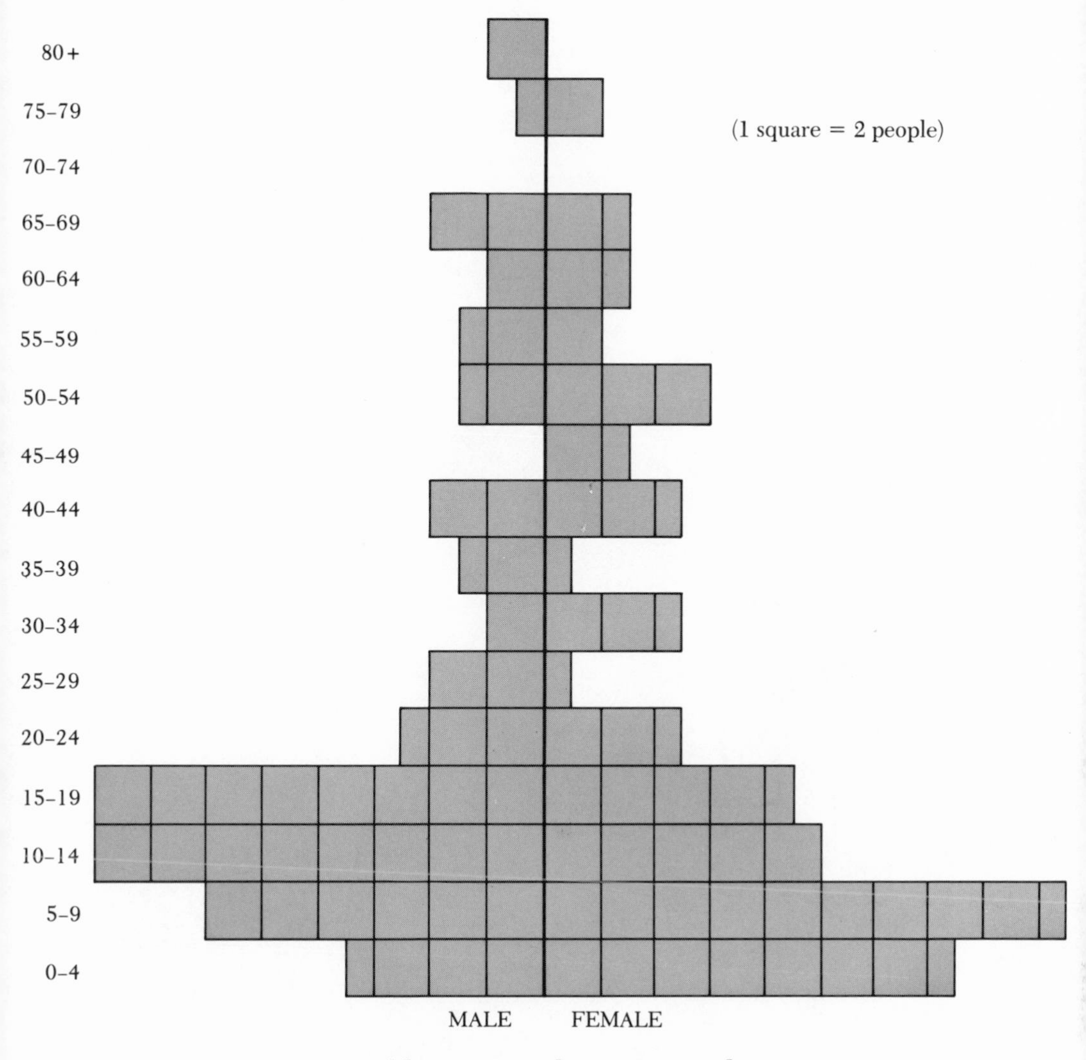

Table 1. Population Pyramid

Houses

Every house in the village is made of adobes except two: one in the placita of *jacal* (vertical poles or boards) plastered over with *soquete* (adobe mud) so that from the outside it looks like an adobe house, and one very conspicuous cement block house on a hill just south of the placita, at present unoccupied. The schoolhouse on La Cuchilla is also of cement blocks. Cañoneros hold adobe construc-

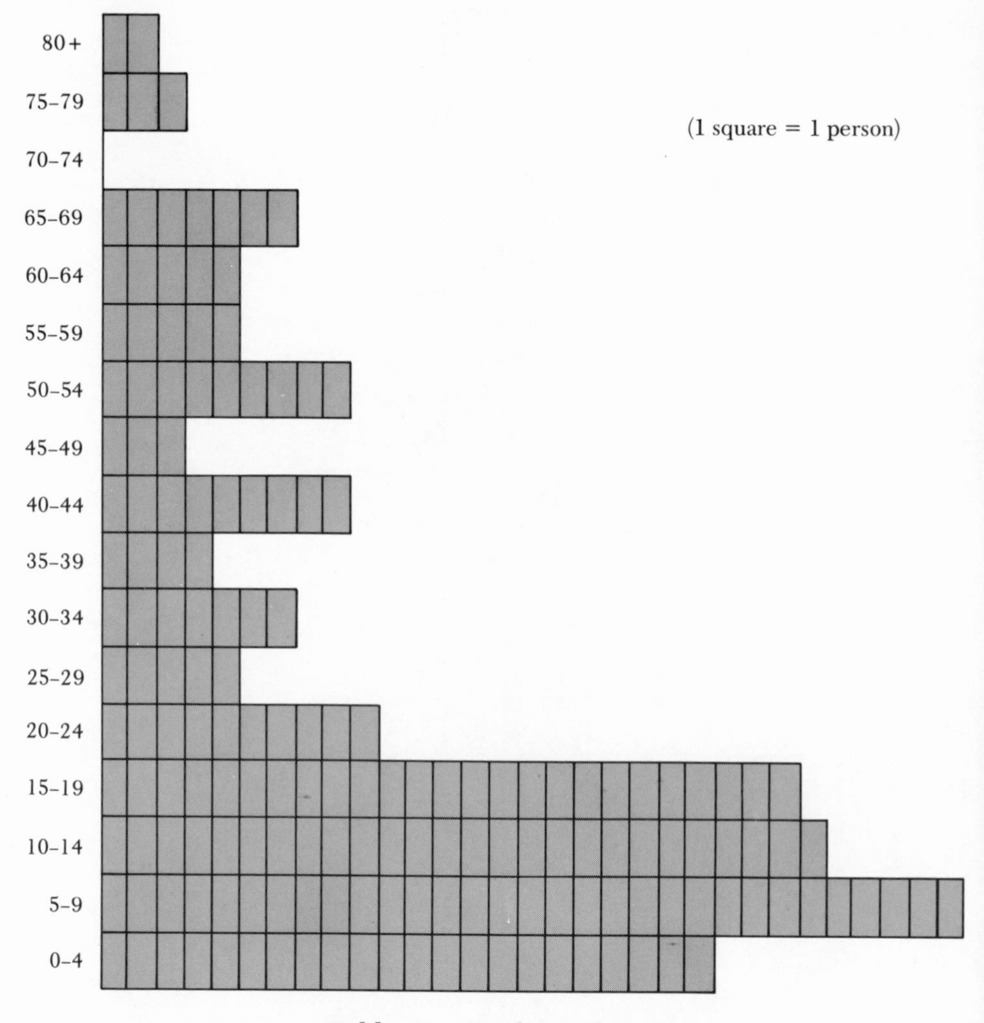

Table 2. Total Population

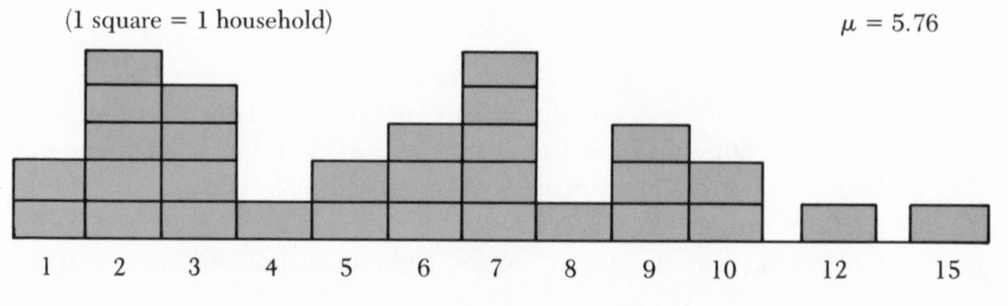

Table 3. Household Size, in number of people

tion to be superior to all other, both practically and aesthetically, and tend to scorn alternatives. The old adage that "an adobe house is like a good woman—warm in winter, cool in summer" is repeated with approval here.

Many adobe houses have been made more durable and more comfortable by adding pitched tin roofs to flat earthen ones, by plastering the outside walls with a coat of cement over chicken wire (which is then tinted while wet, painted, or left gray), and by installing aluminum windows and, occasionally, sliding patio doors. Inside walls are covered in different ways. Enamel over a plaster of fine earth is the most common. Wallpaper is relatively rare now, although widespread a few decades ago. Unadorned white plaster is still seen now and then.

The houses in Cañones tend to be square. In the placita we find none of the so-called gallery houses (one room deep, variable rooms long, with doors onto a porch) so common in other villages in the region. Rooms in the houses follow the Spanish colonial pattern, containing, according to E. Boyd, "fair sized, multi-purpose rooms rather than many little cubicles" in the Pueblo Indian style. "The average house [in the eighteenth century] had three or four rooms, even when there were as many as a dozen members of all ages in the family" (Boyd 1974:7). The same is true today. Distribution in Cañones is in table 4.

The width of a room averages about fifteen feet, the usual length of tree trunks used for *vigas* (ceiling beams). Although their length

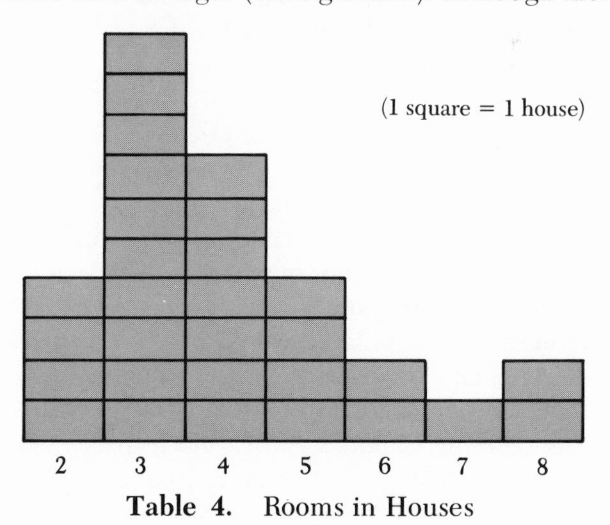

Table 4. Rooms in Houses

may vary arbitrarily, many rooms are only a little off square. One soon comes to appreciate the pleasing proportions of these houses.

Until the recent addition of plumbing, there was seldom any differentiation designed into the shapes and sizes of rooms. Consequently, a room could be put to almost any use, serving as bedroom, kitchen, livingroom, or any combination, and could be adapted easily to changes in family life to accommodate new members, children, spouses, or anyone else who might need special care. Appropriate furniture—including *estufa* (cooking stove) and *fogón* (heating stove)—could be readily moved from one room to another. The older style, of a corner fireplace that served for cooking and heating, died before any of the houses in Cañones reached its present form. One of the adobes was built as recently as five years before the arrival of the field team, another over a hundred years before.

Floors of the houses in Cañones are most often earth covered with linoleum. A few houses have wood or concrete floors, both of which last longer than a hard earth floor, while requiring much less time-consuming upkeep. There no longer seems to be any pride expressed in maintaining these traditional dirt floors.

Working in adobe is done by both men and women. Making the bricks and building with them is men's work, as it has been apparently since the first Spanish settlement. (Men also usually do the outside cementing.) But adobe plastering, both inside and outside the walls, is a woman's province. Anyone who knows a particular village intimately can tell who plastered which wall by the characteristic swirl of her hand. Cañoneras take a good deal of pride in being *enjarradoras*.

The truism circulates in New Mexico that adobe construction is for the poor and for the rich, but not for those in between. The poor count their time for naught, and can afford to spend it making adobes; the rich pile up enough surplus to hire others. But the wage earner has neither time nor money for adobes, and must seek more economical construction. It was estimated in 1967 that a comfortable adobe house could be built for $1,000 in cash for doors, windows, wiring, and other hardware. This is what helps keep Cañones mortgage-free.

The utilities serving Cañones consist of electricity, installed in late 1951 and early 1952, and a community water supply installed in 1961 with federal aid. There is no community sewer system. All but four houses have electricity. Kerosene for lamps is unobtainable in the placita; neither tiendita stocks it. When electricity was offered, a few households refused. Adelaida Lucero, for instance, much prefers the soft light of an oil lamp, and teases her children who cannot find things in the dim light, and burn their fingers on her stove when they visit her. But the prevailing attitude toward the change in domestic lighting was expressed by Antonio Serrano, "*La luz de aceite es triste* (Oil light is sad light)."

Twenty-three houses have refrigerators. One also has a freezer. Three houses have sewing machines, two have electric mixers, two have television sets, although reception is almost nil in Cañones. One house contains a piano.

Drinking water is pumped up to the community tank from wells. It is universally considered to be unpleasant in taste and bad for plants. A number of Cañoneros said they had argued for a tank at the *ojitos* at the base of the Mesa India, which would not only have given the village better water, but would also have served more houses since the elevation at the source is higher. The present tank serves only houses in the placita itself, but even one of those (Eduvigen Lovato's) is too high. Others must drill their own wells or dip from the acequia. Water from the acequia is regarded as of dubious quality, particularly after a rain, when animal remains wash down into it. This perception is at least a century old, and probably much older.

Water in many houses amounts to a single tap with no drain. Sinks are desirable, and are being installed as means permit. Bathrooms are also regarded as desirable, but less necessary than sinks. They cost more because of the need to install additional plumbing and to dig a septic tank. Only seven of the thirty households have bathrooms, and water heaters are rare, although most houses have washing machines. Considering the lack of plumbing, the standard of cleanliness in body and clothing is remarkably high.

Wood cookstoves are all but universal—twenty-nine of the thirty households have them. Two of these households also have electric stoves (or half electric, half wood), and one has a butane-wood stove. The thirtieth has electric only. Most women say they like to cook on wood better than on gas or electricity, a widespread preference in Cañones and elsewhere among cooks who have long experience with wood. The economy of using wood, though, is doubtful. One Cañonero who investigated the matter claims that firewood is more expensive than butane for cooking if you count the cost of gasoline for the pickup truck to fetch the wood. One should bear in mind, also, that there are no longer any adequate sources of firewood close to Cañones, so that villagers must drive anywhere from fifteen to forty miles in search of dead trees. Butane is already replacing wood for space heaters, and will probably be used more widely for cooking.

Transportation and Communication

The access roads into Cañones consist of a lower road that leaves paved N.M. 96 a couple of miles west of the Abiquiu Dam, goes by Jacobo Salazar's ranch, and enters the placita after 3.3 miles; and an upper road that leaves N.M. 96 3.7 miles farther west (closer to Youngsville), and winds its way into and out of arroyos for 6.3 miles before entering the placita (see map 4).

These access roads into Cañones are generally thought to be worse than anywhere else in Rio Arriba county. During most of 1967, only the upper road was open. Both are *puro soquete* (pure mud) when they are wet, and passable only by expert drivers. Cars frequently slide off the crown in wet weather and end up in the ditch. The lower road fords the stream twice—disastrous to brakes until they dry out. Neither lower nor upper road is graveled. Roads upstream from the placita are no smoother, and ford the stream in several places; but the earth is sandy and stony here, so these roads are much easier to traverse than the others when they are wet. Since Rio Arriba county maintains 510 miles of road on $76,000 per year and has no rock crusher, it cannot do much to improve road conditions.

Difficult as it is to get to Cañones by road now, it was much harder in the past. U.S. 84 from Española up the Chama River into Colorado was not paved until the 1940s. (Its state road predecessor was constructed in 1922.) N.M. 96 connecting U.S. 84 with Youngsville, Coyote, and Gallina, and from which the Cañones access road takes off, was itself a dirt road entering U.S. 84 north of the confluence of Cañones Creek with the Chama until 1963 when it became a paved highway crossing the top of the new Abiquiu Dam. Before 1963 visitors drove over twenty miles of dirt road to reach Cañones, and could do so only in good weather.

Cañoneros have at least one vehicle per household, except for those households composed exclusively of the elderly. As a rule of thumb, there is one car per wage earner, and it is as likely to be a pickup as a sedan. Other farm vehicles are not plentiful. There may be three small tractors in the village; only Jacobo Salazar possesses any quantity of other farm machinery. Since the Cañonero is often the last owner of his car, the village is a graveyard of autos. In this respect, Cañones is like any number of northern New Mexico villages, identical to Appalachia, most American Indian reservations, and any other poor rural area in the United States.

Despite the difficulties in getting in and out of Cañones, a very important mode of communication is face-to-face contact through visits. (There are, by the way, no telephones in Cañones. The nearest ones are in Youngsville, ten miles away, and Abiquiu, fourteen. The federal officials at the Abiquiu Dam, five miles away, have telephones, but these are not available to private individuals.) There is a great deal of travel between Cañones and settlements where relatives and close friends live, as well as visits back home from Albuquerque, Denver, and Los Angeles, to which some Cañoneros have migrated. When people are ill, they especially feel the need of visits from those emotionally close to them, and such visits are socially mandatory. A great deal of information is exchanged through this visiting network concerning the entire community, not just the families involved.

Mail comes three times a week to the post office in the Jacobo Salazar home, two miles below the placita on the lower road. Jacobo also has the contract to carry the mail between Cañones and Abiquiu, where it is transferred to trucks in and out of Santa Fe. A few Cañoneros rent boxes in the Abiquiu post office, which has daily service.

But in general the printed word has little impact on Cañones. Only a small handful of families receives any periodicals whatever, and these are religious journals or the cattle association paper. Occasionally they read the *Albuquerque Journal*, the Santa Fe *New Mexican*, or Española's weekly *Rio Grande Sun*.

Nevertheless, English is understood by most adults. Those who deal most frequently with employers and government officials are most fluent in English. (The field team did not get accurate statistics on degrees of competence in English, because we tried to function exclusively in Spanish ourselves.) All of the school children handle spoken English, as school instruction is exclusively in English. Ironically, very few Cañoneros can read Spanish—even those who speak Spanish only. Since schools have not taught in

Spanish for at least twenty years, if one can read at all it is in English. Hence, public notices such as those in the tiendita window are always in English.

Formal education is a privilege of the young. Very few Cañoneros over sixty have had any at all. "We'd have had to hire the teacher and buy the books" is an explanation that several of them gave. There was no public education readily available before about thirty years ago. Boys and girls may drop out of school after the eighth grade or when they become sixteen. As table 5 shows, a fair

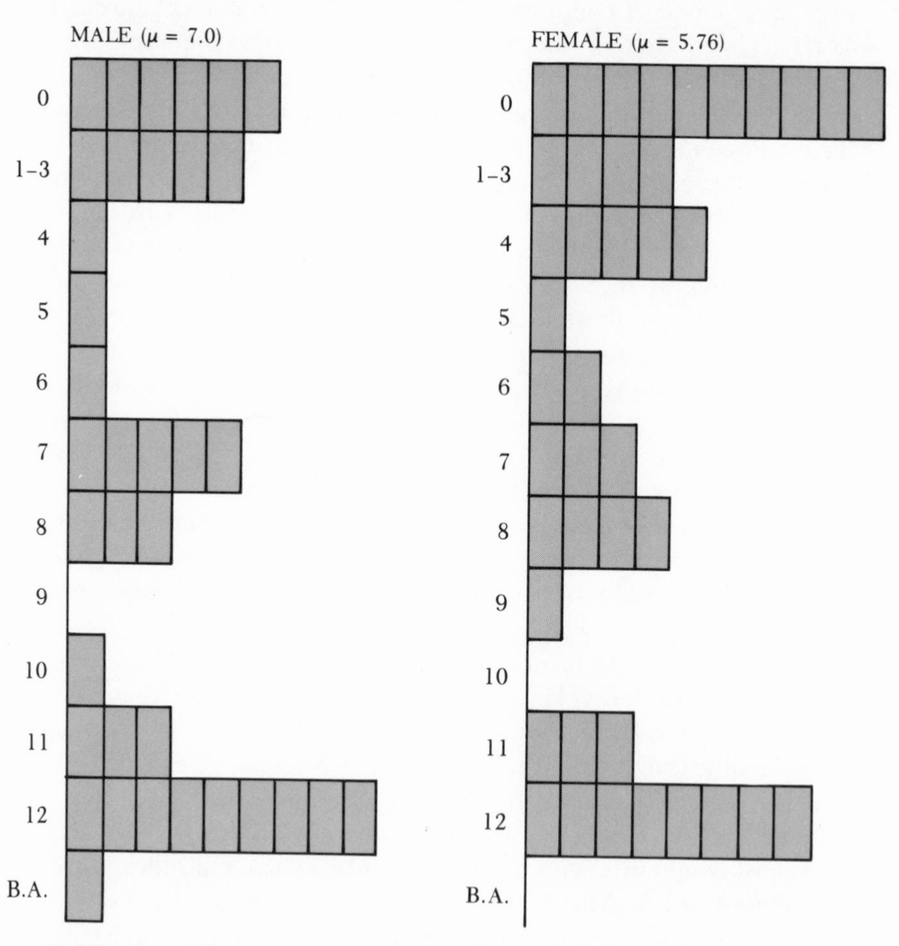

Table 5. Education, in years of school completed
(1 square = 1 person)

number of adults—almost all in their twenties—graduate from high school. The higher average education for males than for females mildly reflects the greater importance placed on professional training for men than for women. (But if the one bachelor's degree is removed, the two halves of the table are not very different.)

Division of Labor

Within the household, domestic jobs are divided by sex and age in a marked but not rigid fashion. Men tend large livestock; women take care of chickens and rabbits. Either or both may care for sheep, goats, and pigs (all of which are scarce in Cañones). Men plow and irrigate the fields; both sexes weed gardens. As we have said earlier, men make adobes and build with them, while women plaster with soquete inside and out. (In some Hispanic villages, men do outside mud as well as cement plastering.) Men work away from home; women take care of the household, cook, put up preserves, wash, iron, mend, and tend the children. Women gather wild herbs somewhat more often than men, but both sexes do it and are likely to regard it as a family outing to the sierra. Men are more active in politics, and women in the Catholic church; but both sexes participate about equally in the Pentecostal church.

Job specialization by occupation is very limited. One man is a better mechanic, another has a tractor and is hired to plow fields. There are no *curanderos* or *parteras* or *sobadores* (curers, midwives, therapeutic masseurs) who work at these trades enough to speak of even as a part-time specialty. There are simply some people who know a little more than most and help out, as Delfinia Salazar modestly put it after assisting at childbirth, "*en caso de necesidad.*"

This division of labor is not absolute. If age and sex distribution in a family, or illness, or jobs away from home, makes it inconvenient to go by custom, then anyone does anything without stigma. Many men and adolescent boys wash, cook, iron, and do other women's chores. Women construct buildings and bridges and do heavy farm work. Fidencia Vialpando, an elderly woman of gusto, and a widow for most of her adult life, is proud of her "male" strength and skills and jokingly boasts, "*Yo soy un Superman,*" joining in the laughter that always follows. Swadesh (1974:178–79) and Mead (1955:164) describe the same flexibility.

Land and its Produce

The 312 acres of irrigable land in Cañones are distributed among 50 owners in 92 tracts on 24 different acequias. The organization of this system is described in chapter 5. While the field team was there, 33.9 percent of these acres was put to alfalfa, 42.8 percent to year-round pasture; 6 percent was in spring grain, 7.9 percent in kitchen garden vegetables; and 7 percent lay fallow (from Van Ness 1979:264–65). That is to say, three-fourths of Cañones farm land was devoted to the upkeep of horses and cows. Since forage is so scarce, it is economic for landowners to devote most of their irrigated land to their livestock, which requires relatively little labor, and to spend their own time earning wages elsewhere.

Table 6 summarizes land ownership by household. Every household owns at least the plot of land the house rests upon. (One elderly couple live in a separate house on land owned by their stepson. They do not pay rent to him and they do run a separate household, so we are not counting them as an exception to the rule of ownership.) Fourteen households own nothing more. Ten own too little land to enjoy so much as a kitchen garden. These households are the poor.

Table 6 highlights a dichotomy between those with property and those without. (Jacobo Salazar owns vastly more land—although not more irrigated land—and cattle than anyone else in Cañones. He is a rancher by any standards short of those of a Texas millionaire. At his request, his exact ownership in land and cattle is not indicated in the tables.) Overt social behavior avoids reflecting this dichotomy, in keeping with Hispanic values that will be discussed in chapter 7.

All those who own irrigated land grow kitchen gardens for their own consumption. No one, including the three households that possess between forty and fifty irrigated acres each, raises any cash crops. If the irrigated land totals more than a couple of acres, the remainder is put to hay or alfalfa.

The labor force on any given plot of land is the owning household, with the help, when needed, of grandchildren, or (more rarely) brothers, or children who have set up their own households. No one in Cañones hires labor, except for the Anglos who live at the head of the canyon.

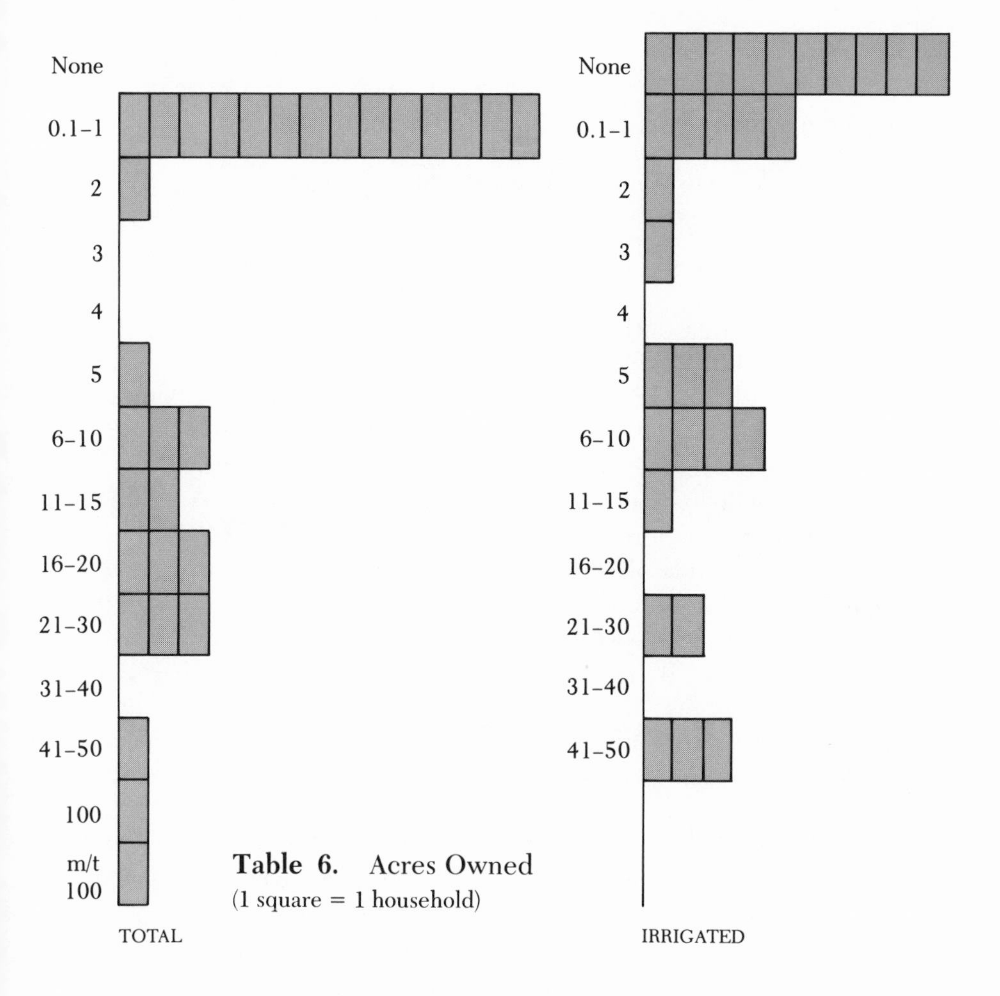

Table 6. Acres Owned
(1 square = 1 household)

There are no mortgages in Cañones, as we have mentioned earlier, and hardly any rental of land. As far as we know, two households rent or borrow plots for their kitchen gardens from neighbors or relatives.

The Tewa Basin Survey of 1935 observed for the entire region that:

> It is by no means fortuitous that less than 5 percent of the farms are mortgaged and that the average mortgage indebtedness for land and improvements on those farms which are fully owned and mortgaged is under $5 an acre on irrigated lands. In those agricultural activities which are well insulated from the price system, the Spanish-American farmer continues to enjoy un-

> changing income from a bushel of corn and a bushel of wheat [i.e., he eats them rather than selling them] and neither speculates in land nor in prices for farm produce.
>
> To the native farmer, land is a permanent possession with a value which changes only as the productive value of that land changes (U.S. Department of Agriculture 1936:30).

In other words, although the reasons may be different in the twentieth century, land is held for much the same reason it was in the eighteenth: for settlement and subsistence, not for speculation.

It seems reasonable to predict that, should the desirability of this land increase and the marketability of these titles improve, land economics will operate to dispossess the present owners. Anglo summer people are already buying land in other villages.

The negative side of nonnegotiable titles is that one's land is not capital in the commercial sense of the word: one cannot capitalize it with mortgages. The positive side is that one is unlikely to lose it in a market gamble. By and large, even failure to pay taxes does not forfeit land, because the buyer who might pick up one's land at a tax sale would not only have to spend an unreasonable sum to prove his title, but also have to face the hostility of his new neighbors.

Land in Cañones is bought and sold within the village, where the quality of the title deed is of less concern. On the internal market, land with water is worth around $100 an acre; land without water $10 an acre. Water rights are not sold separate from land in Cañones, although they are legally separable.

It would be fairly accurate to say that the first benefit that land ownership provides to twentieth-century Cañoneros is a secure place to live. The second is space for a kitchen garden. A skillful irrigator can grow enough on an acre to keep a family of six or seven through the winter. A third benefit is room to grow fruit trees. Table 7 shows the rather even distribution of fruit trees throughout the community. They usually require very little space; only six households lack them entirely.

Although fruit seeds were one of the first Spanish contributions to New Mexico, figuring prominently in convent gardens of the seventeenth century and quickly dispersing among the Pueblo Indians, the largest orchards in Cañones were planted by present owners, and heavy dependence upon home-canned fruit is a fairly recent phenomenon.

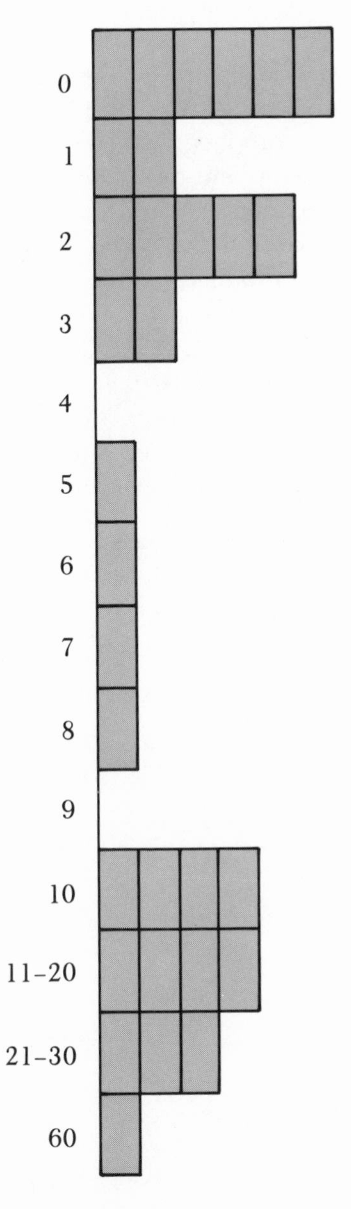

Table 7. Fruit Trees Owned, by household
(apple, pear, peach, apricot, plum, cherry, almond)

The number of bottles of all kinds of produce, including meat, put up by a household (table 8), is the mark of a family's independence from price variations in the market, and its bulwark against hunger. (Until a few decades ago, drying was the only means of preservation, and some produce is still kept this way.)

Table 8, like table 5 on land ownership, illuminates the dichotomy in the village between rich and poor. About half the households have no gardens, and the wives are either too old or too infirm to can a season's produce. So they can nothing, or too little to keep a family, and are very poor.

Those Cañoneras who have rows of shiny bottled goods stored in their *soterranos* (basements or partially subterranean storerooms that are always cool but never freeze) face the winter with some confidence and a good deal of quiet pride. Two of them refer to these rooms as their *tienditas sin dinero* (little stores without money).

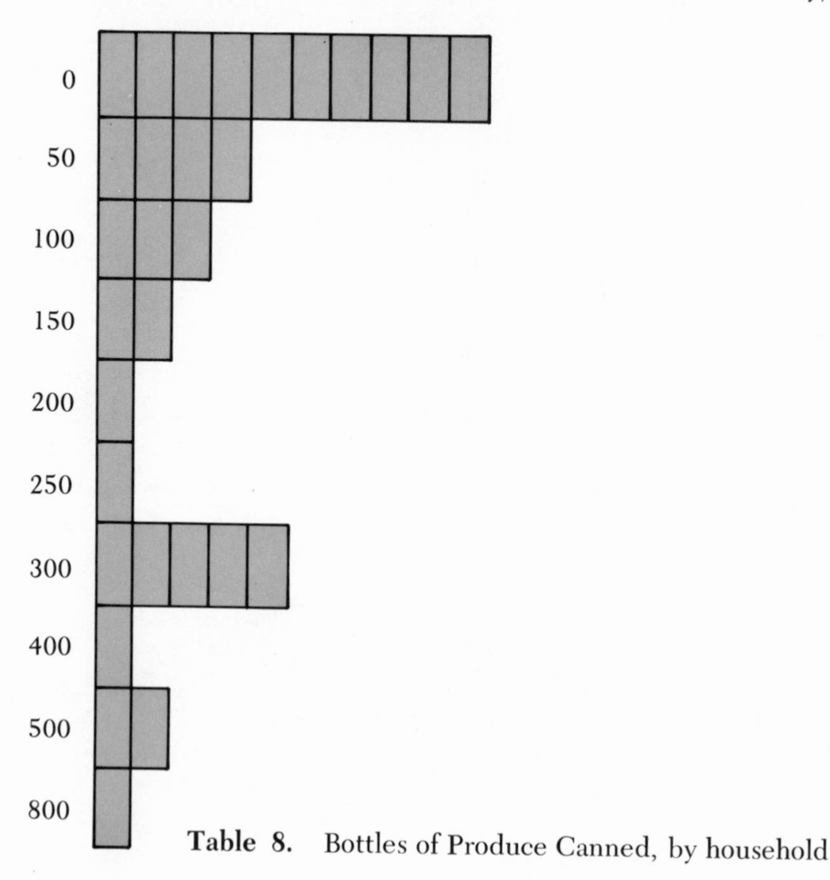

Table 8. Bottles of Produce Canned, by household

This is a bit of "private language" invented by Teófila Vialpando. Her children, she said, would tease her to take them *a la tiendita*. She would reply, "*No tengo dinero.*" (I have no money.) One day her son said, "*Entonces, vamos a la tiendita sin dinero,*" (Well then, let's go to the little store without money) meaning to her private storeroom of goodies. Thus the term became, within the family, a synonym for the pantry or soterrano.

When Kathy Krusnik's mother visited her early in the field work, she discovered the tiendita of Kathy's "foster mother," Luz Valdez (sister-in-law of Teófila Vialpando) when she was invited to stay for lunch. As Mrs. Krusnik noted later:

> She [Luz] said, "I'm going to my tiendita sin dinero to get some food for lunch."
>
> I said not to go to any trouble because we don't want anything fancy.
>
> She said, "Oh, but you don't know my tiendita," and I said, "Well, I'd like to see it."
>
> "Well, no," she said, "It's something that is very private," and she intimated that she never allowed anyone to go in there.
>
> So here came one bottle and then a few minutes later another bottle of food and she brought out about four different bottles; and one was a bottle of canned pickles which looked very delicious, one was a bottle of apricots that were absolutely delicious; then she brought out this combination of meat and green beans with, I believe, a bit of onions in them and they were very tasty. But I think the fruit was the really outstanding food.

Later the same day Luz Valdez did show her guest her tiendita saying "the only things that she buys are flour, baking soda, sugar, coffee, potatoes."

Serafín Valdez, Luz's husband, estimates that if a family grows a good deal of its own produce and burns wood, they can make it through the six months of winter on about $400 in cash.

Nutritionists say that village Hispanos are well fed except for Vitamin C. Chile is rich in Vitamin C only when fresh; when dried, C goes but A remains. As we have indicated earlier, tomatoes do not thrive in Cañones because of late frosts and hail. Citrus fruits are very popular with villagers and are almost always bought in the monthly big shopping with food stamps, but they are too expensive for daily consumption. Marion Hotopp, a physician and a public health officer for the northern counties, advises a Vitamin C tablet which costs only a fraction of the price of an orange. Dr. Hotopp says that pinto beans (called simply *frijoles* here, because no other variety of beans is much eaten) contain enough protein for the daily diet. But as a pediatrician, she says, she worries about children's health when the family is too poor to buy frijoles and must live on macaroni and spaghetti. In this respect, then, New Mexico is similar to Mesoamerica, where frijoles have been the chief source of protein since long before the Spanish conquest.

Three foods feature largest in any Cañones menu: frijoles, flour tortillas, and chile. Frijoles are usually boiled and served with no seasoning except salt. Tortillas are often cooked ahead, to be eaten cold at odd meals. Chile is cooked in a sauce with onions, garlic, and small chunks of meat. It is served separately, to be added to other food as one pleases. In no Cañones home are such "typical" Mexican foods as *tamales*, *enchiladas*, or *burritos* to be found, although everyone knows what they are, and people sometimes enjoy them in restaurants. At times of the year when other foods run short, frijoles, tortillas, and chile remain.

Fried eggs are often eaten at breakfast. Meat, when it is served, is cooked very thoroughly. In the summer a delicacy is *calavasitas* (fresh small summer squash) gently sauteed with onion and sometimes with fresh sweet corn. One or two women still make country white cheese. Dessert of canned fruit is fairly common. Jams and preserves are often served to sweeten tortillas. *Biscochitos* (between a cookie and a tart in Anglo cuisine) and *bunuelos* (sweet fried bread puffed almost like a popover) are cooked for special occasions. Only two *hornos* (beehive-shaped outdoor adobe ovens) are still in use, turning out delectable light white bread. Coffee is the most usual drink.

Cañoneros eat Anglo food along with their native dishes. They like potatoes very much, but buy them rather than grow them. They do not eat or grow much lettuce, celery, parsley, or bell pepper, the salad staples of Anglo households; but radishes are very popular with them.

The villagers gather a number of wild herbs both for seasoning and for *remedios* against illness; *verdolagas* (purslane), for example, is a favorite. A complete list of even the native-grown foods would amount to a lengthy catalog.

Cañoneros are very fond of their diet, and the outsider learns very quickly to share their taste, and to find their food satisfying.

Livestock and La Floresta

Chapter 3 recorded the alienation of most of the grazing and woodlands in the sierra surrounding Cañones—first into the hands of nonresident land speculators and then to the federal government. They are now held and administered by the U.S. Forest Service (called simply *La Floresta* in northern New Mexico). The use of these commonlands was essential to village survival before wage labor appeared to supplement the income from kitchen gardens and small fields, for the commons were used to graze livestock, hunt, cut wood for fuel and construction, and gather wild plants for food and medicine.

These resources are now completely out of community control, and villagers must apply to the forest service for permits to use them. The difference between the villagers' and the forest service's perceptions of reasonable exploitation of these lands has led to misunderstanding, mistrust, and recurring skirmishes, both in Cañones and elsewhere in the region.

Permits to cut vigas and *leña* (firewood) are easy to obtain, but the areas designated for wood cutting may be at a distance of 30 miles or more, making the trip expensive in gasoline and time for everyone, and almost out of reach of the elderly.

Permits to graze livestock have long since been issued up to the carrying capacity of the land as defined by the forest service, which also designates the grazing area. (Cattle are the only important livestock now; goats and sheep were once far more numerous, but forest policy has forbidden goats for many years, while sheep require more attention than wage-earning Cañoneros can spare to them.) Cañoneros believe the forest could carry far more cattle than it does, but the decision is not theirs to make. As a result of their limitation, permits are worth about twice as much as cows (currently $100 versus $50), and are bought and sold privately. One asks a Cañonero not "*Cuantas vacas tiene?*" (How many cows do you have?) but "*Cuantos permisos?*" (How many permits?). At present permits are good for five and a half months per year, and holders are charged 50 cents per month per permit. Cattle are sold in October or November, usually to a buyer who arrives in a truck with portable scales. Fatted cows bring in slightly more than $100 on the average. Three or four households in the placita (not counting Jacobo Salazar) each reap $1,000 or somewhat less per year from this source. The number of cattle indicated in table 9 is very close to the number of permits. (There are also 1 pig, 2 rabbits, 1 goat, and 10 sheep. Seven households own a total of 107 chickens, and 10 households own a total of 27 horses.)

Table 9 also shows the dichotomy of wealth in Cañones more dramatically than tables 5 and 8 do. Eighteen households have no cattle whatever (although one or two of these eighteen are repre-

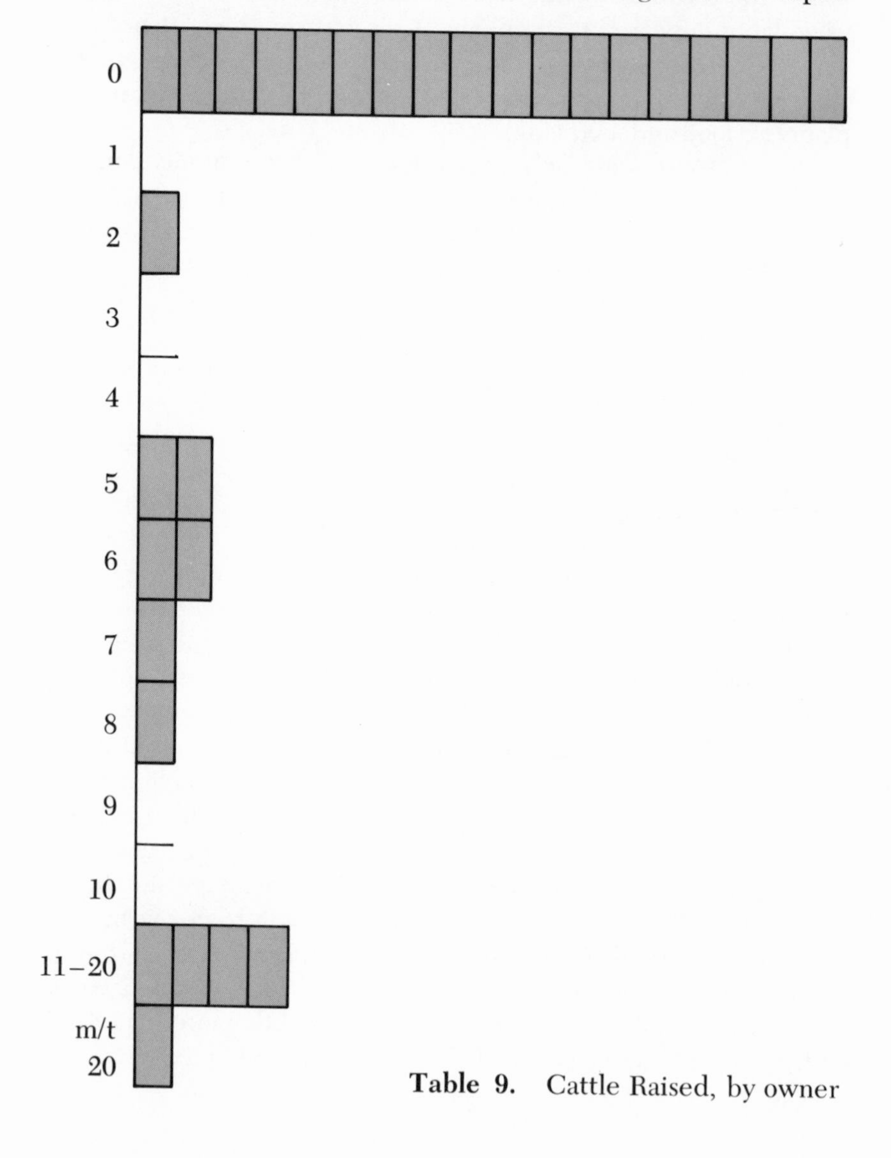

Table 9. Cattle Raised, by owner

sented in the other livestock figures). Only five possess more than ten cows.

Nevertheless, Cañoneros think of themselves more as ranchers than as farmers. This perception fits the self-image of the Hispano as *caballero* (which means both *horseman* and *gentleman*), an unbroken tradition since the Reconquest of the Iberian Peninsula in the late middle ages (cf. Menéndez Pidal 1950; Merriman 1918). A brief anecdote illustrates the vitality of the ranching ideal: Kutsche came back from Santa Fe one day excited about the new "Navajo See Themselves" film project of John Adair, in which they portray themselves in their roles as weavers, silversmiths, and so forth. He described the project to Cristóbal Lucero, then nineteen and son of a family with five horses and eight cattle, and asked what he would show if he were given the opportunity to make a film picturing his own life. "*La vida del ranchero* (the life of the rancher)," Cristóbal replied without a moment's hesitation, and proceeded to give an animated description of the work from horseback of herding cattle, moving them from pasture to pasture—activities that occupied a small proportion of his hours, but accounted for a large proportion of his sense of self. Indeed, the Cañonero on horseback is a graceful and stirring sight. Care of cattle during the summer is a job that boys and young men look forward to—arduous but diverting, requiring them to spend several days at a time on the mesas or in the sierras.

That is the ideal. The reality for many is that they have no grazing permits and thus are effectively landless. The discrepancy between ideal and real drives a number of Cañoneros away from home for long periods of time, or forces them to emigrate entirely.

The reality of outside control of so important an economic and symbolic resource is a constant aggravation. They view personnel of the forest service as rigidly bound to regulations formulated in the Department of Agriculture in Washington, conservative to the point of caricature, ignorant of the culture and needs of the people of the region, and prone to see communism in Hispanic movements to regain land. Forest land administration is predicated on nationally oriented conservation policies and appears to favor the interests of large-scale ranching, commercial timber cutting, and those who promote the use of forest lands for public recreation. These administrative policies are seldom compatible with the subsistence needs of the local communities.

A brief example will illustrate. During our field work, Van Ness had occasion to meet with the Coyote district ranger, and to discuss at some length the administration of forest lands in the Cañones region. His field notes recorded the following:

> It looks as though there is very little communication between the Forest Service and the Hispanos, and there is considerable misunderstanding of each other's attitudes and objectives. The ranger said that in practical terms anything under 100 head was too small an operation to be really profitable and that running the 10 to 20 head that the average Hispano has is ridiculous. He thought that it was more a hobby for them than anything profitable. He also ridiculed the Hispanic concept of land and the way Hispanos use the land. He retold with amusement the standard tales of how vaguely boundaries were defined in their titles. He spoke with disgust of their lack of any notion of soil conservation. None of the Anglo rangers had the least idea why the Alianza [Federal de Mercedes, headed by Reies Lópes Tijerina, latest of a long string of movements trying to regain lost land for Hispanos] were giving the rangers trouble. They definitely felt like they were being picked on.

From Kutsche's notes of an interview in 1969 with James Hall, director of the Ghost Ranch Conference Center:

> [The forest service is] an unmoving bureaucracy which does not act to favor the small landholder. He said the individual forest officers were mostly very decent people and that particularly the rangers were often fine men but that they are going more and more by the book. He quoted a former regional director in Albuquerque as saying that a good ranger is one who knows when to go by the book and when not. But, commented Hall, if the ranger doesn't go by the book it is his own neck that is out.

And finally, Kutsche's notes of a conference on regional development at the Ghost Ranch, April, 1967, attended by forest service officials as well as many others:

> Don Seaman, of the Kit Carson National Forest, got quite emotional in discussing the activities of the Alianza [which included taking over the Echo Amphitheater campground of the Carson Forest the previous October—an activity for which Tijerina was later convicted in federal court and served a term in prison]. Seaman said the issue is criminal. He won't recognize a civil

issue, although he is willing to acknowledge the likelihood that the land was originally stolen from Hispanos by the chicanery of lawyers and others.

Seaman made much of the fact that one of Tijerina's lieutenants is of doubtful sanity, and of his claim that Tijerina will go into a community and stir up the people and then leave. Community people get the idea from Tijerina that they don't have to have permits for their cattle, and they just run the cattle in anyhow. The ranger then kicks the cattle out, and potentially explosive situations are building up.

In other encounters with rangers over several years, we came to understand that since they are rotated every few years throughout the national system, their natural loyalty is to the forest service and not to the region where they find themselves. The forest service appears to have a very limited, if any, orientation program for employees newly transferred to New Mexico. Cañoneros regard the forest service as an enemy against whom they are largely impotent, and which they must accommodate themselves to if they wish to survive.

Records in the Española office of the Santa Fe National Forest show frequent skirmishes between rangers administering the grazing allotments on the Polvadera Grant and the Mesa del Medio, and Cañoneros. Numerous allegations of trespass by village-owned livestock are recorded over the years since the forest service acquired its responsibilities for this region, beginning in the early 1940s. The records also contain accusations against Cañoneros that include breaking forest fences and intentionally leaving gates open. There is little doubt of the truth of at least some of these claims, for at present such charges and counter charges are common. In some instances, then as today, fines were assessed, stock impounded, and grazing permits revoked. Cañoneros generally have no recourse but to bow to authority when these matters come to a head and sanctions are applied. Morally, however, Cañoneros feel their behavior is justified, for at heart they believe that the surrounding sierra is still their patrimony and that they are only exercising traditional rights of usufruct.

In spite of the fact that this issue has been the subject of region-wide investigations by several arms of the federal and state governments in recent years, as well as a topic of loud public debate for decades, it has yet to be resolved. Only the U.S. Congress has the authority to hammer out that resolution.

Wage Labor

Almost all adult men, but hardly any women, have worked away from home for longer or shorter periods of time. Although some entire families go the the San Luis Valley of Colorado during the vegetable harvest, wives and children usually stay home when the head of household goes away. This work-migration pattern does not produce a matrifocal household. The husband regards his absence as unfortunate and temporary, and his wife and children are prevented by the tight network of kin and community ties from a change in status that might lead to female-headed households.

Until the turn of the century, the only wage jobs available to villagers, aside from hiring out as ranch hands, were sheepherding, mining, and railroad building. The first two alternatives still exist, of course, in addition to new options in the forest service, factories, service companies, and building construction.

It is not totally clear when working away is temporary and when it is permanent. As a rule, one is still considered to be working out from home base whenever the family is left at home, or migrates together for seasonal work. An unmarried son is still "at home" even if he works in Albuquerque or Denver. But if a father sends for his family and closes up his Cañones house, or if a son marries and establishes a home away, then they have moved out. All of the Cañoneros living and working in California are considered to have left, even though they return for visits. Unmarried women seldom follow this path, and then only if they have relatives or very close friends to live with while they are away.

A person working away who is still a member of the household contributes part of his earnings (although not necessarily on a regular or systematic basis) to the household in Cañones. Thus in a new sense the economic advantage of a large family continues: in the past, many children shared garden and ranch work; now they share in earning money.

Cañones is poorly situated for commuting, compared to villages in or near the Española Valley, from which many people commute daily to Los Alamos, Española, or even Santa Fe. The jobs close to Cañones tend to be short-term. For example, a number of Cañoneros helped construct the Monastery of Christ of the Desert built by the Dominican Order about thirty miles northwest. Some work seasonally for the forest service out of Coyote. At least one man has worked in a mine near Gallina, about forty miles away. Duke City

Lumber Company is sometimes cutting near enough so that Cañoneros can return home at night.

During our ethnographic present, wages ranged from about $1.60 per hour for jobs in the forest service up to $3 and $4.50 for construction jobs in Denver. Total earned income for 1966 for four men whose income tax forms Kutsche helped fill out was respectively $1,492.50, $1,722.41, $2,915.53, and $4,095.00. Two of these men were heads of good-sized families. Jobs paid monthly, for instance those at the teacher aid or janitor level in the school system, pay much less. So do purely local jobs. One man working for an Anglo on property at the upper end of Cañones Canyon was paid $6 per day, and that figure was generally considered a fair wage. Another, working on a ranch nearby, was paid $50 per month, considered very low.

Almost all Cañones families are absolutely dependent on wage labor or welfare, or both, to provide the cash they need to make it through the year. Here lies an irony that will bite harder in the future than it does now. In our ethnographic present, one must drive a great deal to find a job, and a great deal to get to it. Gasoline is still cheap—30¢ to 50¢ per gallon. How much more expensive it can become before it no longer pays a wage worker to maintain his home base in Cañones no one knows. A similar price rise is probably in store for propane and butane, and possibly for electricity. The survival of Hispanic cultural patterns in Cañones has become in part dependent upon high energy and the most sophisticated industrial technology.

Keeping in mind the above wage and total income figures, it is easy to see how important the school budget looms for the Jemez Mountain district, including Cañones. In many northern districts that figure is larger than all other sources of income put together. Jemez Mountain has two gas companies (Southern Union and El Paso), whose payrolls may rival the school figure. Here are sample school salaries for 1966–67: superintendent, $10,000; principal, $8,400; guidance counselor, $8,600; teachers average $6,616; the uncertified teacher in Cañones, $4,044. [Figures supplied by Harry Wugalter, chief of New Mexico public school finance.] One Cañonero is a teacher. No one else in the village has a school job at a level higher than teacher's aide. Jobs in schools are fought for with tooth and nail, and are closely connected with politics. So far, Cañones has not won these fights.

Since Cañones is too far from sources of wage labor for its men to commute easily, and since it has not learned enough of the political ropes to compete successfully for school jobs, it depends heavily on welfare. Attempts to start cooperative enterprises—growing cucumbers for pickles, and making highway stakes—failed for want of outside support.

Welfare

Several public assistance programs serve the people of Cañones. Twelve households receive welfare checks for old age assistance, aid to families with dependent children, aid to the disabled, or general assistance, in amounts ranging from $37 to $157 per month. Total income to the village from this source for January, 1967: $1,057.

Some Cañoneros temporarily out of work receive unemployment compensation. Figures are not available for the entire community, but one young man had received $36 per week for a number of weeks. The Home Education Livelihood Program (HELP) employs six men in Coyote at $1 per hour, offering training in very simple carpentry. Since their pay does not include any gasoline allowance, the men formed a car pool to commute. A few elderly people receive social security, probably in small amounts since a large proportion of the jobs they had had are beyond the protection of the social security laws.

The Department of Public Welfare of New Mexico also provides medical care on a contract basis for serious illness, crippled children's services, and, occasionally, house repair assistance for a welfare client. It offers some vocational instruction, but no Cañonero is a student. [The foregoing information was provided partly by, partly at the direction of, John G. Jasper, Director, New Mexico Department of Public Welfare.]

Food stamp aid has become important to Cañones. Most families look to it to one degree or another. The amount of aid depends on family size and ability to pay, and therefore varies widely. One family purchases $90 worth of stamps for $16, another purchases $70 worth for $3.

There is a fair amount of political interference in the delivery of welfare, but evidently less since John Jasper became state director. One Rio Arriba county political boss was reported to have got hold of welfare checks over a considerable period of time and distributed them personally, with a cheerful (but incorrect) reminder, "You know where this is coming from."

During the school fight of 1966, some politicians threatened to cut off welfare from the accused parents because they kept their children out of school. Whether the law would have supported such a threat to the well-being of quite young children, or to older children (who were not at issue in the case), is argued both ways. The threat did frighten several Cañones parents, however, for they are quite accustomed to large amounts of political interference in their relations with government.

Cañoneros have suffered from politicians' meddling into welfare all their lives, and resent it. They regard the public assistance they receive as rights of citizenship, not as handouts.

The Cañones View of Economics

The people who live with the statistics we have just reported have two quite different views of their economic positions, and will ascribe to either one, depending on the context.

"*Somos pobres,*" a Cañonero will say, sometimes sadly, sometimes flatly, in the matter-of-fact tone one might once have said, "*Somos mejicanos.*"

Cañoneros do not lack bathrooms, television, and new cars by choice, although their unwillingness to complain about these deficiencies may at first mislead a visitor into thinking that they are either indifferent or even happy about it. Understandably, the more a villager knows of the city and Anglo worlds, the more aware he is that Cañones is poor. Adolescents of both sexes are harshest about the lack of opportunity, economic and otherwise. "There's nothing to do here" and "Nothing ever happens here" are words to the same tune as the refrain "You can't earn a living here." (Young men are often quite ambivalent: they find working away from home exciting as well as lucrative, but sometimes a little frightening. Chapter 6 tells more about their view of their options.)

The other perspective was summed up by middle-aged Serafín Valdez in a *dicho:* "*La vida de la plaza es ganar ganar, gastar gastar. La vida de la placita es pobre, pero somos contentos*" (City life is earn earn, spend spend. Village life is poor, but we live in contentment). Serafín pokes good-humored fun at city people, including ethnographers, for hurrying after what they never quite catch, and for always wanting more. Other Cañoneros make similar statements: "*Aquí es muy pacifico.*" "*Aquí es tranquilo.*" "*Somos muy augustos en Cañones.*" (Here it is very peaceful. Here it is calm. We are very contented in Cañones.)

Fidencia Vialpando, an elderly woman forced by family illness to spend much time in Albuquerque away from her stout snug home in Cienaguitas surrounded by orchard, flowers, vegetables, and quiet, almost always replies to questions about her well-being with, "*No me gusta la plaza. Me gusta nada más* la placita (I don't like cities. I like only the village) [meaning in particular her native Cañones]." And Leonardo Velásquez, a young man leaving his new wife and baby at home while he found wage work away, complained. "*Es duro trabajar afuera* (It is a hardship to work away from home)."

Although the declarations of satisfaction with Cañones are placed in the context of making a living, they are not directly economic. Cañoneros know perfectly well that they have fewer material possessions than their relatives in Española, Santa Fe, or Albuquerque, whom they see frequently. They are proud, but not defensive, in preferring what they have.

The Ceremonial Fund

At the heart of economics and material culture are ways of surviving. But economics is not just about how to survive. It includes the cost of maintaining social organization according to the rules of society. Eric Wolf says of such costs:

> All social relations are surrounded by . . . ceremonial, and ceremonial must be paid for in labor, in goods, or in money. If men are to participate in social relations, therefore, they must also work to establish a fund against which these expenditures may be charged. We shall call this the *ceremonial fund* (1966:7).

Before we list the ceremonial demands of Cañones, we should distinguish between how high status is achieved and the expectations held of those who have achieved it. Although failure to meet expectations may be frowned upon, it does not affect status itself.

Land, particularly irrigable land, is the unambiguous status marker. Cattle and horses are also important, and, of course, depend largely on land holdings. Education is just beginning to become a way of achieving status, but to date it correlates closely with the amount of a household's land. Graduation from high school is at present the realistic goal of parents struggling on behalf of their children. This year a large party was given to celebrate the high school graduation of the son of a high status family. Parents are beginning to talk about sending their children to college. Those simple propositions established, let us consider what one must spend in money and energy to observe the symbolic forms.

Clothing for an adult male consists of a shirt with buttons, long trousers, and shoes for any time he is outside his own home; a woman must wear a skirt, usually with a blouse. For church services one must have somewhat better clothing, and women almost always wear one-piece dresses (head coverings are no longer required.) Church clothing is standard garb for funerals, but for weddings one must wear one's best. For higher status males, the best includes a coat and tie, usually with a white shirt. On these occasions, higher status women wear conservatively cut dresses made of material better than their everyday dresses. Members of wedding parties go all out for color and style, the women in long dresses they have made themselves, the men in rented tuxedos often in white or pastel. These standards of appropriate clothing are understood by everybody. But those who cannot afford them do not stay home on that account. They clean and iron what they have and attend; no eyebrows are raised.

Depending on the occasion, the Cañones menu varies within a fairly narrow range. Sunday dinner may add a chicken or a little more meat to the daily fares, and special tasties may come out of the tiendita sin dinero for guests, as Mrs. Krusnik reported above. On public occasions like the reception for Governor David Cargo and other state officials in June, 1967, the menu was exclusively Anglo. Wedding receptions also feature Anglo dishes. The hospitable offer of food to guests in the house is still a ceremonial necessity, but it is fading where casual passersby are concerned. The burden is so heavy at weddings that the cost, which includes both a feast and a dance, is often shared between the groom and the parents on both sides. At funerals the cost of food is still heavy. During Holy Week relatives from other places come in large numbers and must be fed. The rituals of the cofradía, however, are not in themselves costly.

The condition of one's house reflects status to a limited extent. Condition of inside walls—that is, whether they are freshly painted, or whether they are decorated with pictures or not—distinguishes high from low status households, as does the condition (but not so much the paint) of outside walls. Higher status houses usually have new linoleum on the floors, and lower status houses do not. The number and condition of appliances such as stove, refrigerator, washing machine, and, to a lesser extent, the quality of furniture also reflect status. Indoor plumbing has recently become a mark of status. The size of one's house, within wide limits, is not relevant. Privacy, in fact, is somewhat negatively viewed by Cañoneros. Village gossip about houses more often mentions the quality of housekeeping than the quality of house or fixtures.

Contributions to church are publicly announced by the Catholic priest, and are generally known within the Pentecostal church. Those with more means are expected to contribute more. Names of those who request a mass to be said for a particular purpose are recorded in the church newsletter. The cost of such requests is generally from five to ten dollars.

The need for cash in pocket is greater for the young and less for the old. That is fortunate, since the young find wage jobs more easily. Etiquette in the *cantina* requires a loose hand on the wallet, and all Cañones Catholic males drink. If a friend buys you a drink, you have no choice but to reciprocate. A group of youths in a car buy six-packs of beer in turn to drink on lonely roads. The courting young man also needs a car whose age, lines, horsepower, and appearance carry the same psychological freight they do for Anglo youths—and possibly a bit more, because of the caballero image we have already mentioned. A young man is expected by his peers to spend money on women; what elders expect of him is rather difficult to discern, as they seem to want him to sow his wild oats and to prepare for a solid future at the same time.

The ceremonial requirements for Cañoneros are, in short, very real, but much smaller in proportion to income than they are for Anglos. They center on maintaining one's dignity and the family's respect. Spending too much is worse than spending too little. In general, with the exception of land ownership, status markers are subtle and almost invisible in Cañones. An outsider, in fact, must live in the village for some time before he discovers any class structure at all, for on the surface every adult treats every other adult exactly equal, except to acknowledge differences of age and sex.

Figure 1. On the way to Cañones, with Cerro Pedernal in the background, 1970. Photo by John Van Ness.

Figure 2. The Cañones placita, looking west, 1969. Photo by George McCu

Facing page:

Figure 3. Cienaguitas, horses grazing, 1970. Photo by John Van Ness.

Figure 4. Cañones, the lower placita, 1969. Photo by George McCue.

Figure 5. The schoolhouse on La Cuchilla, 1969. Photo by George McCue.

Figure 6. Catholic church of San Miguel, 1981. Photo by Moana Kutsche.

Facing page:

Figure 7. Altar of San Miguel church, 1969. Photo by George McCue.

Figure 8. Altar of Pentecostal church, 1969. Photo by George McCue.

Figure 9. Catholic campo santo, 1969. Photo by George McCue.

Figure 10. Santo in a Cañones home, 1969. Photo by George McCue.

Figure 11. Veronica Veil for Good Friday procession, 1969. Photo by George McCue.

Figure 12. Elipio García with children Naomi and Elipito, c. 1975. Photo by Jeff Mosco, *The New Mexican.*

Figure 13. The board of La Academia Real: Orlinda Gallegos, Aquilino Serrano, Serafín Valdez, and Lorenzo Valdez, director, 1975. Photo by Natalie Owings.

Figure 14. Luz and Serafín Valdez, 1981. Photo by Moana Kutsche.

Figure 15. Orlinda and Dalio Gallegos, 1969. Photo by George McCue.

Figure 16. Don Francisco Lovato and granddaughters, Delfinita, Anita May, Fernandita, and Bonnie, 1969. Photo by George McCue.

Figure 17. Saquello and Francesquita Salazar, 1975. Photo by Natalie Owings.

Figure 18. (Above, right.) Fidencia Vialpando in her garden, with horno in background, 1969. Photo by George McCue.

Figure 19. (Below, right.) Atiliana Lovato, holding baby Agustín, with her grandmother Eduvigen Lovato, 1969. Photo by George McCue.

Figure 20. Vidal and Delfinio Velásquez, sons of Genaro, 1969. Photo by George McCue.

Figure 21. Tony Gallegos, son of Dalio, 1969. Photo by George McCue.

Figure 22. La Plebe tinkering with car: Emilio Lovato, Sabiñano Lovato, Jr., Nazario Salazar, Ricardo Vialpando, and Arturo Valdez, 1969. Photo by George McCue.

Figure 23. (Facing page.) "Vista Associates" poster. Elipio García, Facundo Valdez, and Pacomio Salazar confer about the community, 1966. VISTA Program.

Figure 26. Alfonso Aragón's trailer in his family's yard, 1981. Photo by Moana Kutsche.

Figure 27. (Above.) Old-style presa, Polvader Creek at left, acequia at right, 1981. Photo by Moana Kutsche.

Figure 28. (Left.) New-style presa at Los Ojitos, acequia at left, stream at right, 1981. Photo by Moana Kutsche.

Figure 29. El Proyecto community building, 1981. Photo by Moana Kutsche.

Figure 30. New mosque at Abiquiu, 1981—a sign of the future? Photo by Moana Kutsche.

Figure 31. Cañones calls on Governor Cargo, spring, 1967. From left to right: Tony Gallegos, Medardo Lovato, Elipio García, Orlinda Gallegos, Preciliana Salazar, Governor David Cargo, Rose Nava, Simodocea Lovato, and Saquello Salazar. Photo by Milo Photographer.

5
Social Institutions

Family

Although we have said as much as needs to be said about the household, we have not discussed family, a quite different matter. A family is a group of people who share social identity. If asked "Who are you?" the members of a single family will answer in nearly identical terms. The family is the unit of inheritance. It is that portion of society which bears the primary responsibility of handing down cultural style. It defines status.

In Cañones every household is part of a family, but every family is larger than a household, and families share fairly specific obligations that transcend household. The Spanish word *familia* is defined by different Cañoneros as broadly as the English word *family*. Sometimes it is defined as including only husband, wife, and children, that is, the nuclear family. Other times it includes married siblings who have established separate households. One Cañonera said her married brother was still *familia*, but that brother's married son was only *familiar* (very roughly, "some kind of a relative").

The effect of wage labor on family structure further clarifies the difference between family and household. Numerous members of every family have permanent residences in cities of the region, but they keep in close touch with home (usually a core household). The family thus becomes a network of kin radiating from the hub of the Cañones placita to Española, Santa Fe, Albuquerque, and as far away as Denver, Salt Lake City, and Los Angeles. Individuals travel along these networks, receiving and giving economic and emotional support to each other, pooling their resources of money and knowledge about the outside world (cf. Kutsche 1979:12). On ceremonial occasions (Christmas, Holy Week, weddings, and funerals) they gather at home, lodging in various family households.

Even in the village itself, the family is sometimes an economic unit larger than the household. Married brothers may work together, particularly if they have not split up their inheritance of irrigable land—if, for example, the total inheritance is small, they get along well, and it is reasonable to work the garden plot together. They may divide the produce, but their wives take their shares to their own kitchens to put up.

Children and grandchildren take care of or at least assist in caring for parents and grandparents who maintain separate households. Sometimes (but not as often as in the past) a grandchild is detailed to live with the grandparents. Examples in Cañones are Tony and Dennis Gallegos, high school students who from time to time work in the fields of Saquello Salazar, their mother's father, and take the major responsibility for his cattle during their summer pasturing in the national forest. Dolores Valdez, nine-year-old daughter of Serafín and Luz, lives about half the time with Grandma Rosita and Grandpa Juan Madrid, who raised Serafín and who live nearby on Serafín's land. She does small chores for them and to an extent is their eyes and ears, as one is nearly deaf and the other nearly blind.

And likewise, if illness or other catastrophe prevents parents from raising their children, the burden falls first on the grandparents, and then on any other relative who is able to rush to the breach. Local standards of responsibility insist that each family absorb its constituent households if they cannot function. Fidencia Vialpando, for example, has had to face a staggering toll of death and disability among her siblings and in-laws, as well as the death of her daughter. As a consequence, she has nursed and/or raised nephews, nieces, and grandchildren whose number is many times the number of her own children. Isabel García got a sympathetic response in a *junta* (business meeting) when he humorously protested against the possibility of having to raise his son Elipio's family if Elipio went to prison over the court battle.

The responsibility of sharing work within a family appears to be stronger than the sharing of money. It may be that public agencies have taken on this responsibility, especially with social security and old age pensions. Married sons are, however, likely to bring gifts to their elderly parents. The offer of electricity that Adelaida Lucero rejected because she preferred kerosene lamps was an offer to pay for the installation out of wages earned by her sons in Albuquerque and Denver.

Crops, especially fruit, are widely shared within the family and also outside kin lines, whether the recipients helped grow the produce or not. Households within the family may feel privileged to request sharing, but those outside may not.

As for family relations, husbands and wives are, in public, work partners. They rarely show affection for each other in front of the children, and almost never in front of outsiders. Munro Edmonson's detailed analysis of kinship in *Los Manitos* may be accurate for Cañones in most respects, but his remarks on sexual fidelity are only partially true here. Edmonson states, "The wife owes the husband absolute sexual fidelity. . . . The obligation is not, however, reciprocal, and a woman is expected to regard the peccadillos of her husband with tolerance" (Edmonson 1957:31–32). In Cañones, a wife owes her husband absolute fidelity, but he owes her (and his family and the community) something as well: discretion. He owes her the right to be respected by the community, the right to act as if she knows nothing about his unfaithfulness (and indeed she may not). Her position is illustrated clearly in Kutsche's notes of an interview with an ex-wife who had been publicly abandoned and was still very indignant:

> Gracia [name changed] was obviously very hurt indeed. She told me emphatically that Isidoro [name changed] had a good family, that he had no reason to throw it away.
>
> "I was a faithful wife to him. I had men friends, but I just talked to them like I'm talking to you now." And about Isidoro, "I knew he wouldn't be faithful to me if he was away from home alone. I wouldn't expect a man to be." But divorce, she said, is something entirely different.

> With a painful wry smile, she added, "I'm going to enjoy being single, don't think I won't." Her smile turned grim and she said, "I'm going to make difficulty for him. He isn't going to get off easy."
>
> I have had other hints, and this is the strongest evidence, that a Hispanic woman who has been publicly scorned and disrespected is a termagant, much to be feared.

By the same reasoning, a man is not obligated to bring all his cash home, nor even to inform his wife about his total income, but he is obligated to keep his family adequately fed, clothed and housed unless he is simply unable to do so. What he does with the surplus is his own affair, so long as he does it quietly. A woman who is seen in bars is severely censured by gossip. A man who is known to earn money but whose family is not taken care of is thought to be not quite a man. Others will happily drink with him, but they will not pay much attention to his counsel in discussing community affairs.

These relations will be explored further in chapter 7 in the discussion of *respeto de la casa*.

A grown man as father is the authority of his house. His children tend to show more fear than affection toward him. Mothers chide children and sometimes impatiently slap them, but less often seriously punish them. Fathers punish. An illustration is a teen-age girl hitch-hiking on U.S. 84 with a girlfriend from another village, and who turned out to be the daughter of close friends of Kutsche's. (He is about equally close to her father and her mother.) When he let them out she had the friend run after him to say, "She says please don't tell her daddy."

Fathers are, in fact, slightly harsher with their sons than with their daughters. If a father wants to be a tyrant, there is no cultural role and no other kinship status that can stop him. Informants in more than one Cañones family have said, "The boys couldn't get away from home fast enough." The father-son relation is surely the weakest of primary kin ties. It may have been the strongest before the sons could expect to find wage labor away from home, for the only way for a son to support a wife and children was through obedience to his father, from whom he would have to inherit, unless he migrated to the frontier. But as the economic dependency is removed from that relationship, the hostility within comes to the surface. Of course, this relation, like all others, varies greatly with families and with individuals, and there are fathers and their married sons who enjoy warm close friendships.

Other things being equal, a father carries more weight in the community than a man who is not a father. One might almost look at him as representing his constituency (his wife and children) to the community.

A grandfather's position on a continuum from authority to affection depends upon whether he still controls the family's land or has given up his control to his children. If the former, he is still more father than grandfather. If the latter, he may indulge his grandchildren, play with them, spoil them. He may treat his sons more nearly as equal grown males, if indeed they are independent of him, or he may well defer to them if he is dependent. Power and authority, in short, are the keys to the way in which an adult male treats and is treated by others in his family.

A Cañones mother is a more complex phenomenon. She is a drudge who feels trapped to the needs of her family and the whims of her husband. She will advise any young woman "Don't get married," or at least "Put it off long enough to enjoy your youth. Be free while you can." She is a prisoner of her house, who feels entirely free to visit only her close relatives, and should have some specific reason to visit elsewhere unless accompanied by her husband. At the same time, she is recognized as the heart, and—so to speak—a part of the head, of the household.

The appearance of the interior of her house, and of at least its outer walls, are her responsibility, as is the quality of the meals served within. In addition, the appearance of her children reflects upon her, as does the demeanor of her daughters and of her very young sons. How the family spends its money is a decision in which she has a great deal of influence, even though the final decision belongs to her husband.

Her relations with her children tend to be warmer than a father's relations are. Recollections by children of their parents almost invariably dwell on the warm, giving, self-sacrificing mother who somehow even in hardship fed her family well and always had a clean shirt for her son every day for school. (This was almost never literally true, but men's memories of their mothers seldom are.) At times she protects her children against judgment by the father by not reporting minor infractions. She is expected to have the major voice in the upbringing of daughters.

As grandmother she still feels herself a drudge, but she is somewhat less subject to the whims of her husband. She will care for grandchildren occasionally even if she does not have their care permanently. The diminutive terms *abuelito* and *abuelita* are more often used for grandparents than the root terms *abuelo* and *abuela*, indications that both categories are regarded with special affection. (*Mamacita*, "little mother," is not used in Cañones.)

Women do a good deal more than men in maintaining the closeness of the extended family and of friendly nonkin ties. It is usually they who take the lead in visiting between houses in Cañones and between relatives who live in other places. Men alone are more likely to pay calls for business. Women pay calls, taking their husbands and sometimes their children, for the sole purpose of sociability and sharing news. Meals are very often shared among kin (less often among nonkin) during these visits. The visiting circuit extends frequently to Santa Fe and Albuquerque, occasionally to Denver, Salt Lake City, or California, and includes the most conservative and elderly Cañoneros. Bernardita Salazar made such a visit to Salt Lake City in her mid-eighties to see her infant great-great-granddaughter. "*Muy pocos alcanzan* (Few attain [that status])," she said afterwards proudly and with elegant economy.

Brothers, indeed siblings of both sexes, are very close so long as they are still in the parental household. Brothers remain close emotionally if they remain close geographically, but drift apart otherwise. They often live together in large cities at work, one making a bridgehead, the others following. The oldest son is head of the family in his father's absence, and is given the form of this role by his mother even if he may be too young to assume its substance. It is he who will represent the family to a stranger. He gives orders to his younger brothers and sisters, who usually obey without question. All of the brothers are responsible for the reputation of all of their sisters, as of course the father is.

Sisters tend to retain their close ties longer. Among women in the family, regardless of generation, there is a certain clinging together of those without power. A great deal of information and opinion is shared between female relatives over a second and third cup of morning coffee after the men have left for work. A great deal of mutual commiseration over their lot in life creates their solidarity at the same time. As mothers of small children, women may be strict; but as mothers of grown daughters they reveal more of themselves, and as adult sisters more yet. In general, the ties between siblings are stronger than any others.

For approximately the past two generations, marriage has been governed by the desires of the *novios* (sweethearts, or fiancés). As recently as the generation of the grandparents of people now in early adulthood, families chose spouses for their children. There appears at present to be a fairly strong tendency for children of families with land to marry into families with land. The rather sharp dichotomy between the haves and the have-nots shown in the statistics on land and livestock ownership will probably become sharper in the future, for with few exceptions those who leave Cañones into skilled labor or professions also come from the families with property, while those from families without land become unskilled more or less casual laborers. So, go or stay, the gulf is growing deeper.

Inheritance is supposed to provide equal shares to all children without regard to sex or age. In Cañones this rule is usually but not always observed. In a few cases the lion's share or all has gone to a favorite child. Resentment follows but litigation does not. The non-inheriting sons usually leave, unless they have the means to buy land. The daughters will, it is hoped, marry landowners. There is no strong tendency for the inheriting child to be of one sex or the other, so far as our data go.

That Cañones does not follow the regional rule has one excellent result: irrigable land is not divided into strips and half strips and quarter strips from ditch to river so thin that they are unusable. Villages between I-25 and Villanueva on the Pecos River show a long succession of such "strips of jerky." Farm and garden plots in Cañones are often small, but they have never reached such a ridiculous extreme.

Ideally, not only land but also houses are divided equally. A child would, according to this rule, inherit a specific room or rooms in the house. The gallery house referred to in the previous chapter might contain a succession of apartments, each owned by a different married sibling. A curious difficulty of translation between English and Spanish turns on this custom. Marcelino Sandoval and Kutsche were resting from work repairing a house one day and exchanging information about families. Kutsche told him that, as one of four brothers, he had inherited a fourth interest (*un cuarto*) in a house after his parents died. "*Cual cuarto?* (Which room?)," asked Marcelino. (*Fourth* and *room* are the same word in Spanish.) In working out the translation, they learned the difference in the inheritance patterns of their two cultures. Some of the houses with common walls in the placita are probably the result of this pattern having been followed in the past, but it does not appear to be followed at present—particularly since the addition of running water inside houses differentiates the use of rooms, so a house is not so divisible as formerly.

One part of the traditional inheritance rule is followed rigidly: inheritance is always lineal, never lateral. If there is an exception, it is when a childless couple have taken a *criado* (one to be raised; sometimes "servant") who may be nephew or niece, raise him or her as their own child, and pass property to that individual. Since this process is adoption in every respect except the legal papers, it does not constitute a real exception.

Other relatives beyond the nuclear family and its lineal extensions are still of importance. Their names and the behavior associated with them are clearly spelled out by Edmonson (1957:27–33); differences in Cañones are slight. First cousins should be mentioned, because they are singled out by terms—*primo(a) hermano(a)*. The term indicates closeness, but is used to denote any first cousin, whether one happens to be on close terms with that individual or not. Other cousins can be distinguished as *segundo*, and so on, but seldom are.

Aunts and uncles are accorded a good deal of respect, probably because they are siblings, and, in a sense, equivalents of mother and father.

Godparents in the Catholic church are more often than not fairly close relatives. This appears to be the pattern in New Mexico (cf. Swadesh 1974:189–92). We do not have statistics for Cañones. They are chosen seriously for three occasions—baptism, confirmation, and marriage. Choosing them is also a warm ritual for the twenty-fifth wedding anniversary, when it is customary to ask the youngest son to be *padrino* and the oldest grand-daughter to be *madrina*. The wedding vows are renewed both at the twenty-fifth and at the fiftieth anniversary. Godparents and the parents of the godchild become coparents (*compadres*), and this relation rivals that between the godparents and their godchildren for closeness. This term, like other relationship terms, is always used in reference. We have even heard the extreme, "*Mi compadre Ignacio* [name changed] *es mal hombre* (My coparent Ignacio is a bad man)." Both sets of parents of a married couple also call each other compadres.

The formal obligations of compadrazgo is an area that the field team explored impressionistically rather than systematically. Padrinos of baptism and confirmation are responsible to the Church for the spiritual education of the *ahijado(a)* (godchild). There has been an ideal that if the parents of an ahijado die or become incapacitated, the padrinos raise the child. No informant could give an example of their doing so; in fact, relatives (particularly parents or siblings of the deceased) take that responsibility. *Padrinos de casorio* (of marriage) are expected to be marriage counselors to the married couple and take this responsibility seriously. *Ahijados de casorio* may be called upon by their padrinos for short-term volunteer labor, and vice versa, very much as relatives call upon each other.

Compadre, like *primo,* is a term sometimes extended to nonrelatives, as a pleasant fiction. Here is an example of one fiction made fact: when Leonardo Velásquez was a small boy, he used to enjoy visiting Simón Vigil, already in his fifties, his neighbor in Cienaguitas. For fun they started calling each other compadre. In fact, they were no relation whatever. When Leonardo married and his first child arrived, he visited Simón again, and proposed, "*Vamos a ser compadres de veras* (Let us become real compadres) [that is, will you be *padrino de bautismo* to my baby girl?]." The invitation was joyfully accepted.

Friendship between compadres dies hard—perhaps not at all. Men and women who become compadres when all were Catholic still address and refer to each other as compadre even though some have converted to non-Catholic churches. Others are very careful to volunteer no criticism of a relative of a compadre in the presence of one standing in such a relation. Thus it is necessary to know the relationship of everyone in the village to carry on a polite conversation.

In summary, the family, and the quasi family of compadres, are both strong in Cañones. Family relations are virtually unbreakable, even though relatives may not personally like each other. But it would be an unwarranted exaggeration to say that the family is the only strong organization of society in the area. Arthur Rubel's statement about South Texas has frequently been misapplied to New Mexico: "The strength with which a person is bound to his family so overshadows all other bonds in importance that it contributes to the atomistic nature of the neighborhood" (Rubel 1966:55). Cañones and northern New Mexican Hispanic society in general are not atomistic, and the family does not overshadow identity gained in the church, in the community, and as an individual. If the family *were* the only important institution in Cañones, it might have been impossible for the community to unite for any kind of action, given the dichotomy of property, the (sometimes latent) hostility between fathers and sons, marriage along class and property lines, and the inequity of inheritance.

Religion

Before the 1930s, a description of religion in Cañones would logically have been labelled "The Church." Since that time the Asamblea de Dios, a Pentecostal group, has been increasing in the Jemez Mountain region (Johnson 1937), and today among the thirty households in Cañones, twenty-three are Catholic, five are Pentecostal, and one is split with the parents Catholic and the children Pentecostal. One family belongs to the Evangelical United Brethren, whose church is in Hernández (a suburb of Española), and twice a month the preacher comes to their home to hold services.

Roman Catholics

Cañones is one of eight churches within the Parish of Santo Tomás, headquartered in Abiquiu. The priest manages somehow to say mass at least once a week in each church and also to perform weddings, funerals, and baptisms. The priest in 1967, Father Robert Kirsch, was assigned this parish during the period of fieldwork. He says his instruction from the archbishop was to try to counteract the influence of Reies Lópes Tijerina's Alianza Federal de Mercedes. He was a U.S. Air Force pilot during World War II, continues in the Reserve, and flies his own airplane from a landing strip near Abiquiu on church business. (Costs of the plane are borne by private donors outside the parish.) He is of Irish and German extraction, raised in Brooklyn, and speaks Spanish well enough to conduct mass in Spanish, including a good part of the sermon. He is a hail-fellow extrovert.

Participation in Roman Catholic activities by parishioners consists above all in attending mass and other services. May, June, and Lent are the intense times of the year. In May, "the month of Mary," and in June, that of the Sacred Heart, rosary is held every day—the responsibility of women of the church. During Lent, starting with Ash Wednesday, the stations of the cross are celebrated every Friday by members of the cofradía. Services are held every day during Holy Week, culminating in a full and dramatic enactment on Good Friday of the stations of the cross from the church building to the campo santo.

Two couples are *mayor domos* of the church each year, their terms beginning and ending in late September at the Fiesta de San Miguel, patron saint of Cañones. Mayor domos are chosen by the priest, and their duties are to take care of the church building. Those who are able make gifts of new fittings for the church, including new garments for the images of San Miguel or of the Santo Niño de Atocha close to the altar. Upon turning over their charge to their successors, the mayor domos collect offerings from members and friends of the parish. Names and amounts are read by the priest during mass. The number of donations that mayor domos can inspire is a tribute to their prestige, although the individual amounts, mostly $1 and $2, are seldom over $5. Mayor domos will draw upon their ties of kinship and compadrazgo for this purpose.

Boys of roughly eight or ten years of age serve as altar boys, and are often asked immediately before mass to serve. Usually they wear no distinctive vestments.

In the public activities of the Catholic church parishioners play passive roles. Mayor domos, altar boys, and the occasional guitarists and singers who lead the music are all chosen by the priest. The style of the mass and of other services performed by the priest are determined by him or by the hierarchy of the archdiocese. Private devotions are optional, and performed by some communicants, not by others.

Private religious behavior, as opposed to religious institutions, is pervasive in the village. "*Buenos días, le dé Dios*" (May God give you a good day), is a common greeting which is somewhat more common before mass than on other days. "I'll see you next week, *si quiera Dios*" (God willing). "*Ojalá!*" (Literally, Allah willing; an interjection followed by the subjunctive, roughly translatable as "I sure hope so." Obviously derived from the Islamic occupation of Spain.) "*Ay por Dios!*" "*Jesús!*" or "*Jesús María!*" (Good Lord! Oh my God!) Daily speech is punctuated by religious reminders. To some, of course, they are empty forms. To others they serve to keep religion conscious.

Private petitions and promises are made with some frequency to particular saints. We have not been able to confirm in Cañones the frequently quoted statement that the statue of a saint is turned to face the wall if the petition is not granted. Pilgrimages to the Santuario de Chimayó, about fifty miles east of Cañones, do take place, always in relation to particular circumstances, such as the safe return of a soldier from war. (See Borhegyi 1956 for description of the Santuario and its healing mud.) These journeys may involve self-imposed hardships: some pilgrims walk the whole way.

Before children leave home for long absences, parents bless them. The child kneels in front of the parent, who gives the *bendición* with hand on the child's head. (This custom will be described in more detail in chapter 6.)

The Cofradía de Nuestro Padre Jesús Nazareno, commonly called the *Penitentes* by Cañoneros as well as by others, has its morada (chapter house) a little removed from the placita. Eight men of the community are members of this chapter, plus a number of men who now reside elsewhere. The principal function of this Roman Catholic confraternity is to lead Cañones in celebrating the Passion and death of Christ each Lent. They do not celebrate the Resurrection. It is the hermanos and not the priest who conduct the *estaciones* (stations of the cross) each week during Lent, and the various services during Holy Week. Neither priest nor any other official of the Catholic church is present at any of these Lenten events. But the community is present en masse, including those who may be rather lax about attendance at mass at other times. For the estaciones on Good Friday, relatives return so that for a few hours the population of the village is more than doubled. Governor Cargo and his family attended in 1967—a participation that was appreciated by the village as a mark of respect as well as interest.

The cofradía make one other major contribution to Catholic religious services. At the death of a member of the chapter or of someone in a member's family, the hermanos conduct the *rosario* (rosary) and the *velorio* (wake). (The priest is usually not present for the rosario because of his heavy schedule.) Officially, it is the hermanos who dig the grave, although in practice this is usually done by younger men. The hermanos also cooperate with the priest in conducting the funeral mass itself, singing *alabados* in procession from morada to church, then from the church to campo santo.

A few women, whether wives of hermanos or not, assist the chapter by providing food when the hermanos have secluded themselves in the morada and by cleaning the building.

The cofradía is, also, a mutual benefit organization, helping the ill or the unfortunate with money or household chores when needed. In some other Hispanic villages are other cofradías—for instance, the *Esclavos de Santiago* and the *Cofradía de San José* in Mora. But the penitential cofradía is the only one popularly known, and it has the most local chapters.

Most of the extensive literature on the cofradía is garbage. But good and accurate descriptions of the organization and its services have been written by Woodward (1935) and Weigle (1976a). Swadesh (1974) describes the social functions of cofradías in the Chama and San Juan Valleys during the nineteenth century, and Kutsche and Gallegos (1979) summarize these functions for the late twentieth century.

Hermanos in the Cañones chapter have asked us not to describe ceremonial details nor the structure of the organization. While the services are open to the public, nevertheless hermanos have suffered so much from sensational publicity that they feel the less said in print the better.

In spite of the fact that the hermanos and others in the community prefer that cofradía business not be shared with outsiders, there is no air of secrecy nor undue solemnity within Cañones. It is even permissible to joke a bit. For instance, in early spring 1967, Isabel Salazar, his son Napoleón, José Vialpando (Catholic and hermano), and Kutsche were cleaning out the acequia that runs above the morada toward the Salazar property. We had stopped to rest. Medardo Lovato, a Pentecostal and former Catholic, was burning off his hay field between the Salazar house and the morada. A breeze was carrying the fire toward the morada, though there was obviously no danger at all to the building. José jumped up, pretending to be very agitated, waved his arms about and shouted to Medardo, "*No queme mi casa! No queme mi casa!* (Don't burn my house)."

Everyone, including Medardo, was convulsed with laughter.

Exactly how most Catholics in Cañones view the official Catholic church now, is a matter that we did not inquire into, and that certainly varies greatly by family and by individual. It is a matter of record, however, that during the Mexican period all of New Mexico had fewer than twenty priests (Swadesh 1974:74, quoting Carroll and Haggard). In the late eighteenth century, when the Cañones area was settled, there were not many more. At times one of those few priests resided at Abiquiu, but at other times that settlement was evacuated in the face of Indian pressure. Communities on the frontier felt abandoned by a Church whose nearest bishop was in Durango, Mexico. So, in effect, for many decades the cofradía provided the only religious activities, structure, and consolation for many villages.

In the nineteenth century, the first Bishop of New Mexico, Jean Baptiste Lamy, was a French cleric directed by the Pope to end what the Vatican regarded as abuses and heresies. Villagers resented being told that the initiative their own citizens had taken to keep Christianity alive was heretical. And to this day the cofradía, its members, and its services are in a number of respects closer to religious practice and belief in northern New Mexico than the Church is.

Since 1947, the archdiocese and the brotherhood have had officially friendly relations. Their concord has improved since then, and now regional representatives meet yearly under the patronage of the archbishop.

Pentecostals

The Asamblea de Dios church is a Pentecostal sect known informally by the Catholic majority as "Los Aleluias," from their practice of congregational shouts of "Amen!" "Aleluia!" etc. It was brought into the Jemez region in the 1930s by Isaaque Morfín of Arroyo de Agua, who had been converted while a sheepherder in Utah. Johnson (1937) describes how Morfín spread the new faith in the region. Johnson's account is badly biased, but its skeletal facts have been confirmed by Morfín's son-in-law, Ubaldo Velásquez of Youngsville.

The six Pentecostal families of Cañones have taken over the former schoolhouse in the center of the lower placita and conduct weekly services there. Kutsche attended their services once, other members of the field team not at all. The following description of their structure was provided by Elipio García, a deacon of the church.

Each congregation chooses its own preacher, called a pastor, by vote of the membership. He is supported by donations from each member of 10 percent of his earnings. (During the start of the Cañones church, the congregation shared a pastor with another church, but now supports its own.) The Cañones congregation has three deacons and two deaconnesses. In addition to donating 10 percent of their income to support the pastor, the congregation collects for missionaries to other parts of the United States and to Latin America, for the church school, and for youth officials in the district.

Beyond the congregation level is the Latin American Council District, covering New Mexico, Utah, Colorado, Montana, Wyoming, and part of Texas. District officials are superintendent, vice-superintendent, secretary, treasurer, and five representatives from the territory at large. These officials make up the council board of directors. Officials are elected for two-year terms by vote of local congregations. Each congregation sends its pastor plus one representative to a general meeting, and both vote. The council maintains a Bible school in El Paso, Texas. Council headquarters is in Albuquerque.

The relation of member to structure is, then, radically different between the Asamblea de Dios and the Catholic churches. Power flows down for the Catholics, up for the Pentecostals.

All of the Pentecostal families, plus the one belonging to the Evangelical United Brethren church, were formerly Catholics. Three of those heads of household were members of the cofradía, and therefore were more than nominal Catholics. Why did they convert? They frame their answers to this question in terms of the Holy Spirit: *here* is the Word of God, not in the Catholic church.

Social scientists tend to correlate conversion to Protestant sects with upward social mobility and/or Anglicization (e.g., González 1969:77; Madsen 1964:62–63). Swadesh states that Roman persecution of Penitentes drove many Catholics into Presbyterianism, at least during the nineteenth century (1974:77). Cañones supports these generalizations only to a limited extent. The seven non-Catholic or partly non-Catholic households tend toward the upper end of the economic continuum, but are not among the wealthiest familes. All but two have land. All but three have cattle. All seven preserve impressive amounts of produce each year. Only one is among the twelve families receiving welfare, and that is old age assistance. The economic interpretation has merit, therefore, but leaves something to be explained.

Cañoneros themselves make a distinction between "*Aleluias*" (Asamblea de Dios) and "*Protestantes*" (Presbyterians and other sects; E.U.B. is Protestant). "*Aquel hombre es Protestante?*" "*No. Es Aleluia*" (That man is Protestant? No. He is Aleluia.) Protestants are relatively mild in their religious behavior and moderate in their social restrictions, while Aleluias shout during services, and forbid drinking and dancing, favorite Hispanic leisure activities. (There are suggestions in theological literature that Pentecostal beliefs are closer to some tendencies in radical Roman tradition than either is to the Protestant tradition stemming from Martin Luther and John Calvin. That line of inquiry will be left to scholars better equipped to pursue it.)

We have already implied, in the section on family, that Pentecostals and Catholics get along well together. There is not the slightest evidence of factionalism along religious lines. Indeed, close friendships cross them. It is a common event for Simón Vigil and Fidencia Vialpando, devout Catholics, to chat with Norman and Manuelita Lovato, nonaffiliated and Pentecostal respectively, before mass. When the bell rings, they quietly separate without embarrassment. Moreover, as further illustration, when Fidencia's flower garden suffered from a hailstorm just before the Fiesta de San Miguel, when she was mayor domo, the Catholic church was decorated largely from Manuelita's garden. No one thought this particularly remarkable. In complementary fashion, Pentecostals go to their church building a few yards away from the Catholic building at their own stated times, equally without comment. Small Catholic children may make fun of the sounds coming from the building, but not to the faces of Pentecostals.

When the Pentecostals put on a children's religious play, the entire community was invited and virtually everyone attended. Nevertheless, at the moment when an individual or a family leaves the Roman Catholic church to join the Asamblea de Dios, an observer might think the village was coming apart. The event is regarded as scandalous by Catholics, especially if the individual had been an hermano, and it is talked about for an extended period of time. Once the furor has died down, however, relations return to normal, religion is simply not discussed with the convert by members of the other denomination, and he resumes his friendships and enmities as usual. In this and in other contexts, New Mexican Hispanos are notable for their ability to accept the world as it is and adjust to it. (A description of religious aspects of the life histories of Catholics and Pentecostals is included in chapter 6.)

Acequias

Of all the social and economic institutions in traditional Hispanic villages, the organization of resources for getting water from stream to field best demonstrates how villagers are accustomed to work closely together in order to live. For without cooperation there would be no irrigation, and without irrigation in such a dry climate there would be no cultivated crops for people or for livestock.

The Hispanos brought with them to New Mexico a constellation of arid land techniques, including both the technology and institutional framework for the orderly distribution of water. This cultural system shared the suppositions common to all Spanish irrigation systems, as follows:

1. Water rights accompany the land, but they are seldom specified in deeds.
2. All irrigators receive water in proportion to the amount of land they irrigate.
3. New ditches may not be constructed above the ditches of those who have prior rights to the water.
4. Each user is responsible for maintenance costs of the acequia system in proportion to the amount of water he uses.
5. The administration of the irrigation system is entrusted to those who know local custom—usually the irrigators themselves.

These principles were embodied in codified Spanish and colonial civil law; however, codified law functioned more to settle serious disputes than actually to arrange water distribution, which was guided by local custom (Van Ness 1979:266–67).

The acequia system in Cañones is complex because of the complex topography of the two small valleys (see maps 5 and 6). A total of twenty-four acequias serve its fields (see list of acequias). Seventeen of them serve fields in the valley of Cañones Creek, of which thirteen derive from *presas* (diversion dams) on the creek itself, three from springs, and one from Chihuahueños Creek. The valley

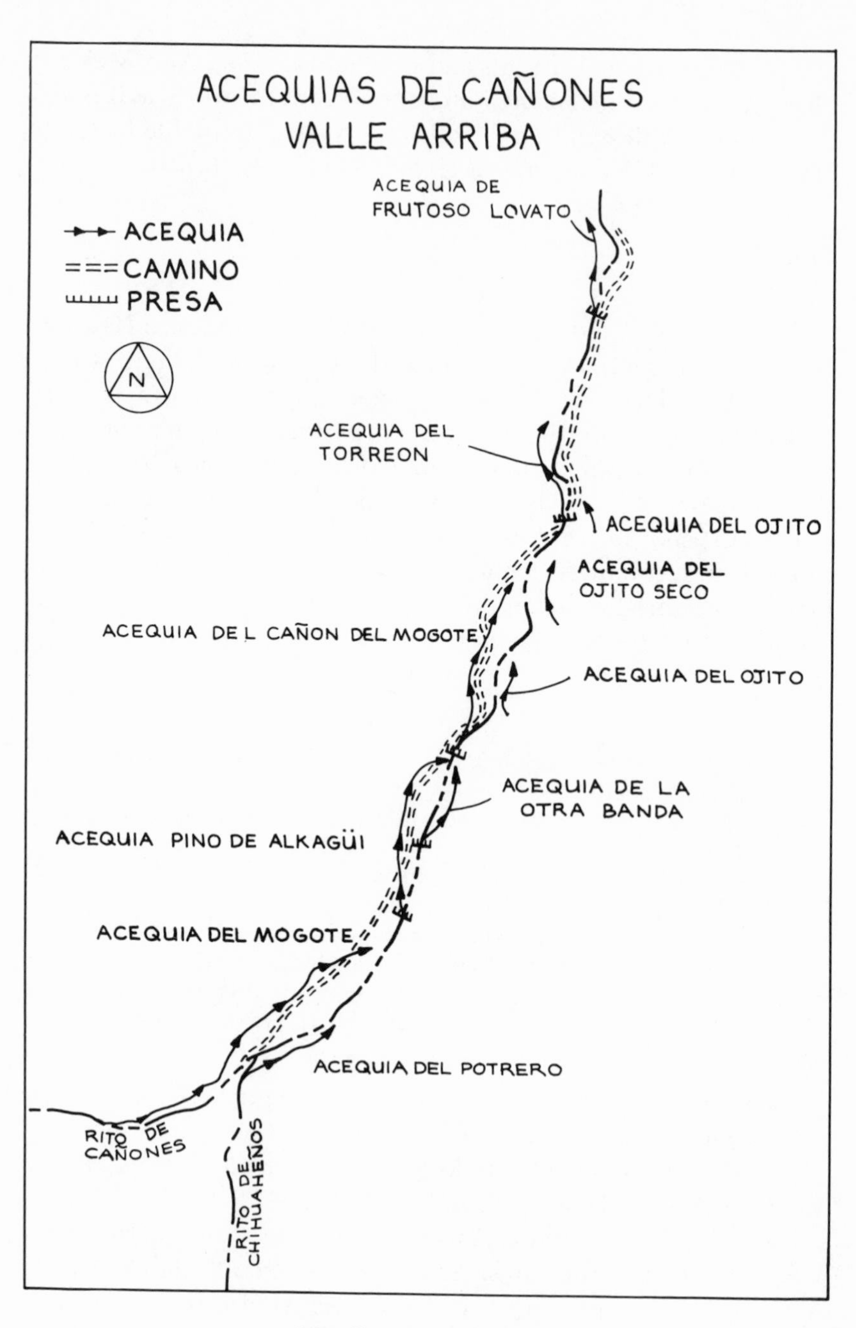

Map 5. Upper Acequias

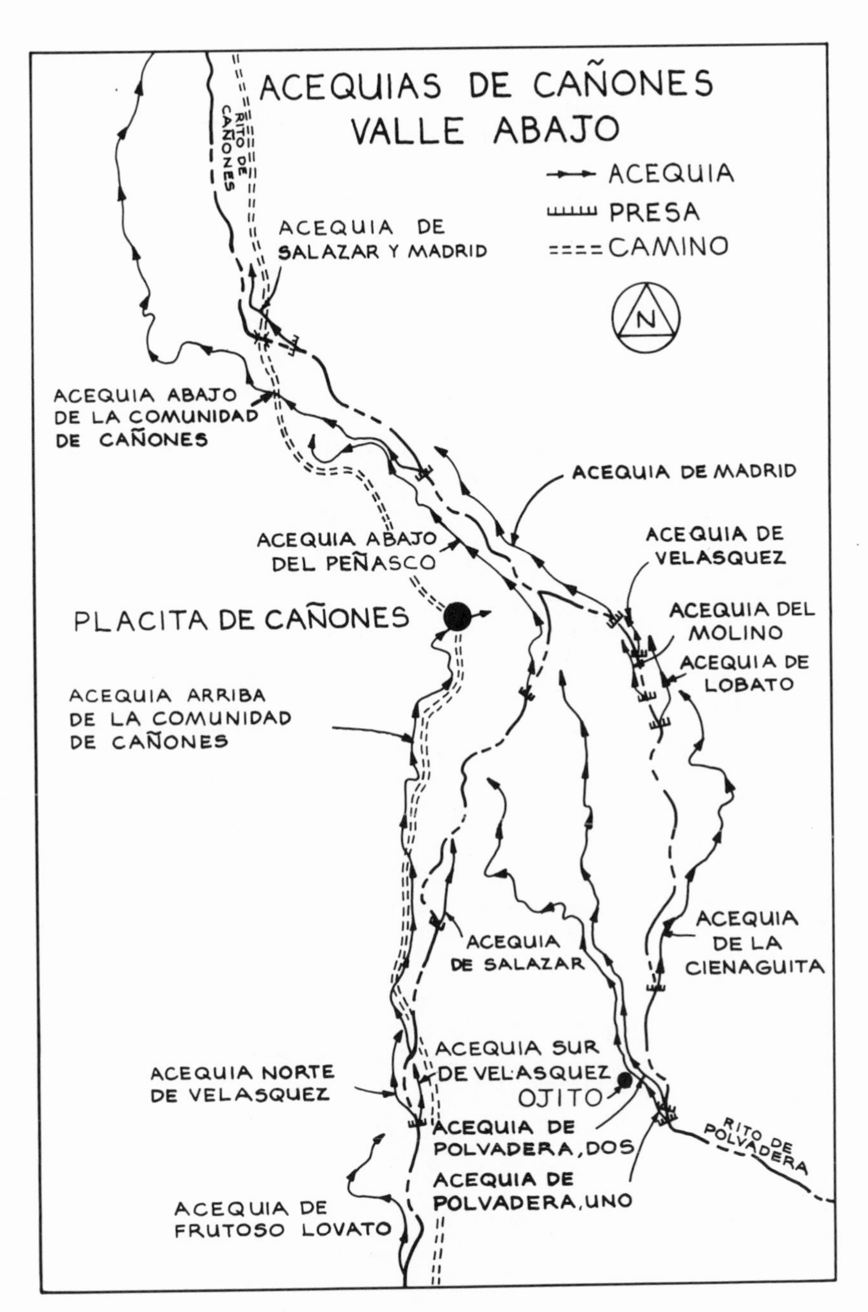

Map 6. Lower Acequias

Acequia 1	• Salazar and Madrid Ditch —diverts from east bank of Cañones Creek —0.3 miles in length —serves 2 tracts (totaling 1.4 acres)
Acequia 2	• Lower Cañones Community Ditch —diverts from west bank of Cañones Creek —2.0 miles in length —serves 13 tracts (totaling 106.1 acres)
Acequia 3	• Abajo el Peñasco Ditch —diverts from west bank of Cañones Creek —1.3 miles in length —serves 5 tracts (totaling 9.1 acres)
Acequia 4	• Salazar Ditch —diverts from east bank of Cañones Creek —0.3 miles in length —serves 1 tract (total 2.4 acres)
Acequia 5	• Upper Cañones Community Ditch —diverts from west bank of Cañones Creek —1.6 miles in length —serves 29 tracts (totaling 57.68 acres)
Acequia 6	• South Velasquez Ditch —diverts from east bank of Cañones Creek —0.3 miles in length —serves 2 tracts (totaling 2.15 acres)
Acequia 7	• North Velasquez Ditch —diverts from west bank of Cañones Creek —0.3 miles in length —serves 1 tract (total 4.2 acres)
Acequia 8	• Frutoso Lovato Ditch —diverts from west bank of Cañones Creek —0.5 miles in length —serves 4 tracts (totaling 15.04 acres)
Acequia 9	• Torreon Ditch —diverts from west bank of Cañones Creek —0.7 miles in length —serves 2 tracts (totaling 13.1 acres)
Acequia 10	• Ojo Spring Ditch —diverts from spring in upper Cañones Valley —0.4 miles in length —serves 1 tract (total 0.4 acres)
Acequia 11	• Seco Spring Ditch —diverts from spring in upper Cañones Valley —0.2 miles in length —serves 1 tract (total 5.2 acres)
Acequia 12	• Spring Ditch —diverts from spring in upper Cañones Valley —0.1 miles in length —serves 1 tract (total 1.2 acres)

Table 10. List of Acequias

Acequia 13	• Acequia del Cañon del Mogote —diverts from west bank of Cañones Creek —0.5 miles in length —serves 3 tracts (totaling 13.1 acres)
Acequia 14	• Acequia de la Otra Banda —diverts from east bank of Cañones Creek —0.2 miles in length —serves 1 tract (total 1.4 acres)
Acequia 15	• Acequia Pino de Alkagüi —diverts from west bank of Cañones Creek —0.5 miles in length —serves 2 tracts (totaling 8.7 acres)
Acequia 16	• Acequia del Potrero (abandoned for some years) —diverts from east bank of Chihuahueños Creek —0.5 miles in length —serves 2 tracts (totaling 7.5 acres)
Acequia 17	• Acequia del Mogote —diverts from north bank of Cañones Creek —0.8 miles in length —serves 2 tracts (totaling 7.5 acres)
Acequia 18	• Madrid Ditch —diverts from north bank of Polvadera Creek —0.7 miles in length —serves 2 tracts (totaling 5.3 acres)
Acequia 19	Velasquez Ditch —diverts from east bank of Polvadera Creek —0.1 miles in length —serves 1 tract (total 0.6 acres)
Acequia 20	• Acequia del Molino —diverts from west bank of Polvadera Creek —0.3 miles in length —serves 2 tracts (totaling 3.12 acres)
Acequia 21	• Lobato Ditch —diverts from east bank of Polvadera Creek —0.2 miles in length —serves 1 tract (total 2.2 acres)
Acequia 22	• Cienaguita Ditch —diverts from east bank of Polvadera Creek —1.1 miles in length —serves 4 tracts (totaling 18.69 acres)
Acequia 23	• Polvadera Ditch No. 2 —diverts from west bank of Polvadera Creek —1.4 miles in length —serves 5 tracts (totaling 17.7 acres)
Acequia 24	• Polvadera Ditch No. 1 —diverts from west bank of Polvadera Creek above no. 2 —1.5 miles in length —serves 9 tracts (totaling 20.12 acres)

Table 10. Acequias *(continued)*

of Polvadera Creek is served by seven acequias, all from presas on the creek. Fifteen of these twenty-four acequias irrigate more than one tract, land held usually by more than one owner. Owners on a single acequia may or may not be closely related, but it seems to make no difference in the smoothness of cooperation.

Some of the acequias formerly provided water to operate gristmills that ground wheat and other grains for farmers from Cañones, Abiquiu, and elsewhere; none is operating now. These *molinos* were communication centers as well as business places during the fall when growers waited their turns at the grinding stones. The Cañones irrigation system has never had any centralized administration. In fact, the first public record of the system was not created until 1974.

The users of a single acequia are called *parciantes* in northern New Mexico, a local variant of the Spanish *parcelante*. Parciantes of the larger acequias are organized with an elected *comisión* of three members, and a mayor domo similarly elected. The largest and best organized of the acequias in Cañones are number 5, the "Upper Cañones Community Ditch," and numbers 23 and 24, "Acequia de Polvadera." Rules for these larger associations are filed with the state engineer's office. Those for the Acequia de Polvadera list eight parciantes.

Water is plentiful, so there is no need to limit each of the eight parciantes to a specific day, except that two of them take out of the *acequia madre* (the mother ditch) close to the presa and are limited to Mondays in order not to deprive lower users. On this acequia each parciante benefits equally and must help equally to clean out the madre acequia and do whatever else the mayor domo designates; the parciante may do the work himself, send a worker (usually one of his sons), or pay $2 per hour so that the mayor domo can hire the work done. Lateral ditches are the responsibility of the individual. The mayor domo is reimbursed for his expenses and for whatever time he has to take away from his regular wage job to attend to acequia affairs. Changes in the rules are made by vote of all parciantes. Acequia rules have been codified by the State Planning Office into a kind of common law in *Las Acequias del Norte* (Lovato 1974).

The Upper Cañones Community Ditch has less water per parciante, and use is computed on a fifteen-day cycle. Each parciante enjoys from one-day to three-day rights, depending upon the acreage he irrigates, adding up to the fifteen. If a parciante fails to turn water onto his field when his turn comes, he cannot make up for it later, but must wait until his turn comes round again. Those with only kitchen gardens have half-day rights, and may take water at any time according to convenience. Because this acequia serves the placita, kitchen garden rights are especially important, and one third of the total water supply is supposed to be reserved for them. Days of water rights equal days of maintenance work obligation, day for day. Owners of kitchen gardens owe half a day of work.

Work parties, like work bees almost everywhere in the world, are fun—an occasion for horseplay and joking—and get a great deal of work done in a short time. Unlike work bees of larger scale, however, these are not accompanied by feasting or drinking, and there is no special term to designate them.

Not everyone follows the rules very well. People sometimes take water when they are not entitled to it, and once in a long while cut off others for spite, using water as a weapon although the real dispute may have nothing to do with water. But the allocation system works well, in part because there is plenty of water even in a dry year like 1967, when only 50 percent average flow was predicted for the Rio Grande Basin (U.S. Department of Agriculture 1967).

In sum, irrigation in Cañones is essentially a closed system under local customary control. Irrigation is and has always been an integral part of farming in Cañones. The system serves to integrate man, water, and land over time and space. That is to say, the system has clear-cut spatial as well as temporal dimensions. The spatial dimensions correspond to the geographical limits of the microbasin. These physical boundaries have always assured the community full control over its vital water supply.

The long-term operation of the irrigation system in Cañones attests to the tradition of mutual respect and cooperation in the village. Any notion such as Rubel's, quoted above, that Hispanic villagers do not readily, even unconsciously, work together in community organization broader than family ties, is incorrect, and ironic in its ignorance of one of the strongest and thickest threads in the fabric of Hispanic rural culture, both in Europe and in the New World.

Drinking Water Association

The town water supply is organized with a president and a secretary-treasurer elected by the users. Connection fee was low when the system was installed in 1961. User fee is $1 per month. There are no meters. At the moment Antonio Serrano is president, Pacomio Salazar is secretary-treasurer. The association has little coercive power, or chooses to exercise little power, and has not cut off delinquent members, even one who is said to have tapped the tank at the bottom to water his cattle, instead of taking them down to the rito like everyone else.

Cattle Owners' Association

At the direction of the U.S. Forest Service, all holders of permits to graze on specific forest allotments form associations. Most Cañoneros graze on the same allotment, but some men from other villages share it. The association discusses round-up and tagging time in spring, when a forest official tags all the cattle to be sent to graze on forest land, making sure each owner holds enough permits for his cows. The association is not in any way indigenous to the village.

School

Church and school are the only visible permanent institutions that focus much of the village's activities. The history of the local school was summarized in chapter 3, and school politics is the subject of chapter 8. This section will describe briefly how Cañones uses the institution and the building.

Title to the two-room cement block structure on La Cuchilla is held by the Jemez Mountain school district. Teachers are appointed by the district, and the curriculum is closely supervised by the state department of education. Instruction is officially in English, although in fact the teachers use Spanish when necessary to communicate with their pupils. The children are not taught to read or write Spanish, for bilingual instruction is still the hothouse flower of a "Demonstration Project" in the state department of instruction, with experiments running in two or three widely scattered schools.

The importance of school for one's children varies widely from family to family. In some, a small child who wants to play hooky need only invent some such excuse as "*me pegaron*" (they [perhaps older boys on the playground] hit me). On the other extreme, some families accept no excuses, keep their children faithfully in school and see that they do their homework. Students may leave school after the eighth grade or at sixteen years of age, whichever comes first. Table 5 indicates roughly that, although some Cañoneros do leave after the eighth grade, those who pass that milestone usually finish high school.

At least one of the teachers in the village school has been local—Wenceslao Salazar, son of Saquello and Francesquita. Most of the others have been regional Hispanos, and some were previously acquainted with people in Cañones. Teachers' aides and janitors are always local people; some of the bus drivers are also, including Elipio García and Jacobo Salazar, Jr.

The schoolhouse is used extensively by the community, with the board's permission. Juntas of various sorts are held there. Dances for all occasions take place there, whether it is the Fiesta de San Miguel in September, the Fiesta of the Santo Niño in January, a wedding dance, or an occasional dance to raise money for some cause. The location of the building, half a mile or so from the placita with no dwellings close by, has a certain advantage for parties, because the noise and the outdoor drinking that invariably accompany merrymaking are less likely to disturb anyone. Birthday parties that do not involve dancing, and baby showers, also are held at the school house. In fact it is the only public building that anyone may apply to use without regard to special restrictions such as churches regularly impose, and its adaptable space is considerably larger than any alternative.

Politics

Politics occupied a small part of Cañones life before the village aroused itself over the school issue, and that small part was almost entirely on the receiving end of political action. The village is a single bounded political entity—voting precinct 55 of Rio Arriba county—but has no other separate political existence. There is neither mayor nor council in the village, and it is a small part of the district for which one of the county commissioners is responsible.

Each political party does have a precinct committee. At the moment, Serafín Valdez is chairman of the Republican committee, Antonio Serrano of the Democratic. There are thirteen Republican households, fifteen Democratic households, one split between husband and wife, and one Independent. North central New Mexico was whole-heartedly Republican until the New Deal, and now generally votes Democrat. Ties of kinship and religion crosscut political affiliation at random, and the widely held belief that the cofradía is a single political unit does not apply.

Patrones and Peones

Both the popular and the scholarly literature on New Mexican Hispanos leads one to expect to find village peones tugging the forelock and bowing to the will of patrones—one man or a few men of power who give orders and who take a paternal interest in the welfare of the common man. Peones are not supposed to be able to make their own important decisions without consulting the patrón. Thus, when we discovered that in Cañones the late Manuel Salazar, father of Jacobo, had owned more than 30,000 acres—the bulk of the Piedra Lumbre Grant—we took it for granted that he had been patrón of the region, and that Jacobo would be one also. What we learned was that although indeed many Cañoneros now living or recently deceased had worked for Manuel, universally respected as a hard-working and upright man, none had thought of him as patrón of the community and no one thinks of Jacobo that way.

There certainly is not, and probably never has been *a* patrón in Cañones. There are, however, many patrones and many peones. A man who works for another man is his peón, and the employer is the patrón. For example, Kutsche and the sons of Joe I. Salazar helped Joe clean a portion of the Upper Cañones Community Ditch in March, 1967, and were spoken of as his peones for the day, although none of them was paid. A Cañonero may work for Duke City Lumber or for the forest service, and speak of his crew boss as his patrón. Nothing is implied but the contract.

Jefes Políticos

The Rio Arriba does, however, have *jefes políticos*, who should be clearly distinguished from patrones. A patrón is an aristocrat whose wealth and power are based on extensive control of land. He also controls the lives of his employees, who reside on his land. He takes responsibility for their education, their religious upbringing, and their behavior in general. He may punish them, but he cannot fire them. The peones owe the patrón fealty as well as labor. We should describe the relationship as feudal, except that the patrón is a capitalist *vis-à-vis* outsiders—a man with surplus produce to sell.

A jefe político is a political boss. The base of his power is knowledge and connections. His service to his clients is to get them jobs, welfare stipends, contracts, or other preference. The clients' obligation to him is to vote for his slate of candidates, and (if he is also in private business) to take their business to him. The jefe's relation to politicians outside his constituency is to deliver the vote, for which he in return expects political preference and jobs. Jefes políticos in the United States appear most frequently when, because of immigration or poverty or linguistic difference, a large group of people lacks access to power and needs a broker.

People of Cañones fit the category of clients who need the help of a broker to obtain the benefits which they are legally entitled to. But within Cañones there are, nevertheless, degrees of political influence between those with property and those without. Those with property in general have more influence outside the village. And in intra-village councils, the word of the propertied usually carries more weight, so long as that word remains close to the consensus of the village.

Cañoneros are cynical about party politics. Their anecdotes are full of distrust of politicians of both parties. Votes, they say, are bought for $1 or $2. Politicians arrive just before an election, make promises, and are not seen again until just before the next election. (That accusation was made to the faces of candidates in the campaign in the fall of 1966, a rare exception to the strict code of personal courtesy.) Certain politicians, according to John Jasper, director of the state department of public welfare, have in the past managed to get hold of welfare checks and distribute them with the implication that they were political favors. As a result, welfare recipients feel vulnerable and unable to be active politically. Cañones believes that it has been neglected since it was founded, except at election time, and it scarcely expects anything more now.

Cañones is also cynical about politics within the parties, but not quite so cynical. Rio Arriba county Democrats are in most cases either *Naranjistas* or *Chaconistas*.

Emilio Naranjo is the most important jefe político. His family has been prominent in New Mexico affairs for several generations, and he has a good deal of influence among Santa Clara Indians as well as among Hispanos. (See Swadesh 1979 for a synopsis of his family's history.) He is the leader of the dominant faction of the Democratic party, and the owner of a successful insurance business. He is a power in state as well as county politics. For a number of years he was the elected sheriff of Rio Arriba county. During our ethnographic present he served as U.S. marshal, a post he was appointed to by President Lyndon Johnson (while his son Benny served as county sheriff).

Emilio Naranjo is no patrón. His land holdings are urban office buildings rather than agricultural fields, and the county government is an important tenant. Prominent among his insurance clients are employees of school systems in the county. He is not concerned with the religious or moral behavior of his clients. Nor does he consider himself to belong to a higher social class than other Hispanos of the county.

The minority faction of the Democratic party is led by Matías Chacón, a lawyer and state senator. He is a jefe político also, but on a smaller scale.

The Naranjo faction is the larger and more powerful, with more patronage to distribute in this county where there is so little cash that is not controlled by some arm of government. Naranjo is accused by his enemies of illegally controlling the welfare rolls and school jobs as well as law enforcement. Insofar as they take sides at all, Cañoneros tend to be Naranjistas. Jacobo Salazar, the one Cañonero with a great deal of land, is a Chaconista. The leaders of the school fight are quite pragmatic, and put their allegiance where they think it will reap the larger returns in benefits to the village.

Politics are active in this remote part of Rio Arriba county only in a way which has not yet touched Cañones: access to jobs in the school and county payrolls. Heads of households in the region scheme vigorously to get even such low-paying jobs as school janitor, bus driver, or secretary. The job of teacher is a large plum. In 1966 very few of these jobs go to Cañoneros. Manuel Salazar, eldest son of Jacobo, teaches in the Jemez Mountain district, and other members of his family are bus drivers. Joe I. Salazar, who owns a fair amount of property in Cañones but resides in Youngsville, secured a bus contract for one of his sons.

How each of the jobs listed above was obtained we do not know. But it is important to point out that from a local point of view there is no such thing as nepotism or unfair influence. The family head who gets jobs for his relatives is acting responsibly in providing for the whole family. Virtue is a personal affair; strict adherence to impersonal professional standards, ignoring all considerations except objective qualifications for job performance, is foreign to local standards and would be resisted vigorously.

6
Cycles

Observance of social form is so important in Hispanic New Mexico that one can think of most aspects of social activity as ritual. Cultural rule, in short, has an unusually big influence on the way Hispanic society conducts its business. In Cañones one can speak of the rituals of the day, the rituals of the seasons, and the rituals of a life history. The outsider who is permitted close enough association with the village to observe people enacting all three cycles, comes to appreciate the skill and stateliness of the social choreography. This has a distinct quality akin to rural European stateliness, and has been little influenced either by Anglo or by American Indian cultures.

The Daily Forms

Daily ritual is quiet, conducted in mellow tones of voice. One starts with "*Como amenecio?*" (literally, how did you dawn?), a solicitous way to greet an acquaintance early in the morning. Or it may be "*Buenos días le dé Dios*" (may God give you a good day). A simple "*Buenos días*" is not counted discourteous, but the more traditional Cañoneros offer the entire greeting. Only one reply is permissible: "*Muy bien, gracias.*" It is considered bad form to burden others with one's ailments unless they specifically ask.

The next move in the ritual of encounter is "*Como está su gente?*" (How are your people?). This question is asked even if (as never occurs in Cañones) neither party knows the other's people. A special inquiry should be made concerning anyone who is ill. If the people meeting each other are close, news is welcome about anyone in the family who has done something unusual, or who is about to arrive or about to leave.

Thereafter, the two exchange a bit of neutral conversation about the weather or something similar. Only after this stage is passed are they free to get down to business, if indeed they have any business.

Breaking off an encounter is equally ritual, aiming to avoid abruptness. The person staying is required to say "*Por qué tan pronto?*" or "*Por qué tan apurado?*" (Why so soon?). No direct reply to the question is necessary, but the departing says "*Llegue!*" (Come with me), or "*Vamos a la casa.*" Finally, the person staying home says "*Vuelva*" (Return).

With so much formality in greeting and parting, it takes a long time to get through an encounter smoothly. If one is walking from one side of the placita to the other, one is obligated to greet everyone he meets, and he may turn up late for an appointment. But the person he is going to meet will understand, because the same obligation rests on him when he is abroad.

Longer separations are treated more formally. The reunion may well evoke *abrazos* and tears from members of both sexes. Men embrace, under such circumstances, only on first encounter after quite a long separation. It depends not only on length but type of separation. The most emotional greetings Cañoneros ever gave Kutsche, for example, came when he returned after a month's hospital stay for a back operation.

Leaving for a long time requires something extra too. "*Que se vaya con Dios*" (May you go with God) is a frequent wish, and "*Que se vaya bien*" (May you go well) is absolutely minimal. To a parent or a spouse, the traveler usually kneels, kisses the hand of the loved one remaining behind, and asks for a blessing.

The rituals mentioned above apply between households, not within a single household, except for the blessing. However close friends may be, if they are not in the same household, they observe the forms. One may think of these rituals as diplomatic relations between sovereign powers. Within the walls of the house, parents order their own children about without ceremony, often scold them, strike them if they feel it is necessary. Husbands and wives are ceremonious outside the house but not inside, and may fight like cats and dogs if no one witnesses. A nuclear family is in effect a single social personality, and its adults treat each other as informally as each treats himself; so do the children among themselves, but not toward their parents.

At the end of the day, when one leaves his companions and goes home, he is as courteous as he was in the morning, and says "*Muy buenas noches*" or "*Gracias por . . .*" whatever favor may have been rendered, such as a ride home.

The rituals just described are all rather stately. But the dance steps of Cañones encounters include metaphoric jigs and polkas as well as minuets. One bit of play carried out between men in their fifties and sixties occurred with due ceremony in the middle of the placita in front of an audience of grown men waiting for a junta to start on a sunny warm Sunday morning in December. Isaaque Lovato came along and went into his brother Medardo's house. Simón Vigil called out to him and chatted a bit. Isaaque put his head out the door, called out to the five or six men in the placita to ask who wanted a cup of coffee. Simón said he did.

Isaaque: "Come and get it."

Simón: "No, you come here."

The banter went back and forth for a few minutes, until Simón drew a line in the dust and said, "My house begins here; bring it over." Isaaque, drawing a line in the dust close to Medardo's house, replied, "My invitation begins here."

This interchange drew rapt attention and quiet appreciation—no guffaws of laughter—from the waiting men. They were enjoying the quality of a dramatic presentation by two well-known masters; whether Simón actually drank a cup of coffee was too insignificant to be remembered.

If an adult is too ignorant or stupid to know the "steps," the other "dancers" sometimes amuse themselves with him. Here is one at Kutsche's expense. He loves to dance, and found one Cañones matron who danced even better than others. Translating literally from the English idiom, he raved about her: "*Consolación* [name changed] *baila como una pluma!*" (dances like a feather). Apparent respectful silence.

Weeks later, after happening to learn that *pluma* is also a slang term for "loose woman," "chippie," and "fart," Kutsche berated Serafín Valdez for letting him make such a fool of himself. Loud laughter from everyone present, especially Serafín. One who is especially good at these "jigs and polkas" has a bit of the *pícaro* in him (cf. Valdez 1979).

In addition to skillful and witty handling of social encounters, the most revealing key to personal relations is the importance of names and titles.

Everyone is expected to remember the name of everyone else, not only in the village but within the whole regional network of people. The exchange of names is no casual in-one-ear-and-out-the-other matter, and if an individual encounters someone he is supposed to know by name but does not, he may be embarrassed by "Don't you remember who I am?" or even teased with, "I'm not going to help you. You should know me."

Titles must be used correctly, including the correct choice of the alternative second person forms of address—the formal *usted* and the informal *tu*.

The rules for using *tu* and *usted* are clear, and still usually observed. Children call each other *tu*, adults call children *tu*, very close adult friends call each other *tu* with an important exception noted below. Strangers and casual acquaintances call each other *usted*, children call adults *usted*. But *usted* carries another shade of meaning which overrides familiarity—it is a term of respect. Thus, compadres address each other as *usted* no matter how close their friendship or degree of kinship may be, because they are required to show respect for each other; in fact, they may have called each other *tu* before becoming compadres and have to shift to the respect form thereafter. Although rare, it is possible for the term of address to change in a single encounter: at Kutsche's request, Medardo Lovato instructed him one afternoon in the life cycle of a member of the Asamblea de Dios church (described later in this chapter). While he was teaching, he called Kutsche *tu* and tried to see that he got the outline straight. When he finished his lesson, and they began to speak in a more relaxed tone of other things, he switched immediately (and, certainly, unconsciously) to *usted*.

Many Cañones conversations, perhaps most of them, discuss people a great deal. The rhythm of these conversations is slow and measured, because every time a name is mentioned, as we have already noted, it is prefaced by a relationship term. For example,

"Ay, pobrecita mi tía María. Ayer cayó y se quebró la pierna."
"No me diga. Y entonces que hizo mi compadre Andrés?"
"Mi tío Andrés la trujo al hospital."

"Oh, my poor Aunt María. Yesterday she fell and broke her leg."
"You don't say. And then what did my compadre Andrés do?"
"My Uncle Andrés took her to the hospital."

Whether one is saying good or bad things about a person, the rule of formality is the same.

The terms of relationship are used in direct address as well as in reference, but are often omitted if a person of higher status is addressing one of lower. If an uncle and his nephew meet, for instance, the nephew will always say, "*Buenos días, tío.*" The uncle will probably reciprocate not with *sobrino* but with *hijo* (son, a term which is often used metaphorically), or with the first name of his nephew.

Since godparents are often chosen from among close kin, many people have two relations to each other. The term of compadrazgo is always chosen over the kin term, by young as well as by old Cañoneros. Adelaida Lucero is a good example. She happens to be comadre to both of her sisters and to numerous other relatives. However casual the conversation, Adelaida always refers to her sisters as "mi comadre Eduvigen" and "mi comadre Manuelita." Compadrazgo is an honor, and one recognizes the honor every time the title is used, whether the person is present or absent, a relative or not. The honor is so important that it outweighs the differences of religion, as we noted in chapter 5.

Another term of respect applied to a single individual in 1967 is *don*. Francisco "Don Franque" Lovato, aged eighty-one, is the only survivor to be called so, for the custom is changing toward less formality and less respect for age. In earlier times, every respectable old man was *don:* the young did not drink in front of him, and in general showed him more respect than they showed to younger adults. Wealth and power have nothing to do with the term; it is not applied to *políticos* or large landowners. Saquello Salazar, sixty-six and very widely respected, is not called *don*. No woman is called *doña*, although several are highly respected and very elderly.

What is the consequence of so ritualizing the casual encounters of daily life? We think it is to keep relations between members of such a small community highly structured, and to remind people constantly of their duties toward each other. Spontaneity might threaten the firmness of social relations. References to the deity (the greeting mentioned above and other daily expressions like "*Si quiera Dios*" and "*Dios le bendiga*") are similar reminders —this is a Christian community, and Christians have obligations to each other.

The Yearly Cycle

Seasonal rhythms, less formally marked than daily encounters or the ceremonies of life, are determined by the weather, the availability of wage labor, and the school calendar.

The first determines when to plant and when to reap. Adult males and young men from families with land may be gone during the winter months tending sheep or working in factories, but they return to Cañones to care for their land and cattle in the summer. Some men who do not need to seek wage jobs, or who are too elderly to do so, rouse themselves from inactive winters to plant and to herd in the summer, helped by their sons, grandsons, or other relatives. At the beginning of summer, during planting and cultivating, the men of Cañones are conspicuously busier than their wives (with the exceptions noted in the preceding chapter on material life). But from late summer through mid-fall, the Cañoneras become heroically busy, drying and canning mountains of produce for the months ahead. The chief service they expect of their husbands at this time is an unfailing supply of fuel for the estufa.

The emotional tenor of the village follows the seasons to some extent, here as throughout New Mexico. Late summer, fall, and winter up to Christmas are fat and happy—the best times for dances and other festivities, and for entertaining visitors. Life slows down after Christmas, belts tighten during early spring, and people long to see fresh greenery again. The bare bones of the barrancas, the dull brown of dry vegas, and the skeletons of rusty junked cars protrude in the winter, seldom masked by snow. Cañoneros open themselves in times of plenty and close in the thin times.

The second determining rhythm is the availability of wage labor. Many Cañoneros lack sufficient land and livestock permisos to make much difference in the yearly budget, and must take jobs when they are available. For unskilled or semiskilled laborers, those jobs are more plentiful in the summer. Most men, and sometimes whole families, pick crops in southern Colorado in season. As a result, Cañones is less populous and more busy in the summer with the increased opportunities to earn a living. (During the summer of 1966, the frequent visits that Elipio García and Serafín Valdez had to make to Santa Fe to negotiate the school battle were a hardship. Elipio, a skilled bulldozer operator, made a considerable financial sacrifice.)

Attention to the daily rituals becomes relatively careless in the summer because of the pressure to work and the absence of many citizens, but increases in fall and early winter, when Cañoneros gather around each other's kitchen tables and catch up on each other's summer activities.

The third factor determining the seasonal rhythm in Cañones, as in most of the rest of the world, is the school calendar. As parents everywhere know, the school bell disciplines the day for whole families, not just for children. During the early mornings of the school year, the placita stirs intensely as children hurry to their school buses or, if they are very young, to the schoolhouse on La Cuchilla. The rest of the day the placita is deserted, while women go about their household activities in more leisurely style. During the evening the returning buses reawaken the placita with youthful noise. But in summer, the placita is filled from morning to night with children playing pickup baseball, shooting baskets, making sand castles, and gossiping—all of this activity determined by their ages, sexes, inclinations, and the amount of work their parents demand of them.

The ceremonial highlights of the year are Christmas, New Year, the Lenten observance culminating in Holy Week, and the Fiesta de San Miguel, patron saint of Cañones, September 25. In the eyes of Cañoneros, the fiesta is the happiest, Lent the most important.

Christmas is a family more than a community celebration. Sometimes Cañoneros travel to visit relatives for the holidays but more often relatives come to them. It is a time of special foods, particularly sweet pastries. Gifts between close relatives are important, but nowhere near as important as among urban families. (The distinction is urban-rural, not Anglo-Hispano. Urban Hispanos seem to make as much of the exchange of gifts as urban Anglos do.) Visiting is of great importance, both within and between villages.

People who ordinarily frown on *paseándose* (idle strolling) walk all over Cañones paying calls on their friends at Christmastime. *Los Pastores*, the Christmas drama enacted in some villages, is not done in Cañones or in other villages in the Chama basin.

Two nonfamily affairs of Christmas belong to the children—*los abuelos* and "*Mis Chrismas!*"

During the novena (December 16 to 24), adolescent boys transform themselves by night into los abuelos (literally, the grandfathers). They go about from house to house in small groups, dressed in bizarre castoff clothing of their mothers, sisters or older brothers, usually wearing stocking masks, scaring little children, begging edibles from adults, and clowning. Small children are genuinely terrified of these anonymous figures who come brandishing rope whips and threatening to punish children for their transgressions. Los abuelos are boogeymen, used by parents to frighten their young children into obedience.

Los abuelos are also boys playing with roles which are normally forbidden, either because those roles are disrespectful or because they are burlesques of female behavior. Field notes of visits from abuelos record pantomimes of obscene activities and singing, questions directed toward hosts that boys would not ordinarily presume to ask, wild dancing, and the expectation of being served liquor. It all stops if the masks slip off, and it is terminated by the courtesies normal to ordinary visits—the copious thanks for time or food and the formal "Buenas noches."

What the origin of this custom may be, no one seems to know. Some local people and others think it comes from the Tewa or other Indians of the Rio Grande, as a modification of the stern-faced punitive kachinas. E. Boyd, of the International Folk Art Foundation, who generally denies cultural connections between Indians and Hispanos, speculates that the custom may have come from *los viejitos* of Chihuahua, when people from that part of Mexico settled in northern New Mexico in the early 1800s (personal communication). *El abuelo* is mentioned in Minton's *Juan of Santo Niño*—a slightly fictionalized account of colonial life near Bernalillo (Minton 1973:53). Informants in Abiquiu say that a generation ago, los abuelos were *jóvenes* and married men, and that disciplining wayward children was a more important part of it. In Coyote, los abuelos continue to be played by grown men. One informant from

Taos said that perhaps twenty years ago elderly men took the abuelo role during the novena in the region of Taos and Arroyo Hondo; they did it seriously, with no clowning or begging.

About dawn on Christmas morning villagers are awakened by children (los abuelos of previous nights, together with their sisters and their younger brothers) shouting "*Mis Chrismas!*" The kids pound on the door full of excitement, squealing with delight and anticipation, expecting candy, fruit, pastries, or whatever the householder has prepared. This is like Halloween trick or treat without the threat. Christmas morning 1966 a total of forty-four children stopped at Kutsche's house in groups of various sizes, having worked their way systematically through the village. No one turns children away at this time (some do turn los abuelos away, or give them goodies only outside the door); many households have baked cookies to hand out. Despite their excitement, children almost always remember to say thanks as they go out the door peering into their paper sacks to see what they have accumulated. The sharp comparisons, the "my loot is better than your loot" which sometimes goes along with Halloween trick or treating, is completely absent in Cañones. (But Kutsche's wife observed some of it in Santa Fe when Hispano children came to the door the same morning shouting "*Mis Chrismas!*")

Mass is not celebrated in Cañones on Christmas Day unless it falls on the scheduled day of the week. If it does, attendance is greater than usual, the church is decorated for the occasion (in 1966, a Christmas tree on either side of the altar decorated with tinsel and blinking lights), and everyone files up to the altar afterwards to kiss a small statue of the Santo Niño (the Holy Child). Clothing worn at this mass is the same as usual, although perhaps people are a trifle better scrubbed and shaved.

The general atmosphere of Christmas in Cañones, as compared to Anglo Christmases in small cities, is of great conviviality and orderly hubbub. Absent is the frantic undercurrent, so expectable in the city, of last minute shopping and wrapping, of housewives overwhelmed by festival meal preparations. The young men more often than not take bottles with them on their rounds of nocturnal visiting and share drinks generously. Christmas dinner gatherings are very large, and in a single room there may be small children playing contentedly by the Christmas tree with their toys (given either on Christmas Eve or Christmas morning, depending on each family's custom), men drinking and visiting congenially by the door, or just oustide if the weather is pleasant, while several women are busily but efficiently and quietly preparing the feast. Callers are even more welcome than usual at any house on this day.

New Year's Eve is celebrated by carolers—adult men and women—who serenade people at home that night and the next day with any songs whatever, seasonal or not. The polite response is to invite the carolers in for a drink. A bonfire is kept going in the placita to warm the carolers between calls, and the occasion is livened by whoops, bells, rifles, firecrackers, and anything else that will add cheer.

New Year's night may be celebrated with a dance in the schoolhouse, as it was in 1967. All of the Catholics and a few of the non-Catholics attend. "All" includes eighty-one-year-old Don Franque Lovato, babes in arms, and everyone in between. This baile is typical of almost all except wedding dances. Before the dancing begins, the sexes separate entirely, from children to adults. Once the men come over to where the women are seated and dancing is general, the sexes mingle pretty freely except for the married women who remain fairly close together, attended from time to time by their husbands and by other men. Married men are in general careful to spread their invitations out equally among the women, neither sticking exclusively to their wives nor to any other one or two women. An enormous variety of steps is danced. The traditional Varsoviana, polka, and waltz are danced by all, though the elders dance them better than the *jóvenes* do. The fox-trot is still danced, and newer steps that are popular with the high school crowd are also enjoyed here. It is all right to smile when dancing—in fact, most people smile broadly—in contrast to the Anglo rural or small town rule that one must dance grimly.

Drinking is an important part of the dances, its form as rigidly circumscribed as those of the older dance steps. Men keep the liquor in their cars and leave the dance to visit at irregular intervals. But alcohol never crosses the threshold of the dance hall. Totally respectable women, particularly married women, do not go out to drink at all. But for a young woman to take a drink inconspicuously at the car of her *novio* or of some other close friend is no great sin.

Fighting is popularly thought by outsiders to be an important part of baile behavior. Cañoneros sometimes fight—again, entirely outside the dance hall. If they do, they almost always use fists rather than knives or other weapons, and third parties quickly pull them apart. Cañones has the reputation of being more peaceful than many other villages, certainly more peaceful than those on paved highways accessible to comparative strangers.

Cañones remains a traditional Christian community, and the peak of its religious year is the Passion. That this peak coincides with the hungriest time of year may be coincidence, but the grimness of late winter and early spring certainly do heighten the dramatic impact of the observance of Lent.

As we have said, the *Cofradía de Nuestro Padre Jesús Nazareno* leads the community for this season. The hermanos of the cofradía may not be prominent during the rest of the year, but their reenactment of the Passion occupies center stage from Ash Wednesday until Good Friday. Their public observances are attended by most Catholics, but by none of the non-Catholics.

If los abuelos are almost unknown to the literature on Hispanic New Mexico, the opposite is true of the cofradía. Marta Weigle published a bibliography of over 1,000 sources on this confraternity (1976b), simultaneously with her definitive review of literature (1976a). There remains little to be said that has not already been included in the section on religion. In this chapter, the Lenten exercises are discussed in relation to the way they focus the village's attention at one point in the yearly cycle. At the request of officers of the Cañones morada, this account will be brief and general.

Northern New Mexico turns soberly and seriously inward during Lent. Self-denial is almost universal. The most common sacrifice is some favorite food or cigarettes. No bailes are held for the forty days, except for St. Patrick's Day, which is a day of festive dispensation. Many people stop drinking for Lent. Other promises of abstinence are made and kept privately, according to the individual decisions. The community regards hermanos of the cofradía as making especial penance on the behalf of the whole village. Often their penance is specifically for an individual or a family, but it may be for the sake of the community or for all Christians.

Much of the cofradía's exercises are conducted in the morada. These are private. Public exercises begin with a rosary on Ash Wednesday, and with the stations of the cross the following Friday, and continue in this pattern until Holy Week. The congregation is small at first, increasing in size as Lent progresses. On Palm Sunday in 1967, the hermanos of Cañones requested and paid for a special mass, at which the cofradía of Coyote were honored guests and attended with their large purple and gold banner labelled *Fraternidad Piadosa de Nuestro Padre Jesús, Coyote y Brazos, N.M.* A gold embroidered cross decorated the banner. Everyone walked in procession around the church after mass, before the hermanos retired to the morada. Before and after this service, hermanos are courteous to others, but hold themselves at a friendly distance. The joking of ordinary times is totally absent. From Wednesday of Holy Week, several public services are held every day with increasing attendance both from the village and from relatives who have moved away. The culmination of these public observances is the stations of the cross on Good Friday, attended by virtually every Catholic who has any connection with Cañones, but not by outsiders, who are unwelcome at this extreme inward-turning time of the year. (In 1967, Governor Cargo had already worked closely with Cañones, and was welcomed as a friend.)

The village concentrates more and more of its attention on the activities of the morada during Lent, and does less and less that is not related to it. Women take turns cooking for the hermanos, who honor one housewife after another with the request to provide food. Every Catholic family brings either food or other gifts to the morada at least once during Lent, with or without a petition that the hermanos pray for a loved one. This total devotion of all the Catholics seems to leave Cañones drained and, in a sense, purified. Little takes place for some days after Good Friday, and then people begin the tasks of cleaning out the irrigation ditches, plowing and planting in earnest.

There is no ceremony to bless the irrigation ditches once they are cleaned out, as there is in some other villages. In June, the crops in the fields are blessed in the name of San Antonio de Padua. A singing procession of many women, a very few men, and a straggle of children, visit all of the fields of the village, coming back to the church for the rosary at about 5:00 P.M. At the head of the procession march a small boy and girl, perhaps ten-year-olds, carrying an arched platform with the santo (a carving or sculpture of a saint), borrowed from another village for the occasion, surrounded by bunches of flowers. Children take turns carrying the burden, which is about two feet long with carrying arms extending another foot in each direction, the whole perhaps a foot and a half wide, the arch two feet high. (Except for the arch, this platform is the same in design throughout the Hispanic world.)

The children laugh, joke, and play, while the women maintain a serious air but ignore the antics of their children. They sing religious songs, some of which they repeat later in the church. On June 13, 1967, the procession arrived at Jacobo Salazar's house a little past mid-afternoon, was met by his wife Severiana some distance from the house, and escorted in for a rest and cooling drinks. With Severiana leading, the procession returned to the placita for rosary.

The happy peak of the ceremonial year is September 25—the feast of San Miguel, the patron saint of Cañones. Crops are in, or close enough so that farmers have a good idea how big the harvest will be. Produce is fresh and plentiful, and some of it has been canned or dried already. The year's harvest of cattle is in hand or in sight to be sold in October. Every village has its fiesta, of course, timed whenever the patron's day turns up on the Catholic calendar. Cañones is fortunate that its fiesta can be a thanksgiving celebration.

The success of the fiesta is primarily up to the mayor domos of the church—the amount of the special collection, the decoration of the church, and the organizing and arranging of the whole ceremony including a dance (usually the last event).

Vespers, on the eve of the Día de San Miguel, begins the fiesta. It is a simple evening ceremony, in the middle of which the congregation forms a procession around the church double-file—women in one line, men in the other—behind a cross and two candles. Vespers in 1969 (ethnographic present for the fiesta, which we did not witness in 1966 or 1967) was lightly attended.

This mass is different from most only in the reading by the priest of the names and amounts of all who have given for the special collection, the announcement of the names of the new mayor domos (a secret until now), and a procession around the church toward the end of mass, San Miguel carried on the platform that bore San Antonio in June. The outgoing mayor domos lead the procession, followed by their successors. Most Cañones Catholics and a few relatives from elsewhere attend. Outsiders are welcome during the fiesta, so long as they behave themselves.

At the *baile* (dance), which in 1969 for the sake of convenience was held after vespers and not after mass, everyone has a thoroughly good time. As at all dances, men and women, married and unmarried, young and old, attend and dance fairly constantly.

For several years, music at dances in several Jemez Mountain villages has been provided by the Camaros, a Cañones combo of guitar, drums, and vocalists, consisting of Ricardo Vialpando, Tony and Dennis Gallegos, and sometimes Cirilo Vialpando or Martín Valdez. These young men took the name Camaro from the Chevrolet model, because they liked the name. The Camaros are equally adept at playing the traditional Spanish dance music and a modern rock beat.

Admission tonight is $1 for stag males, $.75 for stag females, $1.50 for couples, and $.50 for children.

All of the women are dressed in their best, or at least in very good clothing short of what they would wear to a wedding. Some of the men are freshly dressed and shaved, some are not. Everyone dances without inhibition. Most of the men drink outside, and two of them tonight forget their manners and bring their drinks inside. Several fist fights start outside. The leader of the band, after consulting with some of the more responsible adult men, announces over the public address system that unless the fighting and the indoor drinking stop, the dance is over. They do stop, and the dance goes on. Typically, novios spend more time outside near the cars than those who are not yet quite novios, and married men step outside for a drink now and then, but married women do not. The dance lasts until about 3:00 A.M.

It is a good dance. Everyone has been present, virtually everyone danced, no one got hurt, and numerous romantic affairs have been furthered. The outgoing mayor domos are pleased with the entire fiesta, and satisfied that they have discharged their duties to the church and to the community as they should.

After the fiesta, the village works hard at harvest, cuts enough wood to last well into the winter, prepares houses for the cold weather to come, and looks forward to Christmas and New Year's. Once those jobs are done, there is not a great deal that has to be done in Cañones, and people spend a good deal of pleasurable time visiting each other and chatting around kitchen tables over coffee.

From Birth to Death

How one goes through the cycle from birth to death in Cañones depends on whether or not one is Catholic. The basic stages of life and the attitudes toward them are virtually identical, but Catholic and non-Catholic celebrate them differently. This section relies on multiple observations and interviews for its information on Cañoneros in general, and Catholics in particular, and on instruction by Medardo Lovato, a deacon of the Asamblea de Dios, for statements about his church.

The Christian belief in the virtue of having many children is endorsed in Cañones, although table 3, "Household Size," in chapter 4, does not reflect this, since many households are composed of the elderly or of families just starting. Most people seem to think that four children is a small family, and that six or more are desirable. A Cañones woman, therefore, can expect to be taking care of little children until she is forty.

The gap between births in a Cañones family varies from slightly less than a year to several years. This minimum is determined by the traditional advice—reinforced by contemporary medicine—that sexual intercourse should be avoided for forty days after childbirth.

Dictionary terms for pregnancy—*preñada*, *embarazada*, *encinta*, *grávida*—are recognized, but seldom used. In Cañones, one uses the more indirect *esperanda* (waiting, expecting), *enferma* (ill), and, sometimes, *gorda* (fat). *La esperanda* carries on with her usual work. She may attend a well baby clinic, established some years ago by Dr. Marion Hotopp, public health officer for northern New Mexico, who happens to be a specialist in pediatrics. She is less likely to seek the services of a curandera or a partera for there are very few of them left in the area. For specific pregnancy ailments, she may use herbal remedies. Most families use herbs both for eating and for healing, as a supplement to prescription drugs, although no one relies on them as a total substitute.

Babies are delivered in the Española Hospital or at another

medical center. Home delivery is avoided if possible. During the field team's residence, one baby was born at home because the labor was short. The birth went smoothly, thanks to the assistance of an experienced neighbor.

After giving birth, the mother returns gradually to her normal duties. There appears to be no cultural guide to the length of time she will rest. One of the many advantages of a wide network of kin is that women of the mother's own and older generations are available to help, either by coming into the household to work or by taking older children to their own homes.

If the family is Catholic, the baby is baptized at the age of three weeks to two or three months. Although the service may be held during public mass, it is usually private, at the priest's convenience. Padrinos of each sex are chosen from relatives or close friends. Their traditional functions, to guide the child's religious development, and to be available to raise it in case the parents die, do not appear to be obligatory any longer. But the personal affection between padrinos and ahijados is still strong. These padrinos are the first of three pairs that an individual acquires—the others coming at confirmation and marriage. The first pair is usually the most important.

For a baby in the Pentecostal church, the corresponding ceremony is called *dedicación* and is held as early as possible. The child's two padrinos, who may or may not be relatives, take him to the pastor during a regular church service. The pastor dedicates the child to God in the Holy Spirit.

Within the household, the care of babies is shared willingly between the mother and her older children. Boys may be as delighted as girls to handle the new brother or sister. Older girls must; older boys may. The baby is handled by many people. It is the excuse for visits to the parents by relatives and others. The maternal grandmother usually spends a great deal of time in the house; the paternal grandmother often does. The baby is taken everywhere its mother goes, and may sleep in a number of houses in addition to its own. Society is more important than sanitation. Attempts are rarely made to keep a baby away from sources of infection such as the common cold.

Thus at the very beginning of life a pattern is established that will continue until death. One lives in the midst of people. Babies, small children, the elderly, all go to church, to dances, to political meetings, to weddings, funerals, whatever. The only activities characterized as private are the most intimate household behaviors, courting, and those functions of the cofradía within the morada.

The stages of life recognized in Cañones are almost identical to those that Edmonson reports (1957:24–26), but the age breaks differ. Edmonson puts the division between *niño(a)* and *muchacho(a)* at six years. At the other extreme, an elderly Cañones informant suggested thirteen to fifteen years. When pressed, she specified particular grandchildren and the time when they begin to work in the field and around the house. Although her age break is older than others, her criterion is the same—responsibility.

Niño(a)

In Cañones a child is called *niño(a)* from the time it is able to walk and talk until about eight years old. (Babies are occasionally called niño.) A niño is not responsible for his own behavior. He is learning, but has not learned. The niño is subtly encouraged to be adventuresome; the niña is flattered when she wears a pretty dress for mass or dance. If the niño makes an aggressive thrust in play, or the niña plays peek-a-boo over her mother's shoulder, adults may laugh indulgently and exclaim "*Qué hombrote!*" or "*Qué mujerota!*" (What a little man/woman!) Discipline, such as it is, is exercised by both parents, all older siblings, and grandparents, but seldom by others. A niño learns fairly early whose authority supersedes whose; father is final.

Muchacho(a)

A child is a *muchacho(a)* from about eight until late adolescence, when the girl continues to be a muchacha, but the boy enters an equivocal stage when he is sometimes still called muchacho, and sometimes *mediano.* A man may even be called a muchacho, in the same spirit that Anglos use *boy* in "the boys are playing poker tonight." *Los jóvenes* (the youths) are not exactly boys.

Muchachos are workers, small models of their parents performing tasks and jobs according to the sexual division of labor, except when it is necessary to cross these lines because of a shortage of help. As we have noted, women and girls work in the house, men and boys outside. (The conspicuous exception—one which still survives in 1967 but is vanishing—is the enjarradora who plasters outside as well as in). So the muchacho is not expected to feel put-upon if he is asked to do a girl's work, since he knows that his father does women's work when he is away from home as sheepherder or crop picker. As implied above, muchachos may be baby tenders, among their other chores.

A muchacho is a responsible member of the family, and, by extension, of the community. He has learned his social role and must fulfill it. Upholding and, if necessary, defending the family's reputation is perhaps the most important lesson he is expected to have mastered. A muchacho, in the absence of his father or older brother, will play host to visitors, always staying in the room if an adult male is talking with his mother or his sister. He does not leave a baile if his sister is unescorted. He speaks circumspectly to outsiders about family affairs.

A muchacha's responsibilities parallel her brother's but are more passive. Although she upholds the family's reputation positively by her skill in domestic tasks, only a few people will know about this area of behavior. She is best known throughout the community for the things she does *not* do, and these are all in some way or another connected with courting. She is demure, somewhat grave, decorous. She and her brothers avoid careless intimacy. She is so careful never to give any boy an excuse to take advantage of her that she absolutely avoids being alone with one. A muchacha in Cañones is beginning to feel the contrary pulls between the demands of family and village that she be shy and discreet, and those of the school that she be competitive. More of this below, under *mujer*.

Sex education begins at this time. The muchacha learns avoidance. She is taught decorum by her mother and grandmother, but she is not given instructions about her changing physiology by anyone, unless an older sister takes pity on her ignorance. So menstruation comes a surprise, often a shock to her. The muchacho, on the other hand, is tacitly expected to learn as much as he can—at least verbally, if not practically. His teachers are older boys, never fathers and of course never mothers. The verbal knowledge of Cañones muchachos is precocious compared to that of middle-class Anglo city boys. By the age of eleven or twelve, they have learned all the terms for all the possible bodily parts and acts.

The muchachos picking up informal knowledge and skills run together, spend most of their daylight and a good deal of their evening time together. They are the rural equivalent of city gangs, although without the delinquency usually associated with such gangs. Collectively, these adolescents (girls, to an extent, as well as boys) are referred to by adults as *la plebe,* a term that has lost its Latin denotation of "common people" and could be roughly translated as "the kids of the village." The term is humorously disparaging, sufficiently vague in its boundaries so that if the men shooting baskets in the lower placita include married adults, young unmarried men, and muchachos (with a few niños watching), one might with a wave of the hand and a smile call them all la plebe. As a nineteen-year-old Cañonero buzzed the church in his racy car filled with friends, an elderly man chuckled and said, "*La plebe—siempre travieso*" (mischievous). More seriously, if one wakes up in the morning to find minor mischief done to windows or cars, he will conclude it was la plebe who did it. La plebe is a term used about a group and its nonproductive activities. A muchacho at work for his family is looked on primarily as an individual, not as a member of his age category.

What muchachos are expected to master in the progress toward adulthood are livelihood skills, informal sexual knowledge, and the values of vergüenza and respeto. These values are of great importance to Hispanic village culture, and will be described separately in chapter 7.

At some point during this stage comes the ceremony of confirmation and the addition of one's second padrino, a person of the same sex. This padrino may be one of the padrinos de bautismo, but usually is not. A class of people to be confirmed comes before the archbishop of Santa Fe once every four years or so. It is a large ceremony, conducted for the entire parish in the central church (Santo Tomás) in Abiquiu. In acknowledging one's progress toward full participation in church activities, it is very important, but it does not seem to signify much as a stage of life. (One has by his time usually gone through the ceremony of first communion.)

For a child in the Pentecostal church, a much more important life crisis ceremony takes place at about the age of twelve—*salvación,* the point at which the individual makes his decision for Christ. Medardo Lovato emphasized that the dedicación of infants is important for the parents, who accept responsibility to raise their child as a good Christian, but salvación is the decision made by the young person himself. Only after this point can one say, "I am baptized in the Holy Spirit."

At the age of sixteen to eighteen, the Pentecostal child applies to become a member of his church. Membership is not automatic. One applies, in private, to the pastor, who meets with the deacons to discuss the application. Upon passing this examination, one is presented to the congregation at a regular Sunday service for possible examination by the members. The first requirement for membership is salvación. Beyond that, one is examined to see "*Si tiene vicios*" (vices). Medardo Lovato did not volunteer a list of them, covering the subject instead with the comment "*Cualquier vicio que ofende al cuerpo*" (whatever vice offends against the body). Among them, of course, are drinking, dancing, smoking, and irregular sexual conduct. An unsuccessful applicant is still welcome at church. He is likely to have been told that he is not ready yet, but that he can still hope to become a member.

High School Graduation

Graduation from high school is an important rite of passage. In 1967 three Cañoneros graduated in a class of twenty-six from Coronado High School at Gallina—Tony Gallegos, son of Dalio and Orlinda; Isaac Lovato, Jr., son of Isaaque and Margarita; and Viola Serrano, daughter of the widow Teófila.

The ceremony, held in the high school gymnasium on May 24, was more formal than anything short of a wedding. The seniors, the boys in black and the girls in white caps and gowns, marched to the tune of "Pomp and Circumstance." Opposite them sat their parents, fathers wearing red boutonnieres and mothers red corsages, both sexes clothed as elegantly as at a wedding.

The address was given by Lieutenant Governor Lee Francis, filling in for Governor David Cargo who sent a telegram of regrets. Francis, the principal, and other speakers made fairly pointed remarks about various aspects of state and local politics.

After the recessional (to von Webern's "Prayer and March") the seniors formed a reception line against the gymnasium wall and everyone filed past them, shaking hands and giving them graduation gifts. A number of seniors quickly accumulated such a load that a mother or younger sibling would come along to relieve their arms, so they could accept more.

On this occasion the graduating seniors showed the total self-possession of adult Hispanos, not the half-embarrassed giggles of ordinary muchachos and muchachas, and none of the adolescent gawkiness which their Anglo counterparts might have shown in such a situation. They celebrated with a *baile* that evening. Surprise parties, including one in Cañones, were given a few days later for graduating seniors by their proud parents.

Joven

From this stage until adults lose their powers and are put on the shelf as *viejo(a)*, the sexes take such different paths that they must be discussed in entirely separate categories. A *joven* is a young man, no longer a child but not quite an adult. He "graduates" into adulthood when he marries. Edmonson does not mention joven as a separate stage of life. This may be because in the 1950s when he did his field work, the cultural expectation was still for a boy to marry and become an adult without any uncertain self-proving period, although probably such uncertainty was already a part of the experience of his informants. By 1967 both reality and expectation have changed.

After graduating or dropping out of high school, jóvenes spend anywhere from two to five years working in various parts of the West (chiefly cities in New Mexico, plus Salt Lake City, Denver, Los Angeles), enjoying their freedom, visiting home sporadically. Both at home and away, they tend to run together, exchanging information about the job world, drinking, exploring. At the time of our ethnographic present they are not yet thinking of college. In the adult public eye, these young men are not expected to shoulder much responsibility, although they must continue to treat elders with respect and to help their fathers protect their mothers and sisters from possible affront. No work parties to repair the road for them, no sharing the burden of the school fight. They are, in short, expected to be sowing their wild oats.

Only one young man of Cañones ever confided to us his feelings about his place in his own and the wider world, but we infer from him and from observation that this is the time of life when the young Cañonero makes two potentially devastating disoveries. First, he recognizes that as a "Mexican" he will be discriminated against in the job market. He discovers that judged by national standards he has been cheated in his schooling, which prepared him neither to live at home nor to compete abroad. Sometimes, especially away from New Mexico, he encounters blatant racial prejudice. He finds jobs in which the patrones are Anglo, the peones are Hispano. Second, the facade of social equality comes apart. He becomes acutely aware that the heirs of landowners will actually inherit land, and that those who do not inherit will be landless forever, barring some heroic action on their part. In fact, the young heirs are too busy helping their fathers or grandfathers herd cattle and till fields to brood over discrimination. They do go out occasionally to get jobs, but the knowledge that land awaits them at home provides a psychic as well as an economic buffer. For them, there is no separate joven stage of life.

Some other villages of northern New Mexico, particularly those on highways, suffer from gangs of their own aimless jóvenes who rob and beat other villagers. Not so Cañones. For the young Cañonero, this is the period of memorable drinking bouts, of extreme and fairly open sexual boasting, of sudden death in automobile accidents. It can be a time of bitterness, and some landless jóvenes turn to the Chicano movement for identity.

Noviazgo

Novio(a) means sweetheart, fiancé(e), newlwed. *Noviazgo* is still decidedly formal, still firmly set in the structure of family. The novio and novia have numerous opportunities to meet, from the time they are niños if they are both from Cañones, from school days if they are not. Most of their meetings during active courtship (if one or both has already left school) are at dances. Girls and boys go separately and return home separately. They are together only in the dance hall; if a girl accepts a boy's invitation to walk outside, she is already fairly interested in him.

Mothers may keep silent regarding the physiological changes leading their daughters toward womanhood, but they give plenty of social advice. Girls must go to dances with someone safe—at best their fathers or older brothers, at least a group of girls. Kathy Krusnik notes a conversation with a woman who took a motherly interest in her: "She warned me never to go with boys on dark roads, never to go with boys alone, never to go with drunk boys. 'Girls just aren't very strong.' She meant physically."

As recently as a generation ago, the community dance hall was virtually the only place for novios to meet, and marriage was arranged by the parents. Now, novios usually become acquainted at high school in Gallina unless they know each other previously, and a fair amount of courtship takes place in automobiles. None of it took place in the past, nor takes place now, in the home of novio or novia. They use a good deal of ingenuity to find quiet meeting places where they will not be disturbed.

The ideal novia is a virgin when she marries. In practice, nothing the less is thought of her if she becomes pregnant before marriage, so long as the novio is the father (or can reasonably claim to be). As in other areas of Hispanic behavior, what is important is that she conduct herself decorously in public. Families vary enormously in the amount of freedom they give their daughters in the private aspects of meeting and being courted by boys.

Bad courting conduct for a girl consists of *paseándose*—sauntering along the road on foot with another girl of courting age, perhaps smoking, bantering with boys in passing cars, getting picked up. A really worthless person of either sex from joven to adult is labeled *puro pasearse.* Boys will expect to take as much advantage as possible of a girl who "lets the boys do whatever they want." The onus is heavy on her, light on him unless it can be demonstrated that he has made her pregnant. The double standard is rampant in Hispanic courtship.

Parents still play a large role in the announcement of marriage, although they no longer take the initiative to choose spouses. When the novios have made up their minds, they tell both sets of parents. His parents in turn call on the novia's parents to ask for her hand. The novio is not present. (Her parents are likely to be upset if she has neglected to prepare them.) On the spot or shortly thereafter, her parents give their reply, which is almost always yes. Wedding arrangements may be made then or later.

About Pentecostal noviazgo we know little. If a Pentecostal falls in love with a Catholic, one or the other converts—usually the Catholic.

Casorio

El casorio (the wedding ceremony) is a great event, planned for well in advance and talked about for a long time afterward, and may outshine even the fiesta of San Miguel.

The novios set their wedding date in consultation with the priest. (Until the last few years, Cañones weddings were celebrated in the church of Santo Tomás in Abiquiu, but now the priest will come to Cañones.) The work of preparation begins two or three weeks before a big wedding. Relatives or close friends beyond the families of the novios may participate in preparing for the major events, including wedding mass, reception, and wedding dance.

For the wedding mass, the church must be cleaned and decorated with flowers; for the reception, the school house must also be cleaned and decorated with streamers, rosettes, confetti, and whatever else imagination may inspire. In addition, the band must be hired and a meal prepared in a number of different kitchens for the two hundred or more guests. A wedding dance may be held as a continuation of the reception after a break of a couple of hours. If it takes place in a different building—or even a different town—then the cleaning, decorating, and arranging for a band must be done a second time. Relatives from out of town must be housed and fed, and these arrangements as well as preparation for the wedding itself may require many consultations between households. When prominent families are united, Cañones does little else but prepare and celebrate the nuptials.

As for direct wedding expenses, in the past the novio was responsible for the bride's entire trousseau. Today he always pays for her gown, and the padrinos del casorio (usually close friends of the novios rather than close relatives) pay for their own clothes, whether bought, made, or rented. The cost of other special clothes may be paid for by the novio or by others. Entertainment is a very large expense, since invitations are extended not only to everyone in the village but also to others in whatever geographical direction the branches of kinship and acquaintance reach. This cost is borne by the novios and their families, depending on their individual financial resources.

A wedding between two landed families elicited the following observations. Novio and padrino wore tuxedos, as did novio's father. Novia's father wore suit, white shirt, tie. Ushers, others of immediate families, wore sports coats or white shirts without coat. Novia was splendid in long white dress with long train held up by padrinitos— siblings of novio and novia who were still niño and niña. Bride had bouffant hairdo, large veil, carried big white bouquet. *Madrina* and other female attendants all wore long yellow dresses. One of the mothers in white dress and matching coat, white pillbox hat, white gloves and shoes, cut in the understated elegance made famous a few years earlier by Jacqueline Kennedy—stunning, poised, very tired around the eyes from all the work of preparing.

The procession entered the crowded church in the same order as in Anglo weddings, novia last on her father's arm. At the altar she was immediately handed over to her fiance without the ceremony customary in Anglo Protestant weddings. Father took his seat with mother. The ceremony proceeded in usual form for high mass, except that only a few took communion—novios, padrinos, some others. The sermon centered on Saint Paul's injunction to wives to obey their husbands, and on the metaphor equating fleshly marriage with that of Christ and the Catholic church. The husband should love his wife as his own body, consider her welfare as his own. The superordinate-subordinate relation was a solid underpinning to the whole sermon. At least one of the priest's remarks roused comment from others in Cañones that evening at supper: "If a man wants to know how well he has treated his wife, he should look at what he has done to her after ten years or so. Most wives look like old mops." At least one husband said a man might take his mop by the handle and swing it against the wall; his wife replied that wife-mops could swing husbands too, and everyone at supper laughed loudly. But the message during mass was the traditional one of wifely obedience.

The wedding party, grandparents, and other members of the immediate families lined up outside the church afterward to receive the guests. Many guests snapped pictures. (Strangely, no photographs would be taken at the reception.) The novio's car had been decorated with streamers, rosettes, beer and lard cans, messages such as "just married," "*Puro amor,*" "love," and the names of the novios. The sexual allusions frequently painted on cars of rural Anglo newlyweds—"Watch Podunk grow," "Hot Springs tonight,"—were conspicuously absent. Cars made a big horn-blowing caravan to the old schoolhouse for the reception.

The meal was first at the reception, and it was entirely Anglo style, as it almost always is at public events. Nonalcoholic punch was served; guests who wanted stronger drink brought it and drank outside. The line to be served stretched to the door and beyond, but was remarkably well-mannered and good-humored. The bridal party, with novios on either side of the priest, were served separately at a decorated table.

Dancing was next, started by a grand march in which the dancing line passed through the raised arms of the couples before them. There are two or three variations on the grand march, any or all of which may be used. Laughing and shouting and conversation in happy voices constantly accompanied the proceeding. Dancing quickly became general, the band varying traditional Hispanic numbers with contemporary teenage favorites. Virtually everybody danced, regardless of age. When a great-grandfather asked a niña to dance, the crowd found it humorous but not ludicrous. (A good deal of happy laughter surrounds these dances, especially when small girls and boys are pushed by their parents to dance with the novios.)

From time to time a special dance was called, when men were expected to take turns dancing with the novia, and women with the novio, each turn lasting less than a minute. They pinned folding money on the veil of the novia or on the lapel of the novio. A fairly considerable sum—well in excess of $100—may be collected in this way. Today's novia, with her puff of hair and the large veil papered with money folded back over it, and in her composure and stately posture, looked like a Goya portrait of a Spanish *marquesa*.

Gifts were carried to the reception and opened in public shortly after the cake was cut by the novios. Later, after an intermission for supper, the baile began again and went on until about 2:00 A.M. The novia bore up gracefully, but looked increasingly tired as the events wore on. She and the novio alone kept on their wedding clothes; everyone else had changed from suits and tight dresses into clothing that left them freer to dance.

Today there were no fights, for a number of local males with authority stayed throughout the event, and the county sheriff was one of the guests.

During the next few days members of both families cleaned up the mess left in church and schoolhouse. But the event was talked about for weeks afterward, and continued to evoke smiles in the principal families indefinitely.

The Pentecostal wedding is smaller and quieter, but no less public. The entire community is invited unless the couple choose to hold the ceremony too far away for everyone to come. Both Catholics and non-Catholics usually go to all weddings and funerals, and no one of either faith stays away on religious grounds. Following the ceremony in the Pentecostal church is "*una buena comida*"—that is, a meal of more than ordinary size and variety—provided by the families of both novios. It may be held in any convenient place, whether private home or public hall. There is, of course, no *baile*.

Honeymoons may or may not be taken after any Cañones wedding, according to taste and economics. The choice has nothing to do with religious preference.

Hombre

Becoming an *hombre* is the payoff for being a married, adult male in Cañones. (All Cañones males are married, and virtually all have children; *solteros* [unmarried adult men] would be pitied rather than ridiculed.) A man has the greatest responsibility and the greatest prestige. His word is law at home, and even the wildest of his joven sons does not challenge his authority, at least not directly, although he may circumvent it by his behavior away from home—and the wise father looks the other way. Keeping his family fed, clothed, and sheltered is a man's major job.

Among the qualities that men respect in each other are hard work (*muy trabajador* and *muy hombre* are compliments very close in meaning, even though they are not synonymous), and straight upright dealing with others. They are expected to contribute work on community projects such as road work without calculating the amount of their work relative to others. This virtue of hard work must be carefully distinguished from the Protestant work ethic, with which it has little in common. The hombre who is muy hombre is judged by how well he provides for the comfort and dignity of his family and not by the sheer quantity of work he performs; the workaholic would be thought mentally ill, or be suspected of devious motives (see *torcido* below). A sense of proportion was expressed by Sabiñano Lovato when he said of his power saw with a broad smile, "*Es mi peón.*"

Hospitality and generosity with surplus fruit or vegetables are well thought of, but respect attaches first of all to the man who takes good care of his own. The reverse of this coin is summed up in an adjective which is almost an epithet—*torcido* (literally, tortuous, crooked, bent). *Un hombre torcido* is so twisted inside that he cannot deal justly with others. We never heard the term applied to a Cañonero, but only to outsiders—often those from governmental bureaucracies, whose loyalties to their superiors interfered with just dealing. The worst we ever heard a Cañonero call another was "mal hombre." Most other negative terms used locally are humorous, or at least have humorous related meanings—*tonto, loco, pendejo, sin vergüenza, chingado*. One man was called *mujerón* (dangerous to women), but he was not torcido. Other qualities highly valued in men are discussed in chapter 7.

In brief, although Cañoneros have been looked upon as peasantry by the Spanish, Mexican, and United States governments, in succession, there is nothing peasant about the Cañonero personally. He is much more caballero, and the Anglo who deals with him on a relatively equal footing soon comes to realize that he has met an expert at handling personal relations.

If a man seeks prestige, he gains it by being chosen for a leadership position in any of the organizations mentioned in a previous chapter, by a political party, or by an outside antipoverty organization such as HELP, in addition to discharging his domestic obligations in a commendable fashion. Both the assumption and the exercise of such prestige is quiet. The noisy or boasting leader is not admired in Cañones.

Mujer

Females go directly from muchacha to *mujer* (woman) upon marriage, with no such mediation as the joven stage for men. While the adult man is king in Cañones, as in all societies of Spanish descent, the lot of a woman is complicated and contradictory. She has been brought up by her mother to expect little from her adult roles of wife, mother, and lover, beyond the drudgery and pain involved. She no longer has even the comfort of consistency, for the school system confronts her with the egalitarian Anglo expectation that she will compete actively. (At a subtle level it does not, if her teachers are themselves local Hispanos; here may be a source of contradiction within contradiction.) She may advise her daughters to put off marrying as long as possible, but girls tend to marry young because the pool of eligible males in Cañones is small.

A woman's domain is her household, and *dueña de su casa* (owner of her house) is a proud and secure status. Within that domain, her authority is unchallenged even by her husband or children. No one can question her menu or her household skills. Her sons love her far more than they love their fathers, and express this affection openly. An illustration of this affection and respect is the following encounter between an elderly widow and her twenty-odd-year-old son, who was about to leave for a distant city to return to work. He was gently teasing his mother about her old-fashioned ways, and drinking a beer in front of her—a conscious violation of the rule that no one drinks in a woman's house without her permission. In short, he was testing the limits of what a son can get away with when his mother is not backed up by a husband. But the moment of departure arrived. With a serious expression on his face the young man knelt before his mother, kissed her hand, and asked her blessing on his journey and for the time when he would be away. She gave him her blessing, he arose soberly, got into his car, and left. Ritual formality and the emotion that it channels easily conquered the attempt of a young bachelor to act "modern" and independent.

A woman's daughters are a help to her from a very early age and gradually become her friends, although seldom her confidantes. The good conduct of daughters reflects upon their mother much more than the conduct of sons does. While well-behaved niños and niñas are directly their mothers' responsibility, this responsibility lasts far longer for daughters than for sons.

Within the domain of her household the woman takes an important public role, which Alice Reich calls "weaving and reweaving the social fabric of the village, including those who have left but not lost touch, through visiting and conversation" (Reich, unpublished manuscript). Outside her own walls she is seen primarily in relation to her husband. (The one soltera in Cañones lives with her widowed mother and has no roles outside her own household.) Her husband is undisputed head of the household in all of its external dealings; she is the leading subordinate member of that household. Consequently, a proper woman is one whose behavior reflects well on the men to whom she is responsible—her father until she marries, her husband and sons thereafter, her other male relatives all her life. Those men are proud if she maintains the home clean and reasonably presentable for guests, sets a decent table for company (who sometimes arrive unexpectedly), and contributes well from her kitchen to community functions such as fiestas for San Miguel, funerals, and wedding dinners. She must emulate Caesar's wife, avoiding both wrong and the appearance of wrong. There are some women in Cañones so extreme in their propriety that they never leave the house alone except to visit close female relatives, and ask their daughters to accompany them even then. Most women are a bit more confident of their standing and visit fairly freely within the village, but nevertheless a high proportion of their visiting is to relatives. (When accompanying her husband, of course, a women goes wherever he wants to take her.)

With her husband, a woman shoulders her share of community burdens. She takes her turn as mayor domo of the church and as madrina of the births, confirmations, and marriages of her fellow citizens. Her part of the church mayor domo obligation is similar to her household duties—cleaning, decorating, making garments for statues of the saints. As madrina she counsels her goddaughters and occasionally shares work with them. If she becomes *mujereta* (one who does these jobs well), her husband as an individual and her household as a social unit are more highly regarded in the community. All of the women in Cañones who are most highly esteemed—and whose families are as well—discharge these obligations fully and generously.

No woman of Cañones works full-time outside the household, but those who work part-time enjoy as much respect as others do. Orlinda Gallegos is postmistress as well as a leader in the school fight. Fidelia Serrano has worked as aide on the school bus and as janitor. Agueda García, daughter of Jacobo Salazar, drives a school bus. Preciliana Salazar (Jacobo's sister), still very much a part of the Cañones seasonal ceremonies although she lives in Santa Fe, is a soltera who has worked at various jobs during her career. She was helpful to the village during the school fight (see chapter 8). In fact there is some reason to think that a woman's ability to hold down a job is regarded as a virtue, particularly among young couples who must earn their livings away from home. Cañoneros of both sexes are realistic about economic survival.

Whether a woman discharges her duties well or not, she has *dignidad de la persona* (see chapter 7) like everyone else, and will be treated with courtesy. The worst insult that can be paid any Hispanic person is to call his mother or sister a whore. This is an insult rarely heard in Cañones or anywhere else in the Rio Arriba, even when children are born out of wedlock, and such an insult would strip the whole family of dignidad.

The definitive word on Hispanic New Mexican women has not

been written, for honest scholars now differ widely. Frances Swadesh, for instance, says that since the nineteenth century Hispanic women on the Chama and San Juan frontiers have been very nearly equal to men in public and private roles (1974:178–79). Janet Lecompte (1981), writing about early nineteenth-century Santa Fe, tells of women who were highly respected but took lovers and otherwise behaved in ways which would be sin vergüenza in Cañones (see chapter 7). We can only repeat that the status of Hispanic women is complex, and that a comprehensive study is much needed.

Viejo(a)

The old are in an ambivalent position, says Edmonson (1957:26), and in Cañones this would seem to be true. A viejo no longer works productively. He may have given over legal or at least effective control of his land to his sons. He can no longer ride a horse well. His ailments often require frequent visits to doctors in Española or farther off. He is not consulted in meetings. On the other hand, he is respected to the degree that his life as hombre has expressed the qualities valued in Cañones. He may still be independent enough to manage his own household, either as husband or as widower. He will look after his grandchildren on occasion, and they after him. He may retain his grace in dancing, and often his verbal wit. His memory of local history is admired. Don Franque Lovato is such a man.

The ultimate mark of the respect paid to a man is how many people show up for his funeral. For those best loved, the latecomers cannot squeeze into the church.

The vieja, like the viejo, is respected, but she is less likely to continue to wield power than he is. If she is a widow, her land is usually already parcelled out among the heirs. She is visited by her children and grandchildren, one of whom may live with her. To some extent she is petted, coddled, and otherwise ignored.

Death

When Cañoneros feel the end approach, they call in their relatives and friends to visit. The Anglo ideal of quiet and isolation for a seriously ill person is not consistent with the Cañones view of friendship and deference to age. A mark of pride to families of the dying is how many people come to visit, and from how far away. If approaching death turns out to be a false alarm, the recovered himself may recount with pleasure the number of people who came to say good-bye, and the distance they traveled.

After death, the body is prepared by a funeral home, the closest of which is in Española. From this point different procedures are followed depending on whether the *difunto* (deceased) is Catholic or Pentecostal, and whether the family is connected with the cofradía or not. For a Catholic, a *rosario* (rosary) and even mass may be said before the body is brought home.

Back in Cañones, rosary is said the day before the funeral mass. This is followed by *velorio* (wake) during the entire night. According to Benjamín Archuleta of Abiquiu, the present sequence evolved from a simpler one. People came with candles (*velas*) for the velorio. While there, they prayed for their deceased friend, perhaps saying the rosary. Hermanos of the cofradía might figure prominently, depending upon who the deceased was. (This is still the case.) During the night the casket was taken by pallbearers in procession around the placita and back into the morada, followed by mourners carrying candles. The current practice of a formal rosario, followed by all-night velorio, is a natural development. One of the services offered by the hermanos to a deceased member is "*a velarlo*"—that is, to sit up in the wake with candles.

If the deceased was a hermano or a member of a cofradía family, other hermanos will take charge of both rosario and velorio, since the priest is seldom able to perform both rosario and funeral mass. Hermanos are also the official gravediggers, even for Catholic families not connected to the cofradía. Since many hermanos are elderly, however, graves are actually dug by younger men, including the grown sons of the deceased. The family may provide a bottle of wine or other refreshments that are passed among the gravediggers. Digging graves is a very small example of cooperative work, but a poignant one. *Misericordia* (chapter 7) is made up of mutual support within the village at critical moments like this.

The funeral mass is an impressive ceremony, especially if the cofradía is involved. It is also a proper occasion for public display of grief. Males show their grief by weeping; females wail loudly when they pass the open casket, and again when the casket is lowered into the ground.

The most impressive single part of the funeral is the procession on foot from church to the campo santo at the west edge of the village. The priest leads, followed by the cofradía singing alabados. Then the hearse or truck carrying the casket, and the pallbearers and immediate family. At last, the rest of the congregation, completing a procession that may be almost a quarter of a mile long.

The priest's eulogy at the gravesite may be followed by one from a parishioner, depending on whether the widow or one of the children has asked someone to do this. When the casket is lowered into the grave, pallbearers and close relatives toss flowers on top of it, then handfuls of earth. Others in the congregation follow with earth, and then men take turns shoveling to fill up the grave. After most people have left, the grave is mounded over and the remaining flowers are placed on top.

After the funeral, either the immediate family or a close relative serves a meal to the mourners, including pallbearers, hermanos, and those who have come from outside Cañones to attend. People eat in shifts. One of the hermanos says grace—not an ordinary custom at Cañones tables. Three or four women of the community help out in the cooking and service. Conversation at this meal seldom centers on the deceased, and fairly quickly becomes general —the weather, politics, local personalities. This is a reunion of people who see each other seldom, and it takes on the happier character of most reunions.

Friends and relatives make a point of visiting the bereaved during the days and weeks after a death, and take a particular interest in their welfare. The funeral is widely discussed for some time after, including the personality of the deceased and the number of people who came to pay their respects.

The difunto is ceremonially remembered at mass approximately fifteen days after death, and mass will be said for the repose of his soul at the request of relatives or sometimes of friends upon the anniversary of death. Flowers are placed on the grave from time to time. If the difunto died in an automobile accident, as numerous Cañoneros do, a cross painted white, with the name and date of death painted in black letters, is erected on the site. This cross is also then decorated with flowers.

In general, the mode of coping with death appears to be to express grief freely and openly, especially by women, with expressions like "*O mi hijito, murió mi hijito*" (Oh my son, my son died) or "*Hermanito de mi vida*" (My beloved little brother) repeated over and over. Grief thus freely expressed lasts for a time and then the bereaved usually recover without lingering residues.

The Pentecostal funeral, according to Medardo Lovato, is like a regular church service. The pastor talks about the difunto and his life. He mentions significant events in the life of the deceased—the year, month, day he was saved, for example. A hymn is likely to be sung that was one of the deceased's favorites. Burial is in the Pentecostal cemetery, just up the hill from the Catholic church. Otherwise the peripheral events and the solicitous attention to the bereaved resemble closely those already described for Catholics.

The name of a Cañonero who has died is almost invariably preceded by *el difunto*. If the deceased was related to the speaker, the full relationship is expressed whenever he or she is mentioned, as in "*Mi difunta comadre Agapita.*"

Living in Cycles

Thus from morning to night, from January to December, from birth to death, the cycles of Cañones life are orderly, predictable, and ceremonious. The rituals appropriate to these cycles may be played out skillfully or clumsily, and skill in their performance is tacitly applauded. Chapter 1 described Cañoneros as living with style. It is the color and the flamboyance that a Cañonero uses in acting out his roles in the cycles of life that demonstrate his stylishness and his understanding of the endless nuances of his own culture.

7
Integrative and Disintegrative Beliefs

If a community is to be orderly, predictable and ceremonious, its citizens must agree on what actions are good and what ways of living are worth working and fighting for. In this chapter we describe these values, as we perceive Cañoneros to define them. To understand the value system of the village is to understand better the continuity from past to present, and from present to future.

Anthropologists during the past two or three decades tend to regard values as intellectual quicksand, because the data are not firm. Informants do not talk about their values in everday conversation, hence often disagree about what they are, and sometimes are not consciously aware of them. Since it is sometimes necessary to infer values from actions, the ethnographer is led to a good many statements like "It would seem . . ." and "It is reasonable to assume . . ."

We forge ahead nonetheless. The values that Cañoneros live by are the key to comprehending how the village dared to challenge the state department of education over the school-closing issue narrated in chapter 8. In addition, if we distinguish sharply between society and culture, society being flesh and blood human beings organized for survival, culture the understandings and rules that they use to promote their survival, then we can make better sense in chapter 9 out of the changes that Cañones experienced between the ethnographic present of 1967 and publication of this book.

Since values are the centerpiece of this monograph, a concrete definition is in order. We use Clyde Kluckhohn's classic statement, because it leads directly from belief to action: "A value is a conception, explicit or implicit, distinctive of an individual or characteristic of a group, of the desirable which influences the selection from available modes, means, and ends of action" (1951:395. Emphasis deleted.) Kluckhohn and E. A. Hoebel both distinguish between normative postulates (values) and existential postulates ("assumptions as to the nature of existence" [Hoebel 1958:158]). In a well integrated culture like that of Cañones, existential and normative postulates must be consistent with each other; but they are not the same thing.

The starting point of our interest in Hispanic values is conversations with Facundo Valdez in 1966 and 1967, which he crystallized in his pioneer paper "Vergüenza" (1979). Otherwise, all of the data here are our own. They are similar in general to the values described in Munro Edmonson's 1950 study of a village on the western plateau fringe of New Mexican Hispanic settlement (Edmonson 1957). We have not found Florence Kluckhohn's study of values in the same area (F. Kluckhohn and Strodtbeck 1961) to be pertinent to our Rio Arriba village, and Frances Swadesh, who knows Hispanic culture firsthand both in the western plateau and in the Rio Arriba, argues that the Kluckhohn analysis is inaccurate (Swadesh 1972). The similarity between the values of Cañones and those of Spain and other Mediterranean countries, as described by Peristiany and his colleagues in *Honour and Shame* (1966), is so astonishing that we should accuse ourselves of unconscious plagiarism except that neither of us read Peristiany until this chapter was essentially completed. The strong continuity from Spain to New Mexico raises theoretical questions to be pursued in the future.

With that introduction, we turn to describe and discuss the personal qualities that are highly valued in Cañones. The following are commonly recognized, described, and discussed: *vergüenza, respeto de la casa,* and *misericordia. Dignidad de la persona* is recognized by a few Cañoneros, but is not easily verbalized. Fatalism is perceived by outsiders—not by Cañoneros—and is superficial if it exists at all. The values placed on generosity, wit, and style are inferred by us; we have never heard them discussed by people in Cañones.

Vergüenza

In most of Hispanic America, *vergüenza* means little more than *shame.* This is only one of its meanings in New Mexico, where an accurate definition might be *tender regard for the good opinion of one's fellow citizens.* Beyond this, examples will be more useful than definitions. The concept is not mentioned in community studies, with the exception of Mead's brief note (1955:156): "Children are admonished to have '*vergüenza*' (shame, pride, modesty), not to push themselves forward."

A child is born without vergüenza, and must be taught—even whipped, if necessary—so it will acquire this quality. Muchachos and jovenes who may decline to speak in public because of vergüenza —*bashfulness* or *shyness*—are considered modest and praiseworthy, while a shy Anglo youth would be urged to overcome his affliction.

An adult *con vergüenza* will be a traditionalist, because he observes not only the opinions of others in the village, but also the *costumbres* of the past. He will probably make his living according to traditional patterns in farming, ranching, woodcarving, the priesthood, or the civil service. Such a man may also become prominent as mayor domo of the church or of the acequia system. The Cañoneros who led the community in the battle against the state department of education were acting con vergüenza. Politics can be a career con vergüenza, if the político treats his constituents fairly and honestly. It is usually assumed that he will not.

In his home, the man con vergüenza is just and stern. Outside his home, he will challenge authority if he thinks it necessary, regardless of where that authority comes from. Valdez gives the following example of a challenge to religious authority (1979:101):

> A new priest came into a community, didn't particularly like the way his parishioners responded to the service, and criticized them from the pulpit. One man who had never missed mass in thirty years suddenly said, "I won't go to church with that priest, because there is something wrong with him." He said, "*La única dificultad con el padre es que se cree muy padre* (that priest considers himself very priestly and a hot shot)," implying an

> inflated opinion of himself. So the man *con vergüenza* does not shrink from questioning an authority that most people would not question. He knows when to stand his ground. This is another manifestation of his being a private person, one who consults himself and feels no need to find out what people in general think before making up his mind.

Sin vergüenza sheds light on vergüenza, but *without shame* is a pale translation. Valdez states that from vergüenza to sin vergüenza is "almost as if we moved from one type of judgment to another" (1979:99).

The niño sin vergüenza is simply behaving as expected. One speaks of or to him or her, as sin vergüenza more or less affectionately, as one might call him mischievous. In a similar tone, an Anglo parent might say, "That kid! I can't do a thing with him." Such a child has a good deal of energy that, properly channeled, may serve him well later. As a child acquires vergüenza, he or she becomes a muchacho or muchacha who takes responsibility for work in the family and on the farm, and for his or her own behavior as a moral being.

The adult male sin vergüenza is not treated leniently, for he is someone who gets ahead by taking advantage of others. He is *cusco* (stingy) or *torcido* (twisted, crooked). From the village point of view, certain occupations are thus categorically suspect—storekeeping, business, the law, and any other in which one tries to gain a competitive edge.

Men do, however, enjoy a gray area of flamboyant picaresque conduct, which Valdez defines this way (1979:104):

> The *pícaro* gives satisfaction to others because he has found ways of escaping oppressive situations through stylish maneuvering. He is not a Robin Hood, but perhaps we could say that he realizes the fantasies of others. In relation to *vergüenza*, he is not totally "straight" but he never seriously takes advantage of others and he gives pleasure through his wit.

The verbal play reported in the first section of chapter 6 is mildly picaresque. Here are two more examples, from Kutsche's field notes, of a pícaro making fun of himself: Serafín Valdez sat astride the roofpole of a house he was repairing one late afternoon, brandishing a hammer at me in greeting, as if it were the reins of a horse. "*No supe que era carpintero,"* I called out (I didn't know you were a carpenter). *"No soy carpintero. Soy carpintonto!"* he shouted with a roar of laughter. (*Tonto* means fool; the word he made up does not translate.)

A young Cañonero came to a dance alone while his wife was at home in the last stages of her first pregnancy. With a broad smile and immense self-satisfaction the man explained his presence: *"Soy sin vergüenza."* His audience laughed indulgently and with obvious pleasure, although some of them probably disapproved of his not staying home.

A very traditional category of ritual humor is also somewhat picaresque—impromptu verses sung at wedding receptions, combining compliments and advice for the novios with sly remarks about others present. This concert is usually a solo, but the wittiest perform a fast-paced recitative. Simón Vigil, for example, at the reception for his daughter Jenny and her novio Nastacio Gallegos of Arroyo de Agua, sang short barbed verses at the padrino Salomón Martínez, also of Arroyo de Agua, who sang back equally barbed verses to the same doggerel tune. There was never a beat missed between them for about ten minutes, to the enormous delight of the wedding guests.

The examples of picarismo cited above are harmless, and some might even quibble whether they qualify as picaresque. The more usual Cañones definition of the pícaro is harsher than Facundo Valdez's: one who borrows and does not return, one who cheats through trickery, one who robs.

The feminine term *pícara* does not exist in Cañones or, probably, anywhere in the Spanish-speaking world. Women are held more strictly to account, and what might be picaresque for a man would be sin vergüenza for a woman—even a display of verbal wit. In former years, women were not considered entirely responsible for their own conduct. As Valdez says, "If a woman is *sin vergüenza* she has destroyed the manliness of the man; if he had been a man, she never would have become *sin vergüenza*" (1979:102). Although a Cañonera's behavior today is not as likely to be blamed on her father or her husband, nevertheless, the standard she must live up to is not relaxed. Most female behavior sin vergüenza has sexual connotations: such acts include frequenting cantinas, strolling about in public unescorted, and behaving assertively toward men. But joking that would be picaresque in a man is also enjoyed by women. One day while Alice Reich was helping two respectable Cañoneras bake, they made great fun over her ignorance of the double meaning of *biscochito* (a little sweet biscuit; also [*vulg.*] the female genitals).

Respeto de la Casa

Respeto and vergüenza are related values, but Cañoneros distinguish between them. Respeto is typically focussed on the head of the household. The term covers behavior that might be all right elsewhere, but is not permissible in relation to a house (one might almost say *House* with a capital *h*, as when referring to lineage). A grown man will usually not smoke in the presence of his mother, sometimes even his father, unless his parent is smoking. Husbands do not drink in their own homes if their wives object—some object, some do not.

An incident at the home of a friend, edited from Kutsche's field notes, illustrates respeto de la casa vividly:

> In came one of my friend's sons, together with my friend's brother, Juan Pablo, who lives about 100 miles away. Juan Pablo was drunk.
>
> J. P. turned on me as soon as we had been introduced, and acted very belligerently. Who the hell was I? "*Que hace aquí? Viene para chingar a la gente? Viene para fregar a la gente?* (What are you doing here? Do you come to screw the people? Do you come to do evil to the people?)"
>
> I told him where I was from, and gave him the same story I have consistently given, "*Yo quiero estudiar la lengua y la cultura española. Estoy estudiando la historia del pueblo de Cañones.* (I want to study Spanish language and culture. I'm studying the history of the village of Cañones.)"
>
> "Baloney!" he responded. "Bullshit!"
>
> I grew a little indignant, and said, "*Yo tengo un cuento, no más, y es la verdad.* (I have but one story [about my activities] and it is the truth.)"
>
> He quizzed me at some length about who I was, where I was from, what an anthropologist is, and so on, and accepted none of my answers.
>
> My friend and his wife at first laughed it off because J. P. was drunk. Then, as the exchange between us seemed to grow more acrimonious—on my part sort of a retreat upon offended dignity—my friend remonstrated with his brother. He made coffee for him, urged him to sit down and drink it, and then, growing

> more insistent, said, "*No diga riñegos de este hombre aquí.* (Don't say bad things about this man while you are here.)" Then, the strongest statement he made—with some anger, "*Respeta la casa, no diga tantas cosas aquí.* (Have respect for my house, don't say such things here.)"
>
> Juan Pablo went outside to piss, and I thought this a good time to leave, pleading that it was late. My friend, deeply embarrassed, accompanied me to the car. I had never seen him embarrassed before, and speculate that a major source of his pain was his inability to control the behavior of a relative of his, and protect a guest in his house from insult. I doubt that the insult itself figured as importantly.

In retrospect, it is evident that Kutsche's friend's repeated use of *aquí* was a key to his offended value. In effect he said, "Call this man whatever you like, but not while he is under the protection of my house."

Those who dwell in a house can also destroy the community's respect for it. Both husband and wife are responsible. His business is to put food on the table, to care for his family, and to keep their neighbor's respect. One wife describes how her husband's behavior had cost them their respect:

> We fight a lot. He just drinks and drinks and drinks. He is terrible. I never know if he is going to come home drunk, or even if he is going to come home. My children are *malcriados.* I have to tell them all the time not to do this and that.

The wife's responsibility is to cook well, to keep the house presentable and her children neat and clean. When there are quarrels between her and her husband, they are to be kept within the walls of the house. A couple who fought publicly with kitchen knives were widely described as lacking respeto de la casa.

The English expression "letting the side down" comes to mind as an approximate rendering of what happens if respeto is not shown. A wall is breached in the House, showing what is messy, dirty, badly arranged.

Outside the house, people show respeto to each other by speaking well of people and things that are dear to them. No man badmouths a relative or a compadre of the man to whom he is speaking.

No man speaks ill of another's house, village, or *raza.* We are not *gringo*, *gavacho*, or *bolillo* to him; he is not *Mexican* or *greaser* to us. New Mexican village Hispanos fit perfectly the proverb that "a gentleman is a man who is never unintentionally rude." If a Hispano insults anyone, he means it.

Vergüenza and respeto are public virtues. They have to do with one's ability to carry oneself and one's obligations to family and community in a manner that brings public credit to both of them and to oneself. If one wants to take office in the parents' organization to represent Cañones against the state department of education, then he must possess vergüenza and deserve respeto de su casa.

Misericordia

This value lies somewhere between those openly discussed in Cañones and those we have inferred from behavior. We never heard of it until the early 1970s, and then from former governor David Cargo, a native of Michigan, an Anglo, and a Catholic. He said it means *speaking from the heart*. Cañoneros and other local people recognize the word, define it readily as *empathy* and *compassion*, and describe it in terms that helped us understand the sources of village unity.

An Anglo Presbyterian minister who knows the area well said, "Since the word speaks of mercifulness and pity, perhaps 'together in suffering' might be central to it."

Father John Méndez, a native of the island of Cuba, who became parish priest in 1977, said:

> Misericordia is tied up with understanding, the people having gone through so many things together for so long. One person might realize that his friend might not be doing good things, but he can sympathize, can share with him. All of Hispanic New Mexico has a lot of misericordia. I have seen it more in the north, where there is more poverty. People here have more pity. Reflections of misericordia are expressions about people who have had hard lives—*pobre hombre*, *pobrecito*.

"Mercy. They have mercy toward each other," said two women of Abiquiu who know Cañones well. "Cañones has the reputation of living the way people used to, sharing work. When they kill a pig, everybody helps kill, and everybody shares the meat."

And Elipio Garcia described it further as:

> closeness of feeling. For instance, Manuel [name changed] and I know each other so well that each of us knows the other's feeling. The whole community has it, not because everyone is kin to everyone else, but because we have all grown up together, because we all have the same problems. It is partly because the village is hard to get into, with its bad road and all. It is also because we don't have television and telephones. So we consult each other long before we talk with people from outside. Cañoneros share what in most villages is a private, family matter.

Machismo

Machismo is not a northern New Mexican value or word, although the adjective *macho* is used and approved. As noun, macho is a male mule (*mula* is female). A macho human being is *un hombre valiente* (a brave man) according to Isabel Salazar, who says that sexual prowess is not essential to the definition. Munro Edmonson defines machismo as "he-man-ism" in his description of village culture near Gallup (1957:69).

Américo Paredes, the great folklorist of South Texas, writes that the concept machismo properly applies only to sex as aggression. According to Paredes (1972:146):

> With uncompromising Freudian logic *machismo* has been traced to oedipal conflicts arising at the moment when the first Spaniard threw the first Indian woman to the ground and raped her, thus laying the foundations of modern Mexico. Because of this primal act of sexual violence the Mexican sees sex as aggression, and assuming the role of the hated Spanish father he translates his fixation into sadism toward women and symbolic threats of sodomy toward other males.

But in fact, Paredes argues:

> the cult of manliness is not peculiar to the Mexican, nor does the Freudian interpretation of the Conquest explain very much. We can find all the elements of Mexican *machismo* among peoples whose ancestral mothers were never raped by Spanish conquistadors. Yet we cannot deny that in Mexican culture these elements are put together in their own special way. *Machismo* everywhere is characterized by an aggressive attitude behind which there lurks a feeling of defensiveness and insufficiency (ibid.:146–47).

Paredes further associates machismo for the Mexican male with the Revolution of 1910 and the omnipresent threat of U.S. culture to Mexican identity (ibid.:148).

This emphasis on violent aggression and psychic inadequacy does not suit rural New Mexico, where relative geographical isolation has protected villagers from competition, and their national pride is for the United States rather than for Mexico. Here the feeling of sexual adequacy is great enough so that young men can calmly acknowledge that their girl friends preferred someone else. "*No me quería como yo la quería* (she didn't love me the way I loved her)," said one without self-pity. The aggression against other individuals implied in machismo contradicts vergüenza, respeto, and dignidad.

Like Paredes (1972:147), we believe that frontier Anglo America shows far more machismo than traditional New Mexico. We think it is also characteristic of the socially and politically uncertain adolescent gangs of big cities, whatever their origin. One can see it in the urban Chicano movement.

One way machismo may be seen is as an injured response to the loss of dignidad de la persona by social turbulence or some other force.

Dignidad de la Persona

Dignidad de la persona is similar to the Quaker concept of the "inner light." It is the inherent human quality of grace, worth, and psychic autonomy. Every normal adult is assumed to have dignidad.

Since dignidad is inherent, a part of everyone's nature, it is closer to an existential than to a normative postulate. Nevertheless, it belongs in this chapter because the concept determines "selection from available modes, means, and ends of action" perhaps more than any other in regard to how people treat each other face to face. Whereas one must strive as a child to acquire vergüenza and as an adult to maintain it; whereas one must uphold the respeto de su propia casa—one *has* dignidad and cannot easily lose it. One achieves vergüenza and respeto. One is born with dignidad.

Equality of address is central to recognizing dignidad in Cañones. Every adult addresses every other adult, within the two categories of sex and age, with equal respect. Attributes that distinguish forms of address in other societies—land or other wealth, family reputation, morals, past behavior—are ignored. If a man is drunk, he temporarily loses dignidad, and may even be teased if one dares; but one does not remind him later that he was drunk. At the same time, one may say anything he chooses about another person in referring to him when he is not present, for these expressions of opinion are not covered by the concept of dignidad. Some critics call people of Latin culture two-faced because of this distinction.

Dignidad is attributed to everyone, regardless of sex, roughly from the stage of muchacho on up. But in this respect, as in many others, men are slightly more equal than women. A woman must forever watch herself in public; but dignidad provides a protective shield for males endowing them with a very deep-seated self confidence. Behind that shield, as boys and young men, they can experiment with styles of behavior until they find those modes that suit them individually. The terrible fear common to Anglo adolescents of being thought unmasculine seems to be almost entirely absent from young rural Hispanos. The flamboyance that a few of them display—in clothes that are more *gaucho* than cowboy, in riding horses, in personal style in the *cantina,* in dancing, and in colorful use of language—shows not only creativity but self assurance. The remarkable physical grace with which Hispanic New Mexicans handle themselves may be at least in part a consequence of absolute confidence that one is a dignified being. A tendency toward a lack of economic and career competitiveness may be another consequence. One need not compete in order to acquire dignity, since one is born with it. Whether one learns to act con vergüenza and con respeto, is quite another matter.

Some of the guidelines for respecting the dignidad of others are as follows:

1. Greet others in personal terms. Immediately proceeding with the business at hand is bad form. One must pay respect to the *person* before using him or her as an agent. It is proper to ask after the spouse, children, and other relatives of a person one meets after an absence of a few days or more.
2. Treat them with formality and seriousness. If they are not close friends or relatives, a sprinkling of *señor* or *señora* in addressing others is considered courteous. Acknowledge closer relationship by greeting them or referring to them with the appropriate term: *tío, primo, compadre,* however the case may be.
3. Teasing is taboo, unless it is done so subtly that one can

> reasonably deny doing it. Verbal dueling invariably employs such subtlety. A simple example is the Cañonero who, seeing Kutsche overdressed (coat and tie) for a funeral in the village, and knowing him to be slow in Spanish repartee, addressed him with a straight and serious face as "Don Pablo." Paredes's paper on humor (1972) quoted under machismo is itself a masterpiece of subtle barbs. But the jocular informality of Mid-America—greeting a companion on Sunday morning with "Wow, you really hung one on last night!" would be terribly gauche.

Like most other qualities, dignidad can be best illustrated when it is put on the line. Although an outsider might think that being homosexual, which is disvalued, would forfeit dignidad, one finds that it does not. For example, during Kutsche's hospital stay in Albuquerque in 1967, he met a Hispanic homosexual working as an orderly. He was in his late twenties and had a relaxed air toward the hospital and the staff. He did not try to hide or mask his really effeminate ways. Observing this, Kutsche mentioned to him that apparently the homosexual was more accepted in Hispanic society than in Anglo society and that there was no need to pretend to be straight and masculine. He replied that it was so. One could be who one was, and the consequences of everyone's knowing were not hard to live with. Other men simply accepted him without making fun of him. He was aware that in Anglo society this was not true.

On another occasion, Kutsche attended a dance in Cañones where two young and effeminate men from another village were present. They were treated by other males and females like everyone else, with no hint of rejection on or off the dance floor. Two or three weeks later, however, Kutsche met another man from that same village who happened to have the surname of one of the young men at the dance. When Kutsche asked him if he were related—without mentioning anything about the young man's eccentric behavior—the rather indignant reply was that he was not. This episode, plus derogatory remarks made about habitual drinkers—but not in their presence—offers the most convincing evidence that dignidad is a privilege of address.

The reciprocal assumption of dignity inherent in human beings implies nothing whatever about understanding. It is a matter of faith. It extends to geographic and ethnic outsiders whose own values one may not understand at all. This facet of dignidad sometimes leads New Mexican Hispanos to take strangers at face value, and makes it easy for them to get along with outsiders. Generally one does not probe into what makes others different. (Anyone whose appearance or behavior might label him or her "hippie" is an exception, disliked on sight. But this attitude comes from bad personal experience and not from prejudgment. The hippie influx of the 1960s was greeted with hospitality until northern New Mexico villagers began to feel that they were being taken advantage of.)

To withhold dignidad from another, to mock him to his face, is a most serious insult throughout the Hispanic world. Jorge Luis Borges in a one-page story "Los Dos Reyes y Los Dos Laberintos" tells of the King of Babylon who invited an Arab king into his labyrinth "*para hacer burla de la simplicidad de su huesped*" (to make a mockery of the simplicity of his guest), which so enraged the countrified Arab that he later destroyed the castles of the city of Babylon, took its king captive, and left him in the desert to die of hunger and thirst. Similarly, if less dramatically, it is said that the citizens of the village of Questa, New Mexico, took revenge against a gang of motorcyclists who made fun of them with insults and urinated in their streets, by shooting them up when they made the mistake of returning a few days later.

The rural Hispano is no longer protected by isolation from the city and from ignorant insults by non-Hispanos. The city Hispano, who calls himself Chicano, bitterly jokes that "We said to the Anglos, '*Entre en la casa suya,*' and they did." The Chicano replaces the reciprocal assumption of dignidad, which leaves people open to each other, with the protective shell of machismo, which can be seen as a reaction to rents in the social fabric woven by reciprocal dignity. In revolutionary circumstances, the macho male will be secretly or openly admired by those who choose to continue to live in terms of the older values.

Fatalism

Fatalism, like dignidad, is a statement of what is—an existential rather than a normative postulate, hence not a value. But it figures large in the social science literature on Spanish, Mexican, and New Mexican rural society, and from it the observer will infer "conceptions of the desirable" that strongly influence action. Munro Edmonson summarizes the position of many observers of New

Mexican Hispanic society fairly thoroughly in *Los Manitos* (1957:59–61, from which the following quotes are taken). Edmonson says that the Spanish language itself supports fatalism, with " '*Se rompió*' (it broke itself), '*se perdió*' (it lost itself), and other such expressions of fatalistic acceptance. . . ." In health, "Where Anglo Americans spend enormous amounts of money on preventive medical care and life insurance, Hispanos give a characteristic shrug of acceptance of death and illness as inevitable." In weather, "Hispanos accept drought and soil erosion as part of God's inscrutable order of things; Anglos combat them with dry ice, dams, reforestation and soil conservation practices." And so forth.

Edmonson is more right than wrong on the descriptive level. But while he seems to imply that fatalism is basic to Hispanic views of the world, we believe fatalism is a superficial adaptation to circumstances beyond one's control.

The expressions most often used to convey fatalistic acceptance are "*Si quiera Diós*" (God willing) and "*Ojalá!*" (would that . . .; literally, Oh Allah!). But the notion that fatalism is built into Spanish grammar is naïve. "*Qué pasó con la pierna?*" "*Se quebró.*" (What happened to your leg? It broke.) does not carry an overtone of "it broke itself," any more than "*la pierna*" (the leg) carries an overtone less personal than "*su pierna*" or "*mi pierna*" (your leg, my leg). One might as well argue that since Spanish uses a double negative while English uses only one (*No viene nadie*, literally, no one is not coming), therefore Spanish thought is more negative than English.

Debates over the influence of language structure on thought are old in ethnology, and honest scholars argue each side. Charles Hockett (1954:122–23) holds that the influence is minimal—all languages are flexible and inventive and can encompass any thought. Américo Paredes (1977) demolishes with well-sharpened sarcasm the pretensions of Anglo social scientists to understand Hispanic character through analysis of Spanish grammar.

After sharing for several years with Cañoneros their slow communications with the rest of the world, their miserable road, their distance from doctors, their lack of cash, their obligation to drop their own plans in order to give hospitality to virtually anyone who shows up at the door, we offer as follows our own interpretation of their "fatalism."

You invite me to drive to town with you in six days, arranging to pick me up. I say thank you, and tell you I shall be waiting, "*Si quiera Diós.*" You never show up (or you show up and I am not at the appointed place). You may be rained in or prevented by car trouble or sickness. Your son may have arrived from Denver. I may have had an emergency somewhere. Neither of us has a telephone, so we could not let the other know. "Si quiera Diós" makes perfectly good sense.

Another hypothetical example: you and I stand by a hollowed-out log carrying the acequia over an arroyo. It leaks, as such aqueducts tend to do. You say wouldn't it be nice if we had a cement-lined acequia, and a metal pipe to carry water over the arroyo. I reply, "Ojalá!" The expression is used most often when we do not have the means to accomplish what we want, and we are "building castles in Spain."

These two examples are apt because in the decade since our ethnographic present, covered in detail in chapter 9, Cañones has a better road, telephones, and acequia systems improved with cement and metal. Sick and pregnant people more often make it to the doctor in time to be treated. Families are buying life insurance. Appointments are more often kept. Hispanos do not offer "a characteristic shrug of acceptance" when it becomes technically feasible to improve life in some way *valued by them.* The italics are essential, because Hispanos do not always value what an Anglo thinks they should. A number of women, for instance, will not exchange wood stoves for gas or electricity, because they are convinced that food cooked over wood tastes better. We have mentioned Adelaida Lucero, who prefers the gentle light of kerosene to the harsh light of electricity. Virtually everyone prefers traditional adobe houses to those made by any other material; the rest of the region has now come round to that preference.

Edmonson's statements about fatalism were made before alternatives were economically feasible. In our opinion fatalism does not indicate passive acceptance, but unwillingness to get ulcers from frustration. The attitude is the same as that expressed in the well known prayer:

> Lord, give me the courage to change what can be changed
> The strength to accept what cannot be changed
> And the wisdom to know the difference.

Cañoneros know the difference.

Fatalism is a reasonable view of the world for segments of large civilizations that have been impoverished for centuries. It is a psychological coping device that is being shed rapidly in the late twentieth century. It is noteworthy that a major shift on the village level from fatalistic to activist attitudes occurs together with the War on Poverty and other tangible attention to poor people from the federal government.

A different explanation of the behavior labelled fatalistic by social analysts is offered by Hispanos themselves. As we have mentioned earlier, "Si quiera Diós" and Ojalá!", along with the polite form of greeting "Buenos días le dé Diós," are conscious reminders of the religious community, that we are all devout Christians under God. In these respects fatalism is simply a misinterpretation of religious belief.

Other Values

We infer that generosity, hospitality, and style are qualities the Cañoneros value from their attitude and behavior toward people who have them. Generosity and hospitality—always going together—are exemplified by two or three houses in the village that are centers of communication. In those houses visitors are welcomed with a cup of coffee, food, fruit, or vegetables from the garden. Visitors bring their latest news, and receive news left behind by previous visitors.

A contrast between two households throws the value of generosity into relief. Neither has primary kin relations in the village, so others have no formal obligation to them. One of the two households consists of people too old and infirm to collect their own firewood. Nevertheless, they always have a supply because their friends and relatives frequently, if unsystematically, bring it to them. It is generally recognized that not to help people who always show such warmth and hospitality would be sadly unfriendly. The second household, likewise unable to go after its own firewood, is always in want and depends upon the state welfare office for money to buy wood (about $20 per load). Nothing comes from that household by way of geniality or tangible hospitality, and no one seems to care about its well-being.

When the head of the first household died (well after our ethnographic present), people went out of their way to describe him as a "*muy buen hombre,*" and simply "*muy hombre.*" Many people came to his funeral.

In Spanish, Cañoneros make the distinction illustrated above with the adjectives *corriente* and *particular,* valuing the first and disvaluing the second. Corriente means plain, easy, generally received, ordinary, common, acceptable; particular means peculiar, special, private, individual, odd (both according to Appleton's *New Cuyás Dictionary.*)

Style is valued in some activities and not particularly in others. It is more valued by some age and sex categories, less valued by others. Riding horses, driving cars, and dancing, are three very stylish activities. Good horsemanship is admired by everyone, and men of all ages happily discuss details of horses and horsemen. Graceful and imaginative dancing is admired by all Catholics, without regard to sex and age. Virtually all of them try to become good dancers. Skillful driving is valued by everyone, of all ages, sexes, and religions, since everyone must get in and out of Cañones whether the road is dry or muddy. The most skillful drivers are jóvenes and young adult men; they can be quite smug when they maneuver an old sedan past cars stuck in the mud outside Cañones, and bring their passengers home safe and dry. Details of flamboyant driving, especially when skill is shown although the driver is drunk, are discussed lovingly by jóvenes over the disapproval of their mothers.

Competence is approved in daily activities. The well-made house, the neat rows of a vegetable garden, the smoothly plastered wall, are all quietly praised. But there seems to be no stigma attached to jobs done without elegance, so long as the results serve their intended purposes.

These minor values are independent of others. People highly valued in these respects may or may not have vergüenza and respeto. Their dignidad is neither higher nor lower because of them.

There are numerous areas of personal relationships that values say nothing about. A note on some of these areas may help the reader to understand the limits of application of values to behavior.

Maternal attitudes vary widely. A grown woman of Cañones says of her mother, "It was always the dishes and the house first before us kids." That mother is highly respected, as are women who cuddle their children first and clean the house second.

Children may be apt or clumsy at the dance, may be studious or stupid in school, athletic or not. This doesn't affect their social worth.

Musical talent is valued, perhaps because of the pleasure it brings to others. As in other societies, the person who can sing or play the guitar is welcome at private and public fiestas.

Drinking

We end this chapter with two categories that are widely known but heavily disvalued. The first of these is drinking. Virtually all Catholic men drink fairly heavily from time to time. A few drink a great deal. Binge drinking is more common than steady light drinking. One thoughtful elderly man, looking back on a life that included heavy drinking when he was young, explained the affinity for liquor as lifting one onto a plateau of joy. He, for instance, had liked to dance but was shy. A few *traguitos* of strong drink would make him think he was a great dancer. Vergüenza inhibited a young man, but liquor released him from inhibition.

No male behavior upsets women more than drinking—not even wife beating. Why is it regarded as such a threat?

Because proper behavior is largely restrained behavior.

One grants dignidad to others by resisting temptations to treat them in undignified ways. One is formal. (*Formalidad* is a named virtue in Spain, defined as "self-control and strict adherence to the rules" [Aguilera 1978:144]. The properly *formal* Spaniard can drink a great deal without loosening his tongue or otherwise making a fool of himself [ibid.:30]) One attains vergüenza and one upholds respeto de la casa by deliberate and thoughtful public behavior. For women, even more than for men, respectability is achieved by holding back one's impulses. Alcohol is a solvent of restraint. The drinker regularly acts sin vergüenza and may lose respect. One temporarily loses one's dignidad while drunk. Men beat their wives while drunk and spend family money recklessly. All cases of violence in Cañones that we know of involve alcohol.

Drinking is part of a pattern of behavior involving generosity and sociability, which are positively valued by nearly everybody. Sharing beer or other liquor is an inevitable part of friendly interaction between males outside dance halls, and is a frequent part of visiting between households, when the women chat inside and the men outside the house. In a cantina reciprocal buying of rounds is mandatory. Many people in the region see this patterned drinking as unfortunate and destructive. Further, some individuals believe that generosity is likely to victimize the generous, and are more comfortable living *un poco parte*—not, so to speak, always in each other's social pockets. The entire pattern, of which drinking is a large part but far from the whole, is escaped by becoming Pentecostal, for drinking (as well as dancing and some other indulgences) is taboo in the Pentecostal faith.

Brujería

One hears very little about *brujería* (witchcraft) in Cañones. This lack of evidence, plus the pragmatic attitude of Cañoneros toward medicine, accepting medical help from Hispanic or Anglo practitioners impartially depending upon availability and past experience, leads us to conclude that belief in *brujos* plays a small part in their views of the world. Nevertheless, witches are part of the history of Hispanic culture in New Mexico (cf. Simmons 1974, Brown 1978), and however strong or weak the belief in their practices may be in Cañones, it tends to prevent people from close friendship and cooperation. One example will illustrate this tendency: a young wife, mother of two infant children, died. The husband and father believed that the cause of death was brujería by another Cañonero, and accused that person directly and publicly. Years later, the accused came to the widower's house to ask his permission for the hand of one of his daughters as a bride for the accused's son. The father refused. Relations between the two households remained cold.

8
The School Fight

August 29, 1966: Cañones kept at home all of its children in grades four through eight who should have been bussed to school in Coyote. Every school day for the next three months the bus came in at 8:00 A.M. as scheduled, waited in the placita, and went out as empty as it entered. For a short time, this deliberate quiet civil disobedience headlined Cañones in the regional newspapers and on radio and television, became an issue in the 1966 governor's race and other political campaigns, was debated by educational specialists, and inspired Cañones to call on its reserves of values and social institutions to organize into the "Cañones Parents Committee"—a force that dominated village life for about a year.

My residency in Cañones from mid-October, 1966, until August, 1967, shaped my personal bias: I have a hard time thinking of department of education officials as anything but the bad guys in black hats. [Ed. note: During these events Kutsche's role shifted from observer to participant. Van Ness was not yet on the scene. Therefore Kutsche refers to himself here in the first person.] They were careless with their facts once they decided to close the Cañones school. They made groundless charges merely for the publicity it would bring them. They were willfully ignorant of Hispanic culture. They treated natives of Cañones with contempt. And the state superintendent treated my own professional credentials with contempt. All of the statements of fact in this chapter have been checked carefully for accuracy, and sources listed. Interviews were recorded in shorthand and transcribed within a few hours. But my interpretations are those of a passionate participant, not of a neutral observer.

To understand the school fight is to understand the strength of Hispanic village culture, and to learn something of the clash of values between rural Hispanos and a state bureaucracy shaped by Anglo culture. When Cañones challenged the state department of education over the safety and education of its children, vergüenza confronted "making something of yourself," and misericordia met impersonal professional standards head on.

The battle between Cañones and the educational bureaucracy seemed to be a simple one. A new consolidated elementary school in Coyote, designed to accommodate all the village children in the area, had opened its doors. Since high school students had been bussed out ever since the first high school in the region was built as a gift in the 1930s by Arthur Pack, owner of The Ghost Ranch, bussing out children in the first eight grades made perfectly good sense to professional educators. But not to Cañoneros. They lived day to day with the dangers of their access roads described in chapter 2. They wanted to keep as much control over the lives of their small children as possible, and sending them to a school from which they returned home for lunch permitted much better control. The thought of entrusting these children to strangers in Coyote in case of emergency was not welcome. The school itself was one of three visible formal institutions in the village (the others being the two churches), and a source of community pride.

The state department of education in Santa Fe, seeing the implacable opposition of the village and fearing adverse publicity, offered the compromise of keeping the schoolhouse on La Cuchilla open in 1966–67 to the first three grades, bussing four through eight. Cañones refused, and the empty school bus was the immediate result.

The battle was simple on the face of it, and the outcome perfectly predictable. Tiny villages do not win confrontations against the force of state law. But the battle was really not that simple. To describe it adequately, we have to sketch some of the history of public education in New Mexico, and to indicate the values of the state bureaucrats.

History

The Spanish colonial government made no provision for public education. A few children of ricos were tutored and a few were sent to private schools in Mexico. In 1822, during the Mexican period, the provincial government passed a public education law, but little came of it beyond Santa Fe. New Mexico was too poor to support general public education, and the Mexican government was too poor to subsidize its provinces. But some children of the rich still managed to received educations away from home in St. Louis and elsewhere. After the U.S. conquest in 1846, the territorial convention in 1848 and again in 1849 passed laws to establish schools, but they fell to the same fate as the law of 1822—no funds. Various individuals, both lay and clerical, established private schools during the late nineteenth century, and these schools seem to have been greeted with some enthusiasm.

In outlying settlements like Cañones, a few parents would get together from time to time and hire a school teacher for a few months, as funds and the availability of teachers permitted. Saquello Salazar says his father and others did so. Bernardita Salazar says her father personally taught her to read and write Spanish. The first Cañones schoolhouse was an adobe building (c. 1890) in the lower placita, now the Pentecostal church. A few of the more prosperous counties had small and struggling school systems. But it took the efforts of the new Territorial Educational Association, backed by governors Edmund Ross and Bradford Prince, to get an effective free public education law passed in 1891 that provided a system of statewide financial support. (This account is drawn from a summary of early education by state historian Myra Ellen Jenkins [1977].)

But money has never been adequate in New Mexico for education, or for anything else. Former governor Jack Campbell, who took a special interest in education, explained the relation of money to control in an interview in July 1971.

He said that during the depression of the 1930s, the state became desperate for ways to finance schools, and came to an agreement with major taxpayers—railroads, mining companies, cattle ranchers—that a 2 percent statewide sales tax would be levied, earmarked for schools. A ceiling would be placed on the millage rate for real property taxes, as part of the same agreement. A substantial proportion of the cost of public education was to be shifted from local school districts to the state, both for more equitable distribution of funds and for more efficient administration.

Control over the purse has been separate from the rest of educational control since 1923—a situation unique in the United States. In that year, according to Thomas Wiley, historian of New Mexican education:

> The educational budget auditor . . . appointed by the governor, was given control over the approval of all budgets for the school districts of the State. The office continues to this day under the title of chief of the school finance division—with all the original powers. . . . To this day, the chief has full veto power (Wiley 1973:94).

Formally, then, control over New Mexico schools has been highly centralized in Santa Fe since the 1920s and 1930s. But it has also been divided with the budget in the hands of the finance chief appointed by the governor, and the rest of the apparatus in the hands of an elected state board of education that hires the superintendent of public instruction. (Before a change in the state constitution in 1958, the superintendents at both state and county levels were elected and the state board appointed by the governor. Thomas Wiley, quoted above, was the last elected and first appointed superintendent.) Nothing in the rules ensures that cooperation between the state superintendent and the budget auditor will be close.

Despite tight formal control, local politicians sailed through loopholes in the system. In Rio Arriba county one politician seized the awarding of jobs in the school system, and also forced school employees to buy their personal insurance policies from him. The New Mexico Educational Association investigated and published a report with the pointed subtitle "When Public Education Provides Patronage for a Political System" (National Education Association 1964). The report described the corruption in detail although it stopped short of naming the politician.

From the point of view of educational officials, this political influence characterized the "bad old days," when professional standards counted for nothing. In these days, for instance, Rio Arriba county superintendent Siby Lucero defended himself when he was discovered staffing Kennedy Junior High School in Española with improperly certified teachers, by saying "If you read the newspapers . . . you know that every time I transfer a teacher I get sued" (*The New Mexican*, Santa Fe, June 9, 1964). From the point of view of villagers, such fights were remote. They were too poor to buy insurance policies, and they didn't see a problem in staffing schools; they saw a problem in finding jobs for the members of their households and the members of their families, and the value of misericordia—as well as simple survival—dictated that they use whatever connections they had to get those jobs.

Two legislative acts, initiated in 1962 and in 1965 by state senator Gordon Melody, resulted in abolition of all county school boards and consolidation of smaller districts. From this period emerged Jemez Mountain school district 53.

"During all this time the transportation system was improving," said Campbell during the interview of July, 1971.

Kutsche: "Not for Cañones."

Campbell: "It is quite possible the state failed in the case of Cañones."

Consolidation was Campbell's idea. He was governor (1965–67) during a national surge of building. And he was a great builder. In addition to schools, he built the famed Rio Grande Gorge Bridge northwest of Taos. He and the state department of education took the point of view that the sorry condition of the roads in Cañones was an unfortunate but very small detail in the picture of new school buildings, new busses, and improved roads. During the Campbell regime, building was good politics. Environmental issues, bilingual education, and the community control of schools were to come along later. Campbell congratulated David Cargo for seizing on these issues during his own campaign for governor, for by then they were good politics.

In the 1960s, in the eyes of state officials, the elementary school on La Cuchilla in Cañones was a failure on two counts. For one thing, they believed that good education was impossible without a separate classroom for each grade. For another, the building was inadequate. It had looked good in 1948 when it took the place of the original building in the placita: cement blocks, perhaps 40′ x 20′, the east facade all windows, accordion doors at midpoint so that it could be one or two rooms according to convenience, good electric lighting, a tight roof, a butane heater. But no running water: drinking water was brought up from Dalio Gallegos's house below, and two privies were dug at a respectful distance to the west. It had no kitchen, of course, because the pupils all lived either in the placita, half a mile to the west, or in Cienaguitas, over the hill about the same distance to the east, and had time to eat lunch at home.

Whether on balance the new schools were better than the old is a question that dedicated educators could and did disagree on vigorously. The new school buildings of the new Jemez Mountain district were certainly better equipped. The elementary school at Coyote had a separate classroom for every grade, a lunch room, flush indoor toilets, drinking fountains, audio-visual aids, and certified teachers. By 1966 and 1967 the teachers still described assignment to the district as exile to Siberia, and pupils in the new classrooms acted very much as they had in the old: quiet, well-behaved, looking dreamily out the windows.

Since behavior on the busses was often boisterous, especially by older pupils, Cañones parents were concerned about the two hours of unsupervised mixing of adolescent boys and girls. But they were also worried about the physical safety of their very young children traveling on unimproved roads in bad weather. Horror stories circulated: two girls, aged six and thirteen, had to walk home in bitter weather from a stalled school bus near Cuba in 1964. The little one froze to death, and the older one lost both her hands from freezing. Many times the bus to Cañones dared not leave the paved highway, and the high school children had to walk in. That was inconvenient for them, but would be dangerous for little ones. One young woman explained that she never finished high school because of bad memories of waiting in stalled busses in the cold and snow, sometimes atilt when the bus slid off the slick crowned road.

Values of the State Bureaucrats

If, as I said above, the school fight is a clash of values and not just another political fight in a highly political state, then we should try to spell out the "conceptions of the desirable" of state education officials in their own words, just as we did for the people of Cañones. Our classic method of participant observation was not open to us, so I relied on interviews with officials in their offices, minutes of state board of education meetings, our own notes during other meetings, and newspaper stories. The contrast with Cañones could not be more complete.

Ralph Drake, director of elementary instruction, was raised in Lee County in Eastern New Mexico—the area called "Little Texas." A tall, rather athletic man who looks like a cowboy, Drake was trained at the University of New Mexico, Eastern New Mexico State, and Washington State, and received a bachelor's degree in secondary education, a master's in elementary. During our interview Drake endorsed and called attention to the statement of philosophy in the department's official pamphlet *Standards for New Mexico Schools:*

> The broad objectives of New Mexico elementary schools are to educate children to meet the realities of living in contemporary society, to understand thoroughly the values inherent in our democratic way of life, and to use the basic skills effectively (State Department 1965:28).

How, Drake asked, can we prepare the child for his life twenty years from now? How can we prepare him to live better and happier right now? These children won't live in the Cañones environment. They need experiences and activities that will give them knowledge of living in the outside world. That preparation is to be obtained by going to school at Coyote and Gallina, where the kids study with Anglos and Indians as well as with Hispanos. The constant association with each other in Cañones, where no one has any particular educational advantage, is one of their greatest handicaps. Drake repeated several times that the language of the culturally dominant group in the United States is English, and it is important that all school children learn to read and write English. Since the population of New Mexico is only about 40 percent Hispano, the problem of instruction in Spanish for elementary kids is not going to be solved by just teaching in Spanish. (He was not, however, opposed to the new program of bilingual instruction then being demonstrated in several schools in the state.) "Most of these youngsters will not live here all their lives. Since they are going to live in other places, they need experiences that will cause them to be aware very early that other places do exist. Parents have not been able to do much educationally. The school district has not been able to do much educationally either." The example he cited of poor education was the outside privies in Cañones.

Robert Esparza, director of secondary education, was born and raised in Bernalillo, New Mexico, the child of a Mexican national father and a New Mexican mother. At the University of New Mexico, he majored in medieval and renaissance history as an undergraduate, and in educational administration as a graduate student. He had known as a child the ostracism of his New Mexican peers, who criticized his correct Mexico City accent and grammar. Although Esparza agreed with the official position of the department that Cañones children would be better educated in Coyote and Gallina, at the same time he knew far better than his colleagues how the world looks to an isolated villager. He thought Cañoneros quite sophisticated politically, and had a good deal of sympathy for their bitterness.

"Thinking as an educationist is rather new here [in the northern counties]—in the last four or five years only." Esparza's reaction to the Cañones intransigence was more complex than those of his Anglo colleagues, despite his basic agreement with them, and he escaped the "majoritarian" assumptions that came unconsciously to them.

Leonard DeLayo, state superintendent of public instruction, refused my request for an interview. Born and raised in the Bronx, he received a B.A. from the University of New Mexico, and an M.A. from Columbia University. He became state superintendent in 1963, succeeding Thomas Wiley. One authority on state schools said during an interview that DeLayo has not enjoyed the respect shown either to his predecessor or to Harry Wugalter, whose authority over schools perhaps exceeds his in the peculiar New Mexico system. DeLayo is regarded as something of a political chameleon, changing philosophy as the board complexion changes.

Because DeLayo was not willing to talk with me when I sought an interview, I have pieced together his views from other sources, each mentioned in its place below.

During a meeting of the state board of education on December 5, 1966, apropos of the Cañones issue, DeLayo said:

> "I have a certain concern that there may be people in federal community assistance programs promoting civil disobedience to obtain certain objectives. . . .

> "I am genuinely concerned in this regard in that if we do have people on the federal payrolls, or otherwise, stirring up civil disobedience it seems to me to be a matter for the state board.
>
> "I have no specific facts and no details, but I do want to register my concern to the State Board of Education at this time" (*Albuquerque Journal,* December 6, 1966). [Minutes of that meeting add, "He thought that the state board should weigh the matter carefully stating that this was one sure way to undermine our democracy."]

In May, 1972, DeLayo and a number of his aides met with me and seventeen Colorado College ethnography students, and spent half a day with us describing the department of education's service to villages and answering our questions. The students pressed DeLayo and staff on whether the educational system respected cultural differences. To those who asked about his own New York Italian background, he replied, "I can be Italian any time I want. And at other times, I am just a plain American." Concerning Cañones: "I was not impressed with Cañones. Garbage was thrown out of front doors, and their schoolhouse was an inadequate building with no plumbing. We had the alternative of a good facility in Coyote, with a good cafeteria. I hoped that the kids could learn alternatives in Coyote, so that they could choose whether they wanted to return or not."

Harry Wugalter, chief of the public school finance division of the department of finance and administration, was interviewed in March, 1967. He was raised in New Jersey and Pennsylvania. After being mustered out of World War II service on the West Coast, he "got as far as New Mexico and just stayed." He received B.A. and M.A. degrees from the University of New Mexico, and joined the public school system where he rose rapidly until appointed to his present job.

Governor Jack Campbell said that he respected Wugalter thoroughly, that he has an excellent grasp of both finance and administration.

And Wiley said of Wugalter: "He is thoroughly knowledgeable in the field of school finance. While he can wear the dictator's mantle at times, as becomes the office, he has brought to the office an element of service to local superintendents and boards of education to a greater extent than was true in the past" (1973:151–52). Wugalter was a greater threat to Cañones than department of education officials because of his efficiency, his drive, and his veto power over all public school budgets.

During our interview, Wugalter described the patronage system: all jobs in the school system, even waitresses and janitors, are assigned by the local school boards. A villager might beg for a job that didn't pay more than perhaps eighty dollars a month. "You might sit down to chat with a grandfather in a Spanish village and say to him, 'Don't you want your grandson to be in a rocket, to participate in a space program and be one of those men to reach the moon?' No, he doesn't want it. He wants his son to be the janitor of a local school."

Kutsche: "What is *your* ideal, toward which you want to help prepare school children?"

Wugalter: "To take the children into an environment that will open up this world to them."

Kutsche: "What world?"

Wugalter: "The world outside of Rio Arriba county, the world of security and employment, central heating, TV, leisure, reading—yes, reading. We must enlighten the parents, of course. We can't do it like Nazi Germany."

Wugalter endorsed a newspaper story quoting him as declaring that small multiple-class schools everywhere should be closed. "The children would be better off . . . if they were packed up and sent off to boarding school. We aren't running a baby sitting service. The State of New Mexico just won't pay for baby sitting" (*The New Mexican*, Santa Fe, June 9, 1964).

In Wugalter's office suite, where the interview took place, a public address system played soft background music, interrupted frequently with staccato notices of the proceedings on the floors of the legislative chambers. The telephone rang frequently, and Wugalter, fashionably dressed, beautifully poised, barked orders into it to his aides who were pushing bills. This was command headquarters of a confident, dynamic liberal executive with a sense of humor; it was no philosopher's study.

These fragments of insights into what state officials think about education and about Hispanos might be summarized as follows: people should accumulate objects. Geographical and social mobility are preferable to stability. Security consists of a wage job that pays well. Ethnic differences are leisure-time luxuries. Village

Hispanos live in rural slums. They are dirty and lack community pride. Educational standards are universal and ought not to differ according to the social or cultural situation of the people to be educated. A good education can be defined in terms of physical equipment, lunchrooms and flush toilets.

The statements reported above are consistent with mainstream American materialist and melting pot values. If Alexis de Tocqueville were to meet these bureaucrats, 130 years after he scathed us in *Democracy in America*, he probably would have said that nothing had changed.

The field team learned little by little that among state officials, the difference between politicians and bureaucrats is greater than the difference between Anglos and Hispanos. I shall return to that theme at the end of this chapter.

How much did formal education mean to people in Cañones? They seem to have been ambivalent about it. A person who is well brought up in Hispanic values is considered well educated without schooling. Everyone of course recognized the usefulness of reading, writing, and arithmetic, since one should be able to understand the written contracts that employers and merchants make with him. But beyond the skills listed above, and in the absence of instruction in Spanish, a number of Cañoneros sense that public schools pull their children away from their own roots. Textbooks used in the Jemez Mountain district were guilty of such unconscious insults as the following in a geography text (accompanied by a picture of a landscape like most of the Piedra Lumbre Grant): "The desert is an interesting place to visit, but I wouldn't want to live there, would you?"

Monolingual education in English probably violates the constitution of the state of New Mexico; employing monolingual English-speaking teachers certainly does. Article XII, Section 8, states that "The legislature shall provide for the training of teachers . . . so that they may become proficient in both the English and Spanish languages." This provision has been violated regularly for decades.

The Battle Joined

The school in Cañones during 1965–66 still held the first eight grades staffed by two teachers and a teacher's aid. The board of education and the superintendent of the new Jemez Mountain district, planning to consolidate Cañones into the Coyote school in 1966–67, met with Cañoneros to convince them that the decision was wise. They claimed that the condition of the building, especially its lack of running water, was the principal reason for the change. Cañoneros attended these meetings in force, and argued vociferously for keeping the school open. Dalio Gallegos and Elipio García, who live closest to the school house, offered to pipe water to it, but the offers were ignored. As Cañoneros looked back on these meetings, it was always "officials telling us what they were going to do," never discussing problems *with* them.

The district board of education, good local politicians all, dragged their feet when Santa Fe pressed them to close the Cañones school. They remembered that in early April, 1966, sensing that this event would be used as a precedent for permanent bussing, the village refused to let its children be bussed to Coyote for one-day achievement tests. So the decision was made at a budget hearing later in April by Harry Wugalter, with the concurrence of Ralph Drake, Robert Esparza, and Bill Lemon (state director of transportation). Rudy Gutiérrez, Jemez Mountain superintendent, who already knew that his contract was not to be renewed, was present, and so were three board members. They mildly protested, but, as Esparza said in the interview noted above, "Then and there . . . Mr. Drake and I, representing the state department of education, gave our judgment that the school should be closed and the children sent over to Coyote." Wugalter accordingly ordered all items in the district budget that had to do with Cañones to be stricken. (As we have noted, his word in budget matters is final.) The local board members present said they were happy that state officials, not they, had made the decision.

Wugalter and Esparza were emphatic when interviewed that it was they and not the Jemez Mountain school board who had closed the Cañones school. For public consumption, the state superintendent said the opposite was the rule: "Consolidations . . . are recommended only after complete investigation of the systems involved, and nothing can be done until the boards of each system take action" (*The New Mexican*, Santa Fe, February 4, 1969). There is no record in the Jemez Mountain board minutes of any decision to close the Cañones school. Instead, the minutes of September 23, 1966, state ". . . the *New Mexico State Board of Education* has approved the action by the Chief of School Finance to close the Cañones Public School . . ." [emphasis added].

The state department of education offered to provide a bus stop shelter in the Cañones placita, 4-wheel-drive vehicles as school busses, and two-way radios between the busses and the school in Coyote for constant communication between the school and the children in transit. To the suggestion (made much later) that a third radio be installed in a Cañones home, Ralph Drake objected that there was a question whether anyone in the village was trustworthy. The state department also insisted that the Coyote school make provisions to keep Cañones children overnight when weather conditions made this advisable.

The promises contained in the preceding paragraph reveal a further split in authority, beyond the separation of control over budget and curriculum. Although the state department of education had felt free to make numerous specific promises to Cañones, it was not they who could carry them out. In the early 1970s, when Cañones tried to get these promises kept, they found Santa Fe officials willing to confirm what they had promised; but all requests were referred to Jemez Mountain district officials, who had promised nothing. In fact, the shelter waiting station was never built, 4-wheel-drive busses were never purchased (they are not, as it turns out, manufactured in the right size), and two-way radios were not installed. (I did not learn whether overnight provisions in Coyote were made.)

The Cañones reaction to the attitude of education officials was profound. That their wishes were overruled was no surprise, but that state and district professional educators had treated them in public, even to their faces, as if they were too poor, too ignorant, too simpleminded to have a voice in their own affairs, was infuriating. To paraphrase the Arab king of Borges's story in the New Mexican dialect, "*Se buslaron de nosotros*" (they mocked us). Cañones would have lost dignidad in its own eyes if it had accepted the insult without a fight. Vergüenza gave villagers the model for trusting their own judgment and the strength to reject the scorn of others. Outsiders, with their impersonal mainstream Anglo values, never understood the depth of outrage in Cañones.

But fury is not political organization. For that, Cañones relied on the emotion in misericordia, most particularly that intimate knowledge of each other quoted in chapter 7: ". . . not because everyone is kin to everyone else, but because we have all grown up together. . . . So we consult each other long before we talk with people from outside. Cañoneros share what in most villages is a private, family matter."

The organizational experience that Cañones fell back upon was not the family—everyone is *not* kin to everyone else, and a family-based organization (of, say, the families with most land) would have reminded the village of divisions between families as well as unities within them. Nor was it religion, for the hard feelings caused by individual conversions are still present underneath the surface, even though they are not permitted to intrude upon daily relations. The best models available were the acequia system and the memory of communal herding and hunting in the past. They remind people that survival demands they submerge personal grudges while the village works together for common goals.

So the village held meetings. At first these juntas were merely get-togethers to understand the challenge, but gradually they became strategy-planning sessions. As news got around that Cañones intended to fight, people from outside the village offered their help and the benefit of their experience fighting other battles in other villages. Milton Loewe, editor of the weekly *Rio Grande Sun*, came to report and stayed to advise. The most helpful among these assistants was Facundo Valdez, Community Action Program worker on the payroll of the University of New Mexico, a native of Mora and thus no outsider. (He later authored the paper on vergüenza extensively referred to in chapter 7.)

And when the moment came for the village to stand firm—on the first day of the fall term of 1966–67—it made no difference that, of the twelve families whose children were kept out of grades four through eight, nine were Catholic (three belonging to the cofradía), two Assembly of God, one United Brethren; that some were landed and others destitute; and that some were Republicans, some Democrats. Cañones was monolithic in its rejection of state bureaucracy and state law.

The Day in Court

Within the framework of official insistence and village intransigence, there were far too many subplots to record here. Leonard DeLayo, perhaps sensing that he was in for unfavorable publicity, appealed to the state highway commission to take over the Cañones access road from Rio Arriba county. The commission refused, but "instructed its chief engineer, T. B. White, to have the road studied, engineered and repaired . . ." (*Rio Grande Sun*, September 8, 1966). DeLayo also tried to enlist public sympathy for his own position by referring to Elipio García as "ringleader" of a "gang" in Cañones that was stirring up trouble for its own political ends. DeLayo kept his word, however, to maintain the school in Cañones for the first three grades during the academic year 1966–67. Meetings between Cañones and state officials resulted in shouting matches, misinformation from state officials (e.g., from Esparza that children had to walk two or three miles twice a day because they live so far from school [*Rio Grande Sun* September 22, 1966]), the complaint from new district superintendent Horace Martínez that the Cañoneros kept repeating the same arguments, and their shouted reply that they had to keep repeating, because the officials wouldn't listen.

Martínez, a native of Abiquiu, was acquainted with Cañones and its people. He knew how precarious his new job was and resented being thrust into a quarrel designed by others. Wugalter noted that while Gutiérrez was an old-style educational politican, sensitive to local pressures, Martínez made up to the state bureaucracy, in the hope of finding another post if he lost this one; he eventually did lose it, and another superintendency was found for him.

During early fall, the state and Cañones were on a collision course. Education and finance officials, enforcing the professional standards that they had created against such opposition, discovered that Cañones was getting a good press at their expense. "Tiny impoverished village fights overwhelming state power" made irresistible "man bites dog" copy. But the state felt it could not compromise and back off. Cañones was courting, and being courted by, candidates for office in the general election scheduled for November. The village enjoyed its prominence, and would not back off. Instead, it started enthusiastically at the top.

Gene Lusk, Democratic candidate for Governor, was not interested. But David F. Cargo ("Lonesome Dave"), the Republican candidate whose political career lay outside the regular Republican machine, was very interested. Cargo is an Anglo from Michigan, married to an Hispana from Belén, New Mexico, and calls his children *coyotes* (of mixed blood). Perhaps the most important plank in his platform was a promise to right injustices to Hispanos, particularly in the rural north.

Albert Amador, Democrat candidate for membership on the state board of education, was also interested. He is a native of Vallecitos, a village above El Rito, a son of a convert to the Presbyterian church, and educated out of state. Former Rio Arriba county superintendent, he was running on a slate put up by Emilio Naranjo, Democrat boss of Rio Arriba county. Through him, Cañones contacted Edwin L. Felter, a Democrat lawyer closely connected with politics and later a state judge.

Cañones approached some candidates for state legislature and elicited some interest, but nothing as definite as the friendly reception from Cargo and Amador.

The meetings between Cañones and the outside officials remained informal so long as no legal charges were brought. But in mid-October, district attorney Alfonso Sánchez had run out of alternatives, and sent each of the twelve parents of the delinquent pupils a notice of criminal action for violation of the school attendance law. The possible penalty was five to ninety days in jail plus a fine of up to $100. (This is the same man whom Reies Lópes Tijerina and members of the Alianza Federal de Mercedes would set out to arrest in the famous "Courthouse Raid" in Tierra Amarilla the following June 5. Sánchez was generally regarded by Rio Arriba villagers as economically involved with outside interests opposed to them.)

The first reaction in Cañones was shock. As the villagers said, "No Cañonero has ever been in jail." (Disputes between villagers were usually settled on the spot.) The second reaction was defiance and the formation on November 2 of the Cañones Parents Committee, Isaaque Lovato president, Dalio Gallegos secretary, Elipio García treasurer. They expressed their defiance with glee. "The officials didn't expect any back talk from a bunch of poor dirty Mexicans," they said. "We shouldn't be afraid to stand up for our own rights. The only time we should fear is if we cannot protect our rights."

The organization got right down to the business of hiring, and finding money to pay, a lawyer—Amador's friend Felter, who charged a fee of $100 per defendant, or $1,200 for the entire case. The first step in raising the money was a document dated November 2, which said simply:

> *Los siguientes nombres son para respaldar el comité que va a pedir el dinero. La suma de* ——— (The following signatures are to guarantee the committee which is going to seek money. The sum of———) [Not filled in]

The first three signatures were the officers. The others follow, spelled as written:

Mr. and Mrs. Norman Lovato
Miss Kathy Krusnik
Mr. and Mrs. Dalio Gallegos
Mr. and Mrs. Genary Velasquez
Mr. and Mrs. Elipio Garcia
Mr. and Mrs. Sabiniano Lovato
Mr. and Mrs. Antonio Serrano
Mr. and Mrs. Dalio Gallegos [Dalio signed one line, Orlinda the other]
Mr. and Mrs. Sequello Salazar
Leonard Velasquez
Medardo Lovato
Emiliano Aragon
Seraphin Valdez
Mr. and Mrs. Isaac Lovato
Mr. and Mrs. Benicio Serrano
Viviana Vialpondo
Mr. and Mrs. Aquilino Serrano
Trainquilino Herrera
Mr. Simon Vigil
Mr. and Mrs. Pacomio Salazar
Paul Kutsche
Mr. and Mrs. Juan F. Madrid
Mr. and Mrs. Isabel Garcia
Mr. and Mrs. Sebidello Salazar

Kathy Krusnik and I took up residence in Cañones in mid-October. We had been observing, taking careful notes in juntas, but avoiding expressing any opinions. We were both taken a little off balance when we were asked to commit ourselves. Kathy expressed the ideals of a 20-year-old college sophomore in her field notes: "So now I may wind up in the carcel with the rest of them! But, I will contribute money, because I do believe that it takes courage to try to bring democracy back to an individual level." When the document was brought to me for signature, I asked first what respaldar meant, as I had not heard the word before. "That means you're backing us," said one delegate in English. "It means you have to help pay," said the other with a grim put-your-money-where-your-mouth-is look. In the rest of this chapter I make explicit the ways in which Kathy and I (and later John Van Ness) participated and when.

What the committee did with the respaldar note revealed much about the reputation of Cañoneros among those who knew them well. They took it to the First State Bank of Cuba and borrowed the full $1,200, at 10 percent for ninety days, on signatures alone. Raymond B. López, vice-president and cashier of the bank, later explained:

> It's true, a bank examiner wouldn't be delighted with such a loan. But I've been here a summer or two. I know most of these men personally. If they hadn't got the money here, they'd have gone to a finance company, which would have charged them 72 percent annually. I made that loan for moral reasons, and because everyone who signed that note [and the respaldar note] had a moral obligation to pay.

Fired up and financed, Cañones rejected several attempts by intermediaries to settle out of court and claim a victory in the newspapers. The last of these attempts was turned down at a junta November 5. After that meeting recessed and Milton Loewe and Facundo Valdez left, the village took its organization in a new direction. A blackboard was set up in the front room of Emiliano Aragón's home, and the merits of candidates for office in the election to be held November 8 were discussed boisterously and without inhibition.

The consequences of this discussion became clear the following week, when election results were published precinct by precinct. Cañones cast fifty-five votes for David Cargo for governor, six for his opponent. For other offices the vote was almost as lopsided. This tiny precinct, with a grand total of less than seventy votes to spend, had at last made its *grito* (shout) heard. That the shout was loud enough, was acknowledged by Cargo when he visited Cañones as governor of New Mexico the following June:

> I want you to know that I certainly appreciate what you did for me, because when I ran for Governor I had all the votes up here with the exception of a very few, and I think that those six people we've converted. [from a tape recording]

The voice of Cañones began to be heard at the county level also, and in the local school district. Cañones votes had gone predominantly to Naranjista candidates for county office, including Emilio Naranjo's son Benny, who was elected sheriff—a job he had been appointed to when his father, then incumbent, became U.S. marshal. Benny Naranjo showed Cañones a number of favors the following winter, during the dispute over the road, and delegates from Cañones to the next Democratic county convention pledged themselves to the Naranjos.

At the local level, the votes of Cañones elected a member—not a Cañonero, but friendly—to the Jemez Mountain board of education in February, 1967, and managed to get Dalio Gallegos of Cañones appointed to a vacancy later. A school bus contract was also awarded for the first time to a Cañonero, Elipio García, in 1967.

The mood in the placita after the election ranged from quiet joy to loud jubilation. Happiest of all was one Cañonero who bet his cattle money, two hundred dollars, on Cargo and won.

On the fourteenth, subpoenas to appear for the trial arrived, scheduled for the seventeenth at 1:30 P.M. in Santa Fe. The list of defendants (only one of each married couple) and their delinquent children or wards was printed in full on each subpoena:

> Mrs. Dalio Gallegos for Amada, Debra and Toby
> Mrs. Angelina Lovato [wife of Sabiniano] for Clara and Rosenda
> Mrs. Eduvigen Lovato for Agustin [her grandson]
> Mr. Norman Lovato for Lydia and Norman, Jr.
> Mr. Isaac Lovato for Juan
> Mr. Pacomio Salazar for Abade, Alfredo, Nazario and Rose Mary
> Mr. Antonio Serrano for Jose Leon, Mariana and Rosa
> Mrs. Teofila Serrano [a widow] for Antonio and Steven
> Mr. Serafin Valdez for Arturo and Martin
> Mr. Genaro Velasquez for Aurelia and Samuel
> Mr. Leonard Velasquez for Flora [his sister and ward]
> Mrs. Viviana Vialpando [wife of Jose Dolores] for Ricardo

The trial was postponed until November 25. Felter was not always available when he said he would be, because of court appearances and other business, and the leaders of the fight were becoming more and more frustrated with the entire proceeding. Felter never found time to visit Cañones, and this added to the clients' apprehension.

Friday, November 25, at 2 P.M., the trial took place in the courtroom on the second floor of the Santa Fe county courthouse. The room is a large, square, imposing place with a large hall leading up to its carved double doors. (Seven months later the same hall would be crowded with Alianza supporters before hearings for Reies Lópes Tijerina, and would pulse with the cry of "Viva la Raza!" [See Peter Nabokov, *Tijerina and the Courthouse Raid*, 1969.])

The people of Cañones and their friends filed rather timidly in for State *vs.* Gallegos et al., 3907. Adult men tended to sit together on the right, the young bachelors behind them. Women and small children sat in the center section, with small groups of older children and teenagers here and there near them. The left section of benches was mostly empty, but later filled with the press. On the front row of the right section sat witnesses for the prosecution. Dalio Gallegos and Elipio García sat with their wives in the center section. Whispered conversations. Nervousness. The air inside the building was very hot. Children were unnaturally quiet, looking around.

Journalists present were from United Press, Associated Press, the *Albuquerque Journal*, and *The New Mexican*. The story was by now front page news both in Albuquerque and in Santa Fe. A friend of Kathy Krusnik even heard about the case on the radio in San Francisco.

The proceedings were heard before Samuel Z. Montoya, district judge (later associate justice of the New Mexico supreme court). The prosecutor was E. E. Chávez of the district attorney's office. District attorney Alfonso Sánchez was present during part of the proceedings, but did not examine witnesses. Also at the prosecution table was E. P. Ripley, the state board of education attorney, a dapper urbane man. He consulted with Chávez quietly, but did not speak. The defense was conducted by Edwin L. Felter alone.

The twelve defendants assembled before Judge Montoya, who took great pains to be sure that they understood the proceedings, and that their rights were protected. The judge asked if anyone needed an interpreter. Felter replied on their behalf that they did not, at least now. The judge said he would have an interpreter standing by, and did so.

Did all of the defendants understand the charge?

All nodded yes.

Did they all understand the consequences if they were found guilty?

All nodded.

How did they plead?

Not guilty.

Judge Montoya appeared to hesitate a little before he accepted Felter's plea. Reading of the charge was waived. The judge asked the defendants to take seats in the jury box, which was standing empty because Felter had decided not to ask for a jury. The trial began.

Prosecutor Chávez got up to call his first witness. Chávez was a small man, perhaps in his fifties, who did not appear entirely comfortable in the aggressor's role. He called Jemez Mountain superintendent Horace Martínez to the stand. My field notes describe Martínez as "Extremely ill-at-ease, wet lips constantly. Dressed in conservative brown sports jacket. Age perhaps mid or late 30s, compact figure, rather good looking, black hair very slightly wavy." A careful, defensive man, under pressure.

Martínez testified to the absence of the children since the beginning of the school year. He was stopped short when it was shown that he had neglected to bring his records with him. Judge Montoya leveled an impatient look at Chávez and excused Martínez to get the records. A recess was called.

The Cañoneros weren't sure just what a recess was ("We're tired of all this resting"), but they soon took them in their stride.

Robert Esparza was called for the prosecution. "*Chaquetero* (turncoat)," ran an angry murmur around the Cañones part of the audience. From the americanos you expect hostility, but from a mejicano there is no excuse. Esparza testified that he had visited Cañones about eight times, talking with people there, trying to convince them to send their children to school. It was he who offered the state's compromise of keeping open the first three grades. He testified that budget director Harry Wugalter had cut off money for the Cañones school at the budget hearing in April, because the school was substandard. No attempt to hide behind the local board. Esparza showed slides of the upper road, arguing that it was perfectly passable. Some Cañoneros in the audience were amused, others indignant, that his pictures were all taken of the mile or two closest to the highway, where the upper road crosses a dry flat portion of the *joya* (open field), and is perfectly passable. Nothing of hills, arroyos, washouts. Under cross-examination Esparza admitted that the road might be hazardous in wet weather, that he had driven it only in good weather, and that he had no special knowledge of roads. Felter conducted the cross-examination in a clear resonant voice.

Another recess was called, for what reason the audience couldn't tell. A Hispano acquaintance walked by the bench in which Kathy Krusnik and her foster mother Luz Valdez were sitting, and said to Luz, "Your bed in the *cárcel* (jail) is ready for you." "Had she not had such a good sense of humor, I think she might have cried," Kathy noted.

Nervousness was changing to restlessness when the trial resumed. People began to shift seats, so hardly anyone spent the whole afternoon in the same place. Children began to tease each other.

The state called Agueda García, daughter of Jacobo Salazar, and wife of Pete García who had the contract for the school busses to Cañones. She drove, for grades nine through twelve, a 1964 Chevrolet with a seating capacity of 24 to 30. Sitting nervously in the witness chair, swinging it back and forth on its swivel, she testified that she was able to reach Cañones every day this fall except for two or three— and then her husband drove. She admitted under cross-examination that the children had to walk to the center of Cañones to catch the bus, a distance of about a mile for those from Cienaguitas. (The point of this question was the state department's contention that it took longer for children to walk to the school in Cañones than to ride the bus to Coyote, and that the hardships were greater. Felter got her to acknowledge that children who lived in Cienaguitas had farther to walk to the placita to catch the bus than to walk to the schoolhouse.)

Pete García was called, and testified that he had driven the bus four days this fall. He agreed with his wife's testimony that the road was hazardous when wet.

Jacobo Salazar, Jr., gave the same testimony. He drove the 18-passenger 1955 Chevrolet panel truck that was supposed to transport the smaller children. He said that he arrived at the placita every morning since September 7, at 8:05, waited until 8:15, and nobody got on. He was suspected of being the source of the story that Elipio García had pulled children off the bus one day in September. Today, in response to Chávez's questions, he said nobody had attempted to remove children from the busses. He had come to the placita every day except two when it was muddy. Jacobo, Jr., or Jacobito as he was commonly known, was cross-examined about his age (eighteen) and his license. He admitted he lacked a chauffeur's license. Felter reminded the court that one is required under state law. Jacobito agreed with his sister and his brother-in-law that the road was dangerous when wet.

And that was as far as the trial went for the first day. A faint air of letdown among the Cañoneros to have spent a whole afternoon seventy miles from home and accomplish no more. But the afternoon had seasoned them all to the unfamiliar proceedings. The men found that they understood what was going on better than they had expected. The women had more trouble with the legal English. Children were more restless as the trial went on. The little ones (up to about nine years of age) stayed with their mothers, the older ones migrated toward the back rows of the middle section to socialize, once their awe of the court was overcome. The young men stayed close to the grown men, the young women with the married women. Maybe their awe had disappeared, but this was no Saturday night dance.

Since the trial was scheduled to reconvene at nine the next morning, everybody left quickly. Most of them had to drive home, and get up early the next day. Only those who had friends or relatives in Santa Fe or Española managed to avoid the long expensive journey. In the crowd, in addition to the Cañoneros, were David Waide, Delfinio Valdez who coached basketball at the high school in Gallina, Rio Arriba county sheriff Benny Naranjo, numerous friends of Facundo Valdez, Paul and Marie Brown of Lindreth, and others who were neither Cañones residents nor state bureaucrats.

Saturday morning, greetings outside the courthouse were friendly but reserved. A number of Cañoneros were speaking English, even though they used Spanish exclusively at home. There was little or none of the joking that precedes most group meetings in Hispanic villages—even before mass.

Today the seating was more mixed inside. Some of the men sat on the left with the reporters. Teenagers sat in the last half-dozen rows in the center with some older youths. The defendants went directly to the jury box. Everyone stood without prompting at nine, when Judge Montoya entered.

Horace Martínez was recalled with the records of school attendance for 1964–65, 1965–66, and the first part of 1966–67, plus the exchange of letters between him and Alfonso Sánchez. The testimony was dull, but essential to establish that the crime had in fact been committed.

The state then called to the stand one child from each defendant family. Judge Montoya handled each of them with sympathy, and with care to make sure each one understood what it meant to raise one's right hand and take an oath. Their testimony was virtually identical. "My parents don't let me go to school." "Because my mother and my father don't let me." There was no cross-examination. The Cañoneros relaxed a trifle after the last one had testified, for they had been afraid some of the children would forget what they were supposed to say.

District attorney Sánchez then testified that he had sent letters to all the parents advising them of the consequences of failing to send their children to school. "I used a mimeographed letter which I send in all cases of this nature." Some of the audience registered surprise that failing to send children to school is common enough to warrant a form letter. He entered copies of his correspondence with Horace Martínez into the evidence.

The state rested its case.

Then Edwin Felter called up a list of witnesses to testify about the road. The first of these was sheriff Benny Naranjo. He said the road has been dangerous since the opening of school August 29. A car loses its brakes after it fords the stream. The judge broke into the questioning to ask if this were a county, state, or just what kind of road. Well, said Benny, right now it seems to be a semiprivate, semicounty road. It's a county road, but a private individual seems to own part of it. (No one in the courtroom so much as smiled at this answer, which could be regarded as broad satire of the confused state of land condemnation.)

The private individual was Jacobo Salazar. A state highway department crew, attempting to improve the lower road, had sliced off the top of a little hill, thus rerouting the road by a few feet. The new route crossed some of Jacobo's unirrigated land. Jacobo sued for reimbursement (at $100 per acre value) and pending resolution of the suit had bulldozed rocks onto the road, leaving just enough room for one vehicle to pass. This passageway he closed with two posts and a padlocked chain. The bus drivers—his son, daughter, and son-in-law—had keys. No one in the placita ever asked for a key. Benny Naranjo's testimony contained a further subtlety: Jacobo Salazar was a Chaconista like Horace Martínez, i.e., a supporter of the anti-Naranjo faction in the Rio Arriba Democratic party.

A Mr. Ortiz, of Chimayó, foreman for the New Mexico state highway department, testified that he worked from October 10 to November 4 on the lower road with a crew of six, four dump trucks and two blades. He said that they had bladed and widened the road, and put a culvert in the lower creek crossing, which had previously been impassable.

"And how would you judge the road since your work?" Felter asked.

"It is still hazardous," Ortiz replied. "We put down no gravel."

David Waide brought pictures of some bad stretches of the road, to refute Esparza's claim that the road was good. These pictures were obsolete four days after he took them September 1, Waide testified, because a storm made the road worse. Both roads were a mess, he said.

Facundo Valdez's boss John Arango, director of the Center for Community Action Services, Bureau of Business Research, University of New Mexico, took the stand to show motion pictures of the road. Chávez cross-examined him more on the cost of the film than on the accuracy of the pictures, trying to establish that his evidence was gathered at taxpayers' expense. Arango was ready for him, and swore that his pictures were all taken at his own expense. Chávez and DeLayo seemed joined in their attempt to discredit any assistance offered to Cañones from outside the village. Arango was the first to offer any argument that the road is not so good dry either.

Facundo Valdez was next. As he had predicted, Chávez asked him if he had advocated civil disobedience. He started to answer that he advocated it only if other appeals to regular authority failed, when Judge Montoya cut off Chávez's line of questions as irrelevant to the case. Montoya was running his own show, and seldom waited for opposing lawyers to take the initiative in making objections. Facundo repeated Arango's testimony about the condition of the road.

Delfinio Valdez testified the same way, saying he took basketball players home to Cañones almost every evening, and couldn't make it November 8. He forgot to mention that some players had to walk home from the paved highway recently because the road was completely impassable. The case was conspicuously barren of concrete examples of danger or difficulty, and full of "potentially hazardous when wet" arguments. No one thought to ask Facundo about election night, when his car stuck on the hill going into the placita, and Kathy Krusnik had to rescue him in her Volkswagen bug.

The last witness before the recess at noon was Andrés Martínez, engineer for the state highway department. He had supervised the work on the lower road from October 10 to November 4, gave the specifications of widening—from twelve or fifteen feet to an average of twenty feet. But the road is still almost as dangerous as it was before, when wet, he said.

Cañoneros seemed a little dejected as they filed out for lunch, realizing that their case did not come across as strongly as they thought it would.

I was the last defense witness from outside the placita. I testified that the road was dangerous when dry too, and said something about the tight blind curve on the hill, and the impotence of the field team's new four-wheel-drive Travelall in the face of mud and a high-crowned road. Chávez started to ask me whether the four-lane divided highway to Albuquerque were not dangerous too when it was wet and slick. Montoya ordered me not to answer the question, and rebuked Chávez. He had, I think, already decided what the case added up to, and wanted to get on with it.

Felter called only two of the defendants to the stand—Pacomio Salazar and Serafín Valdez. Pacomio testified simply, through the interpreter, that he refused to send his children to school on account of the bad road. Serafín also asked for the interpreter. Both of these men speak English, and no doubt used the opportunity the interpreter presented of giving them time to think their answers over carefully. Serafín was the first to testify that there have been accidents on the road this fall. But his testimony came too late to have the maximum impact. He cracked a couple of jokes that I did not catch and that were not translated. The audience laughed sympathetically. Serafín's wife Luz was in no mood to laugh at jokes. She gasped when her husband was called, and breathed shallowly and nervously while he performed in this role she had never seen him in before.

"What *would* satisfy you people?" asked Chávez on cross-examination.

"A good road," Serafín answered simply.

Chávez then insisted that these defendants wouldn't be satisfied until they had a four-lane highway.

Felter called no more witnesses. Someone explained after the trial that he feared the district attorney's office would be able to shake some of the more timid defendants into admitting they were just going along with the crowd. Since not all of the defendants owned cars, it is entirely possible that they were.

Chávez called one rebuttal witness—Horace Martínez. He testified that no school busses run anywhere in bad weather, that his principals have a standing order to cancel school then. At the judge's request, he listed the schools and their locations. Under cross-examination, Martínez admitted that he would as often as not be sending children home after bad weather developed. No one seemed much impressed.

A recess was called, after which each side summed up. There was little movement during this recess. Most of the audience just sat in quiet anticipation of the final acts.

Felter argued that the villagers of Cañones were treated like substandard citizens, with a substandard school and a poor road. He said that the state board of education had admitted that it had compromised its standards in the quality of instruction and of building that it allotted to Cañones. In the face of this kind of treatment, he said, citizens had the right not to obey the law. He cited seven cases in precedent, from New Mexico and other states, demonstrating that no crime is committed if necessity prevents compliance with the law, that citizens are excused from complying with the law if they have exhausted their avenues of recourse, because the natural common law gives parents the right to defend the lives and health of their children. Further, he argued that the bus driver was not legally qualified to carry their children. This was a particularly strong point, but, unfortunately, he brought it into the case very late.

The judge followed Felter's citing of cases very closely, checking Felter on case citations, and at one point asking "which state?"

E. E. Chávez summed up for the state. His point was that the children of Cañones were merely being used by their parents to help fix the road. The real aim is not the school but the road. It is true the road is not very good, he admitted, but parents cannot be allowed to set the minimal standards for school attendance. These people have made up their minds that their kids aren't going to school until the road is fixed to suit them. He cited school law, section 73:13:10.

Judge Montoya, sharply: "What does that have to do with transportation?"

Chávez: "Not that section, but some other."

Judge: "Where is that section?"

Chávez: "I believe it's 73:13:3."

Judge: "That's it. I found it."

Chávez: "Anytime a school is more than three miles from home and no transportation is provided, parents are excused from sending their children to school. When conditions are not extremely hazardous, children must attend school. The defense has not shown that accidents have occurred. Transportation is provided."

Felter rebutted only briefly that section 73:13:3 is limited to lawful transportation, and for the sixth grade on down, transportation is not lawful.

Judge Montoya called only a ten-minute recess to arrive at a decision, further suggesting that he had already made up his mind.

People were tense during those ten minutes. Women smoked in the hall, which is unusual for them in a public place. Teenagers paid little attention except to their own affairs. Younger children bought penny candy at the concession stand on the lower floor. One child smuggled in a bag of potato chips that crackled loudly during the reading of the decision. The young men and women were all business, acting on this occasion like grownups.

In the row behind me, officials of the state department of education exchanged quiet comments: "I didn't know the road was so bad when we went over it, did you?" "All this talk of special vehicles and trucks not being able to make it. . . ."

When the judge returned, the defendants rose in the jury box looking almost embalmed, the crowd in the audience almost as sober. The defendants had only a moment to sit down before the solemn "Will the defendants please rise?" The judge spoke very slowly, and the interpreter translated phrase by phrase, so it was possible to record his decision verbatim:

> The court has considered the evidence and arguments and finds the defendants guilty as charged. [No change of expression in the defendants] The evidence is not sufficient to constitute

legal justification for noncompliance with the statute requiring that children be sent to school. The fact that school children are being transported from your community to Coyote and Gallina would indicate to this court that the road is in such a condition as will permit the transportation of children to the Coyote school. You may sit down. [Still no facial reaction]

The court sympathizes with your feelings that you are entitled to a better road. This is not a matter for the court to determine. There are authorities for you to appeal to. The court declares that the school authorities will have to see that legal transportation will have to be provided, and replace those not qualified. That of itself is not cause for you to keep your children from school. The evidence shows that your decision not to send your children to school was because of the condition of the road, not the qualifications of the bus driver.

I was born in a small community, and knew children who went seven miles to school on horseback, rain, snow, or shine. If you want your children to have the opportunity they deserve, you should do everything humanly possible to see that they have an education. To me, it is a poor family that doesn't do everything it can in order to give their children an education.

The court is going to defer announcement of judgment and sentence to Wednesday, at 10:00 A.M., if you can show good faith by sending your children to school immediately. The court has ample authority under statute to compel you to send your children to school. I want to assure you, because of my strong feelings about education of children, that I will use that law to its fullest extent to see that you send those children to school.

The court will make its remarks available to the county commissioners and school authorities so that you, with them, can try to solve your problems. I know of the feelings of people in small communities about the consolidation of schools. I represented some of them against consolidation of schools when I was practicing law. But that power is for other authorities. The decision has been made by those with the authority to do so. The court has to take the position that the moving of children from certain grades to Coyote was in all respects lawful, and you will have to accept this position for the sake of your children. The children are the important ones in this situation. You should look at it in this light. Because in denying your children education for two months, you are denying them the most precious heritage you can give them. You want your children to grow up and compete, earning good livings; and the way you can assure them of that is to afford them an opportunity to do that. Don't deny them that.

Defendants may be released under their own recognizance to Wednesday, at 10:00 A.M.

That final hearing, the next Wednesday, was a quiet and tense affair. The press appeared in greater force than before, with television cameras in the corridors shooting the defendants as they arrived and mostly turned their backs, from vergüenza at the thought of appearing in the public news. The defendants took their place in the jury box.

Judge Montoya asked for a report on school attendance. Both lawyers rose and Chávez spoke first. The Gallegos children had not registered in Coyote, nor had Genaro Velásquez's children nor Leonardo Velásquez's young sister Flora. Felter announced that Amalia, Tobías, and Debra Gallegos are enrolled in the Santa Fe schools, Aurelia and Samuel and Flora Velásquez in Española. These three families had had to leave Cañones when they learned that the village was not about to get a good road. All of the other children were enrolled at Coyote or Gallina, for 100 percent compliance. Felter paused for emphasis on his last sentence.

The judge asked Orlinda Gallegos, and Genaro and Leonardo Velásquez, to confirm Felter's assurance. Orlinda said her family had already moved to Santa Fe. Genaro and Leonardo said they were about to move to Española. There was another pause, while the judge let this evidence of community dissolution sink in. Then he spoke slowly and quietly, through the interpreter:

> Will the defendants please rise.
>
> As you have previously been advised, you have been found guilty of a charge the possible penalty for which is a fine of not less than $5 or more than $100, and imprisonment in the county jail for not less than five or more than ninety days, and in addition, you can also be subjected to a writ of mandamus for ten days from the district court for failure to send your children to school.
>
> The court in this case is going to defer the pronouncement of judgment and sentence, either fine or imprisonment; but it is going to do so under certain stated conditions.
>
> The court is going to defer pronouncement for six months for each and every one of you. The deferment is on condition that all of you comply with the school attendance law, which means that the children will have to be and remain enrolled in school for six months. If any of you fail to comply with these conditions, you will be brought before the court, and the court will then pronounce sentence. The court is also going to defer judgment of costs.
>
> You may sit down.

> The court is not going to make any statement other than it made the other day. The court understands the nature of your problem. The court has already sent a copy of its remarks to the county commissioners, to the superintendent of public instruction of the state, and to the local school authorities in Coyote. The court appreciates the difficulty and possibly even the great sacrifice that you might have to make to send your children to some school other than Coyote; but there is no sacrifice too big for parents to make for the benefit of their children. The court appreciates your showing of good faith, and I know it is for the benefit of your children, and ultimately of all.

All the defendants and their friends went over to my house in Santa Fe for coffee, to celebrate the end of the whole long business. There was courtly behavior toward my wife Marianne, motherly cuddling of my three-year-old daughter Moana, and the warmth of misericordia for everybody. Several of the women went to the kitchen to help Marianne.

Coffee graduated into a junta, and the general topic of discussion was how to keep the community organized in the future, so that the momentum of the trial would not be lost. Everyone was conscious that the degree of unity and action that Cañones had achieved was unusual for villages without formal government and with little experience in manipulating the political world. The ditch associations were mentioned, and the drinking water association, as permanent groups the community could build upon for other projects. Felter's suggestion of a petition to the governor was seconded and heard respectfully.

Aftermath of the Court Appearance

Cañones changed in a few tangible and several intangible ways as a result of fighting the Goliath of state civil servants. It basked, of course, in the favorable publicity in newspapers and on television. Both *The New Mexican* and the *Albuquerque Journal* had kind words. *The New Mexican's* lead editorial on December 6 said:

> [The people of Cañones] purposely took the drastic action of willful disobedience of the law to bring their plight to a head after failure to find a solution in their many meetings with public officials from the school district level to the state level.

> . . . the plight of the Cañones' parents deserved high priority consideration. It deserves such consideration even more so today as a result of the court action.

The state highway commission continued to lend help from time to time for the Cañones road, although it had not become a state highway. The new sheriff, Benny Naranjo, gave substantial help; his father Emilio had cut a ribbon in 1964 for road construction, but that was the end of it.

Politicians from the local board up to the state level took note of a precinct that bloc voted, and courted the village in and out of juntas for the year that bloc voting lasted. Cañones was no longer an entirely forgotten backwater.

During the late fall and early spring, Elipio García contacted various organizations in the hope of starting cooperative industries in the village: growing cucumbers for pickling and making posts for highway fences, for example. Cañones was willing, but the outsiders disappeared before contracts could be made. After he was inaugurated as governor, David Cargo and the village pushed plans for a state park at Los Ojitos. The advantage to the village would be twofold: first, a trickle of income from visitors to the park who would need supplies, plus wages for Cañoneros as park rangers; second, a state law requiring that roads leading to state parks be state roads. Cargo succeeded with such a plan on the Pecos River below Villanueva with benefit both to the village and to the state. Unfortunately, the state legislature "shorted me out," as Cargo put it, and the Cañones park idea died after he left office. In any case, not all Cañoneros wanted the influx of outsiders using what was now good grazing land.

In speeches to the state board of education that were reported in the Albuquerque papers, DeLayo fulminated again about outside agitation. On December 5, he repeated the question whether "Facundo Valdez was inciting the community to civil disobedience" that he had raised October 31, but despite the authority the board had given him to conduct an investigation, he never did so. About what he had and had not done for Cañones, Valdez said in an interview in 1971:

> I provided organizational assistance to the village. I didn't call the shots, but influenced the direction they took. . . . Serafín Valdez and Elipio García went with me to Albuquerque and

> managed to get a good story into the *Journal*. We also made it a point to attend political rallies and conventions. . . . In matters of trying to get legal services . . . they went too fast, and hired Felter before I could make recommendations [to locate free help]. We held a number of mock court meetings to organize information for the court. We made an effort to approach the archdiocese for support, but without success. We held conversations with the county commissioners about the road . . . people in Cañones never gave up the idea of getting help from them. They put a sign on top of the hill that leads into Cañones, about the time of the primary campaign of 1966, but I had nothing whatever to do with it. It said, "*Aquí no queremos cabrones políticos.*" [We don't like damned politicians here.]
>
> I recommended the bloc voting . . . and I also advised them not to bloc their votes for one party or the other, but switch back and forth. I never advised them which candidates to vote for.

The initial reaction of people in the village to losing the battle in court was that they had lost everything. For a few days one heard recriminations in the placita against those who had testified against the village position, against the lawyer. But that died down quickly and people went on with their daily lives. Women seemed to feel freer to speak out in public than they had before. Certainly people talked more with each other, with less inhibition and somewhat less formally, somewhat more eagerly.

On February 4, 1967, the note to the bank was to come due, and the meeting to pay it revealed the village in yet a new way. The total, with interest was $1,218 (evidently the bank lowered the interest to 6 percent). This meeting was held February 2, at 7:30 P.M., in the Aragón tiendita, and for once everyone arrived on time. President Isaaque Lovato announced "*La junta está en orden,*" and treasurer Elipio García read aloud the list of people who had pledged contributions. The total came to $346.50, in amounts from a dollar or two to $40. Webster and David Waide and I were the only contributors who were not Hispano residents of Cañones (Kathy Krusnik had left in December.) Small amounts from a "pig raffle" and the "Republican Fund" added to the individual contributors. Each defendant (plus Elipio) now owed $77.63.

The atmosphere in this junta was high, although no one had been drinking. Voices were raised several notches above their usual pitches, and laughter was louder and more shrill than usual. It grew higher and more nervous as the meeting progressed, and as Elipio's wife Antonia and her sister Vitalia Aragón added figures on the tiendita's adding machine. The pledged money was checked carefully against the list to make sure the totals balanced—a prosaic contrast to the oratorical flights of other juntas, and to the usual acceptance of others on faith. After the $346.50 came out right to everyone's satisfaction, Orlinda Gallegos (acting as secretary for her husband who was in Utah herding sheep) made a gesture of putting the envelope with the bills into her pocket and walking off with it. High loud laughter and cries of "Stop her before she gets away!"

The laughter had not died when Elipio began to call the roll of participants. First Orlinda, then the others, one after the other, pulled wads of cash out of their pockets and paid up in full, $77.63 apiece. Some paid all but the last few dollars. (The arithmetic does not work out, because of the inability of some defendants to pay in full. The amount they did pay, plus contributions, came out almost exactly right.) Five did not have the money then, but would get it before Monday. No one in that room had ever seen so much hard cash in one place at one time, an impressive pile of small bills, the largest a twenty. A usually cynical young dandy's hand trembled as he counted out the money his mother owed. The one or two who wrote checks signed with unsteady hands. Voices were by now almost hysterical, as if very private affairs had become public.

When everyone had paid and the money was counted, the store emptied at once. There was suddenly no one left but myself, Elipio, and a mound of money.

"Where in the world did all that cash come from?" I asked in total bewilderment. "Most of the people here don't even have jobs."

Elipio turned to me with a look that seemed to say that Anglos aren't the only people who can pull dollars out of a hat. "*Cosa muy curiosa, qué no?* (Strange thing, isn't it?)" And those five words were all the explanation he ever gave.

The drama of the school fight was to have only two more scenes, played in June, both attracting a certain amount of public attention, neither leading to concrete action. They were designed to keep the schoolhouse on La Cuchilla open to the first three grades another year. DeLayo had said that if the road did not improve he "might" recommend that it remain open for the smallest children. Preciliana Salazar, who often acted as liaison between her native village and the governor's office during the whole matter, carried word back that Governor Cargo might welcome some pressure from the village. So another junta was called, to draw up a petition to the governor and to the superintendent of public instruction. The content was the village's, the wording was mine:

> We, the undersigned citizens of Cañones, hereby petition you to assist us in keeping our community school open for the first three grades during the school year 1967–68.
>
> When twelve of our parents were charged last year with keeping their children out of school, our defense was that the road from N.M. 96 to Cañones was unsafe for small children. Although we lost that suit and have abided by the court's decision, the road is still unsafe for small children. The work done by the Rio Arriba County Road Commission is not enough to make it an all-weather road, and we know from life-long experience in this part of the country that little ones would still be endangered if they had to fight their way through snow, hail or sleet from a stalled bus to Cañones.
>
> We are confident that the specific objections of the State Department of Education to our school—water supply, toilets, condition of the building, certification of the teacher—can all be met if we are permitted to work out the solutions together with the State and the School District.
>
> We therefore petition you, the responsible State officials, to help us retain our community school for the smallest of our children during the coming school year.

Orlinda Gallegos got fifty-seven signatures on each copy. She was careful not to let anyone sign the petition except Hispanos living in Cañones. I was not asked, nor were Webster and David Waide. The offer of friendly Anglos in another part of the school district to sign was refused. No one who did sign seemed to be very sanguine over its prospects. "What is there to lose?" was the general feeling. Both copies were mailed June 5.

Governor Cargo received his promptly, and said later that he called Leonard DeLayo to ask what response he intended to make. DeLayo denied receiving it, so the governor immediately sent him a photocopy, with a strong recommendation that the state board honor the request. DeLayo put the matter on the agenda for the meeting scheduled for June 29–30.

The petition had two results. The first was a visit from Governor Cargo, with a large retinue of state officials on Tuesday, June 20. The second was the presentation of the petition to the state board of education.

Every household was notified of the governor's visit and invited to attend to discuss roads and schools. Women of the village prepared a cold-cut lunch and other refreshments. Everything was ready for the visit—but no one had a key to the schoolhouse. So a deputation went to Bill Hatley, president of the school board, who was agreeable. But Horace Martínez had the key and was at home in Española. So they tried a janitor in Gallina who was thought to have a key, but without success. In the end, they had to break into the building. The difficulty was petty, another in the endless string of insults to the dignity of the village. But people were beginning to take such things in their stride, and to use them politically.

The morning of the twentieth came on dull. Rain drizzled all day and fell in downpours a couple of times. Cañoneros were delighted, although the state police who came in early worried whether the governor could get in, and if he got in, whether he could get back out. Cañoneros joked with the policemen, said they would be very willing to have the governor simply stay. A *Washington Post* reporter attended the meeting, but filed no story. (In the spring, Tom Wicker of the *New York Times* had been in Governor Cargo's office when a delegation came from Cañones, and wrote a column on the village.)

There must have been more people at the schoolhouse than the total population of Cañones. The whole placita turned out, from crying babies in arms to the oldest citizen. And numerous Cañoneros who lived elsewhere came in for the occasion. Rose Nava (sister of Sabiñano Lovato), who gave the village frequent help from Santa Fe, was there, and Wenceslao Salazar drove up from Española.

The honor of giving the governor the official village greeting was assigned to Francisco Lovato. Don Franque greeted the governor in Spanish.

The party moved indoors, and the governor took charge of the meeting. John Van Ness (who had arrived in the field only about a week before) stationed himself near the governor with a tape recorder.

The governor, of course, had his audience with him from the beginning. He spoke slowly, in phrases translated by Reginaldo

Espinoza, state highway commissioner for District 5 and a Cargo appointee:

> Ladies and gentlemen, I'm very happy to be here today, and I apologize for not being able to bring my regular interpreter, but my wife is afraid to come over the road and in addition to that we're expecting another *coyote* [laughter] in August, and she had to go to the doctor this afternoon. But she did come up here one Sunday [actually the previous Good Friday, when they attended the last part of the estaciones, including the procession from morada to campo santo] with me last winter. So now you've had the governor come twice and the first lady come once, in three hundred years. [laughter, applause] And I enjoyed it very much up here, and I'm going to put all the policemen to work on your road. But I wanted to come this afternoon because I have received your petition, and I've been up here before, and I know that you have two problems that you're very much concerned with.

The governor then introduced Espinoza and the other officials who came with him: Harry Wugalter, Leonard DeLayo, and Father Robert García (head of the Office of Economic Opportunity for the state). The applause was evenhanded for each guest, in keeping with Hispanic courtesy. Cargo drew loud laughter as he presented García:

> So even if he can't get you out of poverty, he can help you pray. So, I'm very happy to be here, and today I'd like to have you ask questions of the people that I brought, and I want you to know that I certainly appreciate what you did for me, because when I ran for governor, I had all the votes up here with the exception of a very few, and I think that those six people we've converted. If they haven't converted, I urge them to go down to the church, and Father García will hear their confessions.

It seemed that Cañones was suffering an attack of that vergüenza which inhibits young people from speaking up, and Governor Cargo filled in long gaps with encouraging monologue. Finally someone set off a flood by asking point blank whether a school could not be maintained in the village. The question was referred to Horace Martínez, who replied in Spanish:

> What we heard in Tierra Amarilla from Mr. Wugalter, when he gave money to keep the school open here, was that we were not to expect anything for the following year. And, according to

> what the governor has just said, the road is going to be fixed. Since this road is going to be fixed, we expect that next year the small children will go to school in Coyote, including the first grade, and the older children to Gallina.

Leonard DeLayo spoke in English shortly after Martínez had finished, and Robert Esparza translated for him. He spoke loudly, clearly, and with apparent conviction:

> Before Governor Cargo became governor, and before Mr. Espinoza was placed on the highway commission, I appeared with Mr. [Elipio] García and other people from this community before the highway commission to get your road improved. I asked them to declare this road a state road. They said they could not declare a state road, but promised to improve it. I will admit today that the road needs some improvement. [applause] I would like to join the governor in his personal appearance before the highway commission, and try once again to get the road improved. Now I shall attempt to answer the question. The state board of education has disapproved this school, which means that it will be closed for the fall. I believe the state board of education made the right decision, to close this school, and I believe with all my heart that we can do a better job for these boys and girls at the Coyote school. I have your petition and I will present it to the state board of education a week from Thursday.

DeLayo's flat statement might seem to have ended discussion on the chance to keep the school open, but questions were now flowing. Wenceslao Salazar asked DeLayo to express his own philosophy of education, specifically why the education in Coyote would be better than in Cañones.

Esparza answered for DeLayo, first asking in Spanish how many of the people did not understand English. Orlinda Gallegos answered with some spirit that many did not, "And I don't either." Laughter greeted her remark. They were speaking at cross purposes, and Orlinda was aware of it. Esparza wanted to get on with the business of the meeting, and regarded the constant translation as an annoying game played for the amusement of the Cañoneros, who had showed by their responses to the governor's jokes that most of them understood English perfectly well. Orlinda regarded Spanish as a symbol of the identity of Cañones, to be respected by translation, even at the expense of slowing down the meeting.

Esparza proceeded in Spanish:

> You ask why. First, because here there cannot be more than one teacher for several grades. In Coyote there is one teacher for each class. The children can learn better. Second, the services of the school, advising the students, physical examinations, providing lunches in the dining room, well-planned hot meals. Everything is handy at the school. Moreover, the cost of taking the children to Coyote is less than continuing the school here.

There was some muttering at Esparza's reply, but no challenge out loud. (After the meeting was over several Cañoneros said they were outraged by this speech of Esparza's, which implied that the school system could feed their children better than they could in their own homes. Esparza's remark was factually inaccurate as well as insulting. Despite the widespread belief among Anglos that the rather limited village diet must be inadequate, medical opinion holds that it is nutritionally well-balanced. Pinto beans are richer in protein than most other vegetables, and cultivated or wild greens provide a good supply of vitamins.)

Most of what followed was not picked up by our machine. Children had started to become restless, babies were crying louder than before, and the questions came faster from farther down the room. The governor, sensing that the meeting had accomplished as much as it was going to, and that the attention span of the younger members of the audience had run out, took the chair again, and with political grace brought the formal meeting to an end. Lunch was served. During it, Cargo said privately but with heat, "If only I could sell those guys in the department of education on a system of graded schools, with perhaps four different levels of school!" Each level, he said would be geared to a particular economic and ethnic situation.

Jacobo Salazar offered to unlock the gate on the lower road so that the governor's car could exit more easily. The governor accepted and soon left, with almost no fanfare. Others struggled out over the thoroughly sodden upper road.

Cañoneros were unhappy about the outcome of the meeting. They did not feel their real grievances got aired. They appreciated the friendliness of the governor, but complained that the school officials acted as if they hadn't wanted to come, and had given cold, stiff, and unsympathetic answers to their questions. Several commented on what they called a sour expression on DeLayo's face the whole time. Several were full of anger over Esparza's insult about the quality of home food. Some of the men said yes, but they hadn't expected much from these officials. There was enthusiasm about Espinosa's optimistic prediction for the road, even though Espinosa had not promised anything definite.

The very last scene of the legal battle was the state board of education meeting June 29, at which DeLayo had agreed to receive the village's petition to keep the school open. I took a more active part in this event than I had in any previous episode—with entirely unsuccessful results, as the account will show.

We decided to base our presentation on the argument that state department of education employees had given false or misleading information to the board about Cañones, and on the assumption that if the board had correct information it would vote to keep the Cañones school open at least one more year. We drew up a list of thirteen errors, reduced them to three double-spaced typewritten pages, and ran off enough copies for members of the board and the journalists we estimated would be present.

The delegation was a small one, consisting of Saquello Salazar, Orlinda Gallegos, and Genaro Velásquez. (This was almost a family affair, since Orlinda is Saquello's daughter, and Genaro his brother-in-law.) We were all very anxious, and suffered a virtually silent ride.

Item 10, the Cañones petition, came up about an hour after the board meeting reconvened for the afternoon. Our friend Albert Amador was not present. DeLayo told the board that he had visited Cañones with Governor Cargo on the twentieth and that, although he thought the school ought not to open for students in the fall, he was prepared to reserve judgment. If the road were not improved before September, he might recommend that the school remain open for the first three grades.

(According to the board's published minutes "if the roads were not improved by September he *would* ask the state board to reconsider the matter" [emphasis added].) He had no recommendation to the board now concerning the Cañones petition.

President Virgil Henry told us courteously, but in a businesslike way, that since our delegation was not on the agenda, we really ought not to be heard. (We had been shifted from the twenty-ninth to the thirtieth of the month, without our knowledge—since we had no telephone. So we arrived on the twenty-ninth, to find ourselves no longer on the agenda.) Delegations were usually received only if they made requests ahead of time in writing. But, since we had come from a distance, he would permit us to make a brief presentation. Would I please limit myself to fifteen minutes.

Quite thrown off balance by this unknown rule and unexpected time limit, I clutched like a graduate student delivering his first paper before the American Anthropological Association, my throat went dry, and I spoke much too fast to crowd in all thirteen points, completely forgetting to introduce members of the delegation until I had finished.

Our argument consisted of a point-by-point refutation of the state's contentions about the inadequate building, inadequate local diet, and the unsanitariness of outdoor privies (which public sanitation experts assured us are not inherently better or worse than flush systems), as well as accurate information about actual distances to the school from various parts of the village, the sloppiness about proper chauffeur licensing, the lack of improvement in the road, and the failure of the district to supply promised sports and other equipment. Only the licensing and equipment issues made any impression on the board.

Finished with the list of errors, I tried to defend Cañones as trying to establish community partnership in the education of its children when school officials would only talk *to* the village, not consult *with* them. But what should have been an indignant and eloquent speech came out as merely nervous and defensive. I failed in my attempt to label state officials as incompetents who could not read the odometers in their cars and who did not bother to look at maps of the village.

DeLayo rose to the attack the instant I concluded. Loudly, in his Bronx accent, he said, "I think the state has matured to the point where we are not in need of professors from the universities of Colorado or Texas to help us solve the problems of New Mexico. I think the state board of education is perfectly capable of deciding what needs to be done" (quoted from *The New Mexican*, June 30, 1967).

The Texas reference was a sly attack at Governor Cargo who, in the crisis following the Alianza's raid on the courthouse at Tierra Amarilla June 5, had called on Clark Knowlton, professor of sociology at the University of Texas at El Paso and an Alianza advisor, to be a liaison between the raiders and the state government. Right-wing New Mexico opinion was critical of Cargo for this move, and was well represented on the state board of education. DeLayo knew his board well, for no member challenged his irrelevant remark.

This flank attack, so totally unexpected, finished me off as the champion of Cañones. My only response was a stuffy, "I don't believe a remark like Mr. DeLayo's deserves the dignity of a reply."

Horace Martínez then rose from the audience and said in an agitated voice that his job had been made much more difficult by Dr. Kutsche and by other outsiders working up the Cañoneros, setting them against the people of Coyote. (According to Cañoneros whom I queried later, there was no animosity between adults of the two towns.)

Ralph Drake jumped in: the controversy over the closing of the school has been publicized too much. The Cañones school story has been one of political intrigue, a fight over the Cañones road and special university studies which have completely overlooked the most important thing—the education of the children.

State Representative Benito Chávez now demanded to be heard, saying he disagreed with DeLayo about New Mexico not needing advice from elsewhere. "We need people from outside to come and help us with our problems. Personally, I would like to see more of them." If the road were not fixed, Chávez said, he would be back to the state board in the fall to demand that the Cañones school be kept open. Chávez's support was remarkably generous, considering that Cañones had voted against him 50 to 6 the previous fall.

President Henry thanked me for my presentation. He said that the board was confident its employees had done a good job, and had studied the situation for a long time.

Member Thelma Inman, of Hobbs, repeated DeLayo's charge. Outsiders are interfering with education in New Mexico, she said. She and other members came from districts in which little kids were bussed much farther every day—up to 60 to 70 miles in some cases.

H. M. Mortimer, a physician from Las Vegas, asked the president what the position of the board would be about keeping a school open for twenty-three pupils if the building were in good condition and the road were all right. "I'm asking because I just want to get this decision into the context of what we would do elsewhere in the state." Henry replied that he believed the days of the old red brick one-room schoolhouse were over, and that education was better in the consolidated schools.

As the presentation came to an end, DeLayo turned to me in a pleasant tone of voice and asked me to introduce the others in the row containing the Cañones delegation. They were Carlos Colina, Gerry Greig, and Sue Sheila Horwitz, VISTA workers in Cañones and Coyote. Carlos and Gerry had driven to Santa Fe with us that morning. I had not seen them before at the board meeting. I couldn't imagine why DeLayo wanted me to introduce them, and was too tired to think fast, so I simply introduced them. Carlos told me later that DeLayo winked at one of his staff members when he made the request. Only outside in the lobby did it dawn on me that DeLayo set me a simple little trap of demonstrating that even more outsiders had come to the region to "agitate the natives."

The board went on to other business and the delegation left. All of us depressed, we said little, except to answer questions by Vina Windes, the *New Mexican* reporter who wrote a sympathetic story about us the next day. Milton Loewe, whose story in the *Rio Grande Sun* was even more sympathetic, went out with us. Before she left us, Rose Nava asked, "Why does Cañones always have to lose?"

The delegation drove straight out of town, stopping only in Española for a couple of the members to buy groceries. I felt I had let Cañones down totally, and had nothing to say at all. To brighten me up, one of the others said, "*Mira, Pablito, usted es un Cañonero.*" They showed me a small box on the front page of the day's *New Mexican* reporting that a delegation of citizens from Cañones was to appear before the state board of education after lunch. Since no mention was made of anyone else accompanying them, I was suddenly "from Cañones." I felt a little better.

In the placita when we arrived was the usual motley collection of children and a few adults. They crowded around the car to find out how the meeting had gone. Orlinda answered them so flatly that there was nothing more to be said.

"*Cañones perdió otra vez.*" (Cañones lost once again.)

Saquello Salazar, full of years, wisdom, and vergüenza, quietly brought home to me later the parallel between my treatment at the hands of DeLayo and his aides, and the treatment that Cañones had been subjected to during the entire fight—and long before—by various district and state bureaucrats. "*DeLayo no quiso platicar con usted, y los oficiales no quisieron platicar con nosotros. Es el mismo.*" (DeLayo didn't want to talk with you, and the officials didn't want to talk with us. It's the same thing.) Our dignidad had been cut down equally.

Politicians and Bureaucrats

García and de la Garza comment in *The Chicano Political Experience* that "underrepresentation in elected offices is worsened by the fact that Chicanos are equally underrepresented in bureaucratic positions . . ." (1977:110). During an interview on July 31, 1978, Chris García added that bureaucracies in New Mexico are even more likely to underrepresent Chicanos than political offices are, because at the levels where power is held and policy made, "it is a case of professionals," and professional training is less open to Chicanos than political office is. Further, the politician is responsive to his voters, the overwhelming majority of whom are Hispanic in northern New Mexico, while the bureaucrat is responsive to his professional training, which appears to override his own ethnic background. The only state civil servants who spoke sympathetically about local control of schools were two whose work officially recognized cultural differences: Henry Pascual, a Puerto Rican in charge of foreign language instruction (and later of bilingual education), and Ellen Digneo, Anglo director of the Small Schools Project, which at the time of the Cañones battle was running highly successful demonstration projects in bilingual education financed by the Ford Foundation in Pecos, Las Vegas, and Albuquerque. (See Digneo 1965–66.)

We have some evidence that Hispanic education bureaucrats who grew up in villages themselves suffer a good deal of ambivalence. One of them said to the field team, "When I got my bachelor's degree, the people I grew up with nicknamed me '*El Educado*' (the educated one)."

The politicians who were involved with Cañones, whether Anglo or Hispano, listened much better to Cañoneros than any of the professional educators did. Governor Cargo's relations with Cañones are documented in this chapter and in the next one. He added, in an interview in 1971, "Everybody is entitled to his own religion, his own way of making his living, and, by God, his own system of education." Former governor Campbell, after stating the views already quoted, went on more reflectively, "It comes down to basic values. Do you want to preserve the villages and be romantic, or do you want to help the young people get a college education and a good job?" A thoughtful pause and then, "Of course, once they get the education, they won't come back."

And then a second afterthought, even more reflectively: "If you look very frankly, comparing let us say Chicago or New York, and ask whether public services are rendered more efficiently there with impersonal bureaucracy than they are in New Mexico through political manipulation, I don't think you can honestly say that the bureaucracies are better."

Toward the end of interviews with them, two bureaucrats crossed the line to make political comments. Harry Wugalter said that one of the biggest problems in northern New Mexico is that New Mexico's leading politicians, including the Hispanos, find it expedient to keep the north poor and dependent. And Robert Esparza's answer to the question "Why has there been no bilingual education long since in New Mexico?" was succinct: "Anglo domination."

9
The Last Fourteen Years

Since 1967 much has changed in Cañones. Some of these changes are the local reflections of what has happened in the nation. Some originated in the village. We shall try to handle these changes systematically by first simply describing them (ignoring the question whether they should be labeled technical, social, or other) and then analyzing the changes in culture that result from these changes in the circumstances in which Cañones lives. For this purpose, *culture* means new existential and normative postulates, new conceptions of the way the world is and the way it—and people—should be. We shall find that a long and seemingly drastic list of changed circumstances produces a short list of changes in culture.

The first new event was the VISTA volunteers who arrived in the summer of 1967 to tutor children who had missed school during the lawsuit. Where the field team had come to learn, VISTA people came to teach, so their impact was more immediate.

Near Cañones, a long-range change started that affected Cañones a little less immediately. In April, 1967, a conference held at the Ghost Ranch indirectly set in motion increased attention to the Rio Arriba by public and private agencies. Sponsored by the governor's office, the Museum of New Mexico, the archdiocese of Santa Fe, and the Presbyterian church, it called itself "Consultation on Human

Resource Development." Governor Cargo and Alex Mercure (of HELP) initiated the conference, and the governor opened it. Kutsche attended as an observer. The five-day meeting was remarkably free of political posturing, full of enthusiastic discussion of present problems and potential solutions, and remarkable for the range of participants. They included regional forest service officials, state welfare director John Jasper and some staff members, Facundo Valdez and Tomás Atencio, former governor Jack Campbell, Eugene Foley former head of the Small Business Administration, Office of Economic Opportunity people, and an economist from the Chase Manhattan Bank in New York. The state department of education was conspicuously absent. Out of that meeting came an expansion of HELP and successful organizations to train Hispanos in making and marketing the crafts of their own tradition. Truchas and Taos benefited particularly. Cañones got HELP programs in carpentry, sewing, and other skills. The more perceptive of these participants recognized that large-capital economic development was meaningless for northern New Mexico, and that to engage the skills of the large labor pool was far more important.

There were disturbing notes in the April meeting: forest service officials, from the regional forester in Albuquerque on down, seemed to have "instructions from the Department of Agriculture that give them no lee-way in negotiating with political elements like the Alianza Federal de Mercedes, and their departmental rigidity is quite likely to find itself unable to bend, and the target of violence" [quoted from Kutsche's field notes]. They refused to acknowledge a valid civil protest in the Alianza Federal de Mercedes. There had already been some violence in October, 1966, when the Alianza had occupied Echo Amphitheater on Kit Carson National Forest land. The other disturbing note, from Facundo Valdez, was "that the rumblings he hears lead him to think that considerable ugliness may come up this summer."

It did. On June 5, the Alianza, having been harassed during meetings in Coyote and elsewhere by District Attorney Alfonso Sánchez, raided the Rio Arriba county courthouse in Tierra Amarilla in an attempt to arrest him. He had already left (see Nabokov 1969). Cañones, although sympathetic to the Alianza, was thoroughly frightened, especially when state police came knocking on doors looking for Reies Tijerina. Before that ugliness subsided, it became an issue in Santa Fe and in Washington, and spurred the flow of federal money to the area. As we noted in chapter 8, Leonard DeLayo made political profit out of it.

Cañones, having so recently been front-page news, continued to receive occasional coverage from *The New Mexican* in Santa Fe, less often from the Española and Albuquerque press, and happily received its share of the increased funds.

David Cargo kept his promises to Cañones throughout his two terms of office—a noteworthy fact in Rio Arriba politics. He pressured Reginaldo Espinosa, the state highway commissioner responsible for the district, to give aid to the lower road into Cañones and, according to James Rankin, district five engineer, "We just went in and helped." Little by little state and county graders widened and graveled it. The ford just below Preciliana Salazar's house was bridged in the spring of 1970 with state and county cooperation, and the ford opposite Jacobo Salazar's house a little later. The right-of-way dispute between Jacobo Salazar and the county was settled in court at the going rate of a little more than $10 per unirrigated acre, whereupon Jacobo made the upper road impassable, reclaiming it as part of his ranch. A sign pointing to Cañones was erected by the state in the 1970s at the turnoff of the lower road from N.M. 96. Cargo had said in 1967 that it was a special insult to the village not even to show the way to it.

During the lawsuit, Cañones became Naranjista, and when Naranjo forces dominated the county commission, graders were seen more frequently in the village. A new road bulldozed toward Elipio García's house gave him easier access, and even the road to the end of Cienaguitas was cleared of the worst rocks.

Telephones reached Cañones in spring 1972, and by 1980 twenty-two Cañones numbers were listed in the directory. Since the system is connected west, not east, calls to Gallina and points in between are local, but calls to Abiquiu are long distance. When the high school students had to go to Coyote and then to Gallina, Cañones got further removed from its mother Abiquiu, and marriage patterns shifted. The new telephone connections gives Cañones another big shove in the same direction. Nevertheless, direct long-distance dialing connects Cañones with its relatives wherever they have moved.

A television antenna went up on the Mesa Blanca in 1976, paid for by the Save the Children Federation (described below in connection with El Proyecto). Most houses have sets, but only one station comes in well.

Late in 1980, Adelaida Lucero gave in and permitted her family to wire her house.

The Cañones post office was moved June 8, 1968, from the home of Jacobo Salazar up close to the placita into the home of the new postmistress, Orlinda Gallegos, as a result of a petition signed by virtually everyone in Cañones. Simultaneously, the U.S. Congress pulled in the purse strings for the post office department, and the brand new post office was scheduled to be closed August 2 of the same year. Fortunately Cañones was still in the public eye, and letters to Postmaster General Marvin Watson from Governor Cargo, Senator Clinton Anderson, and Senator Joseph Montoya saved the new post office, which is still receiving mail three times a week at the time of writing.

A surprise of the 1970s was population increase. Dalio Gallegos, and Genaro and Leonardo Velásquez moved their families out only briefly in 1966. They moved back, and the village suffered no loss of population. In fact, sons and daughters began to buy mobile homes when they married and to park them in their parents' yards. Map 7 shows thirteen new trailer homes, plus a few new adobe houses. Wenceslao Salazar's architect son Eliud added a solar greenhouse to his grandmother's house. Guesses from people in Cañones in July, 1980, are that the population has increased from its 1967 total of 175 to nearly 225. (The 1967 census has not been repeated, so comparisons between those figures and 1980 are largely impressionistic. Map 7, however, was made systematically by Eliud Salazar so as to provide a house-by-house comparison for the two years.)

Among the new residents are former Cañoneros who now find it possible to live there because of road improvements. An example is Modesto Vialpando (no. 69), one of the several nephews whom Fidencia Vialpando raised. He left Albuquerque and bought Fidencia's house and land, when she and her son-in-law Simón Vigil moved to Albuquerque on account of health. Modesto and others like him bring back to Cañones their formal education and their experience of how to cope with government and business outside the village. A clearcut example of how the new households located themselves is seen by comparing Serafín and Luz Valdez's house plot between 1967 and 1980. They sit in spacious isolation in

CANONES 1980: a key to residences in the placita

ED. NOTE — Houses owned and occupied by the same heads of households as in 1967 are indicated on the map, but are not numbered or keyed. Number 5 is an exception to this rule. House 46 is not indicated on this map, but is situated below number 69, on the other side of the road. (Map 3 is on page xxv.)

1. Severiana Salazar
3. vacant (ruins)
5. James Harrill
8. Lilian Madrid
10. Arturo Valdez
11. vacant
14. Marcelino Sandoval (demolished)
21. Bernardita Salazar
23. Juan Velásquez
24. Román Aragón
26. José Dolores Vialpando
29. Asamblea de Dios parsonage
31. Marcelino Sandoval
32. Abenicio Serrano
38. Ricardo Madrid
39. Guillermo Salazar
40. Ricardo Lovato
42. Sabiñano Lovato
45. Ricardo (son of José) Vialpando (trailer added)
46. vacant (Modesto Vialpando)
47. Francesquita Salazar
48. vacant (Sabiñano Lovato)
50. Juan Chacón
51. Felipe Madrid
52. Ricardo (son of José Dolores) Vialpando
53. (trailer) Alvaro Martínez
54. (trailer) Eloy Martínez
55. (trailer) Martín Valdez
56. (trailer) Alfonso Aragón
57. (trailer) Billie Martínez
58. (trailer) Lonicio Vialpando
59. Bonifacio González
60. (trailer) Genaro Serrano
61. daughters of José Dolores Vialpando
62. Felix Valdez
63. (trailer) Ricardo Madrid
64. (trailer) Guillermo Salazar, Jr.
65. (trailer) Vidal Velásquez
66. (trailer) Francisco (son of Sabiñano) Lovato
67. Cañones community building
68. (trailer) Tobías Gallegos
69. Modesto Vialpando
70. vacant
71. Stanley Nava

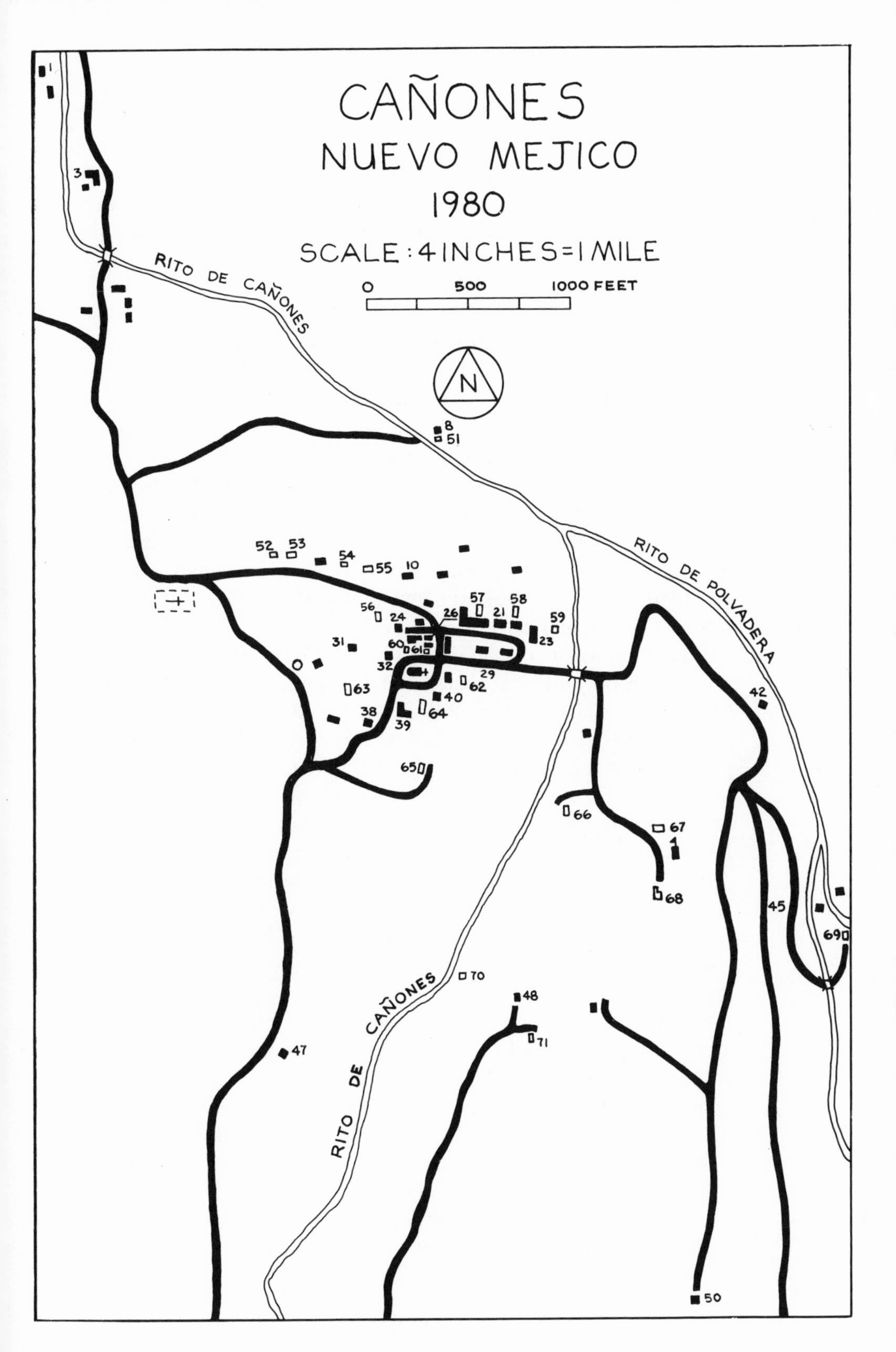

Map 7. Cañones Placita, 1980

1967 (map 3, no. 9), but in 1980 they are surrounded by the houses and trailers of their sons Martín and Arturo (map 7, nos. 55 and 10), and by the children of friends (no. 52, 53, and 54) whom they permitted to build on what some people jokingly are calling the "Valdez placita."

A higher proportion of the adult males commutes to work—an impossibility until the road became more or less reliable. In 1980, for example, four heads of household carpool to work in Española and two to Los Alamos, about sixty miles each way. They leave Cañones at 6:00 A.M. and get back around 7:00 P.M. Each drives one day a week. The price of gasoline has reached $1.20 per gallon, but that figure is not yet prohibitive.

The number of working women has increased, particularly among those who were children in 1967. Serafín and Luz Valdez's daughter Igenia, for instance, only seven in 1967, was trained as a carpenter in the late 1970s and is now working in construction for excellent wages. Several other women have clerical jobs both inside and out of the village.

Education has increased markedly. In 1967 only Manuel Salazar, son of Jacobo and Severiana, had a college degree. Wenceslao (Ben) Salazar already had both B.A. and M.A., but was teaching Spanish in Española where he had a home. In 1980 a handful of younger Cañoneros are in college or have graduated. The road to higher education is still usually the road out of Cañones, but not always. Dennis Gallegos, son of Dalio and Orlinda, teaches in the Jemez Canyon High School close to Jemez Indian Pueblo, but is active in Cañones Catholic affairs and coauthored a paper with Kutsche on the cofradía (Kutsche and Gallegos 1979). Ben Salazar's son Eliud graduated from the University of New Mexico with a bachelor's degree in architecture in 1980. Eliud and his father both live in Francesquita's house in Cañones now, taking care of the cattle and crops since Saquello's death in 1975, and practicing architecture and teaching in the Jemez Mountain High School, respectively. Several other people now living in the village have gone past high school. Several children of Cañones families are now in college or trade school, and may or may not return to live.

As more people work for wages outside, more houses add bathrooms. The community drinking water supply is adequate for the placita so far, but there is no community sewage system. Each new bathroom requires a septic tank, and one of the new sights on the placita is the truck that comes periodically to pump out the septic tanks.

Another result of the tighter connection between Cañones and the world outside is that the tienditas have closed and have not been replaced. Bode's Store in Abiquiu gets more Cañones business. A dismal result of road improvement is that Cañoneros now have more opportunities to be killed on the highways. Adelaida Lucero lost her husband Luis that way when he was only fifty. Of their three sons, only Epimeneo survives: Cristóbal and Miguel died in car accidents in their early twenties. Other families have suffered similar losses.

The Anglos have arrived to stay, although in what numbers is not yet clear. David Waide turned land developer in the 1970s, subdividing his acreage toward the head of Cañones Canyon into lots for summer homes for businessmen in Española and elsewhere. The expectable disputes about water rights are beginning to emerge. Because these Anglos live far upstream from the placita, they do not have any other impact on Cañoneros so far. One Anglo bought land on the lower Cuchilla and built a conspicuous white cinder block house. He never moved in, and at this writing is trying to sell it. For about a year a group of young adults whom Cañoneros labeled hippies rented Preciliana Salazar's house. Since 1974 the house has been rented to James Harrill, a painter in acrylics who comes from North Carolina and sells his work through galleries in Santa Fe, Scottsdale, and elsewhere.

Cienaguitas Land Transfer

Chapter 3 notes the boundary between the Polvadera and Juan Bautista Valdez land grants along Cañones Creek, cutting the microbasin in two, with the result that people of Cienaguitas and La Cuchilla were technically squatters on National Forest Land, even though they had held their land for generations. This was the situation in 1967, tolerated uneasily by the village and by the forest service. The Presbyterian church succeeded in the mid-1970s in settling that problem where the federal government had failed. (Information in this section is primarily from an interview with James Hall, director of the Ghost Ranch Center, June 30, 1980.) The complexity and expense of the process helps explain why any single village, or even groups of villages, have been totally unable to deal with the federal bureaucracy, and may help explain why Hispanos periodically resort to violent movements like the Alianza Federal de Mercedes in their own attempts to cope with the government.

The Ghost Ranch interest in the question arose not long after 1955 when Arthur Pack donated the land to the Board of Christian Education of the Presbyterian church for a conference center. Pack founded the Ghost Ranch Museum for desert ecology on the property and installed as director Bill Carr, who had designed the very successful Sonora Desert Museum, also founded by Pack, outside of Tucson. Legally the new museum belonged to the Board of Christian Education, but the board discovered that budgeting for both the museum and the center was awkward. So a separate corporation was tried, which also proved awkward, and Pack proposed that the museum be split off and given to the forest service, which already owned a part of the exhibit—the Little Beaver National Forest, smallest national forest in the country. The forest service was delighted.

Jim Hall, then as now director of the conference center, knew that numerous parcels of land in the area were disputed between settlers and the Kit Carson and Santa Fe National Forests (the first north, the second south of the Chama River), and convinced the Board of Christian Education to request a land exchange. The board would give to the forest service title to the museum land and buildings, plus other land, a total of 330 acres. The forest service would give the board title to disputed lands equalling the appraised value of the museum and land, and the board would in turn transfer title to the settlers. The regional forester in Albuquerque was hard to convince, but finally agreed after persuasion by Gene Hassel, then head of the Carson Forest. Hall insisted that the forest service and not the Ghost Ranch develop the list of parcels. Hassel's list started at Tres Piedras, and came down to Ojo Caliente, including a number of claims upstream from Ojo Caliente in and around La Madera; a strip from Trujillo Hill down toward Abiquiu on the Chama; Tierra Azul on the Chama River from the intersection of U.S. 84 and N.M. 96 below Abiquiu on the upstream end, almost to Medanales downstream. John Hall, head of the Santa Fe Forest, included only Cañones. More than 110 owners with about 120 parcels totalling 1,060 acres made up that side of the trade.

The Ghost Ranch set up a three-person land panel to deal with each of the disputed parcels: Juan Griego of Chamita, chosen by the Carson claimants; Karl Bode of Abiquiu, chosen by the Santa Fe claimants; and the chairman, Vicente Martínez of Taos, chosen by Jim Hall who was not a claimant. The Ghost Ranch provided the panel with the services of William Gilbert, Santa Fe attorney, and of Joe Luján, Española surveyor—a considerable financial contribution, although both Gilbert and Luján charged less than full tariff.

The forest service "got very nervous" as the exchange proceeded, said Hall, and decided it lacked authority under existing legislation to carry out the exchange. So it drew up a bill that was introduced into the U.S. House of Representatives as H.R. 10857 by Manuel Luján, Jr., June 16, 1972, and into the Senate by Clinton Anderson. The bill was passed, and signed by President Nixon in October, 1972 (*Albuquerque Journal* November 3, 1972). The transfer was completed in 1975 except for a few residual disputes that are now in the courts. As a result, all of the owners of disputed house lots and farm tracts in Cañones now have title to their land, although the status of the Polvadera common lands has not altered.

The resources of money, political clout, and professional skills involved in this exchange were, of course, totally beyond the command of any local entity. The influence of the Ghost Ranch, the Presbyterian church, and Arthur Pack, in Philadelphia, Washington, and New Mexico, were all employed.

A foot note to the complicated process was that at the celebration at the Ghost Ranch in November, 1972, a delegation at least partly made up of Alianza members came from Coyote to announce that although the idea of the transfer was a good one, the Anglos should remember that the Piedra Lumbre Grant land really belonged to the people, and that one day all of the outsiders would be thrown off.

La Academia Real

The public elementary school in Cañones did not reopen. But elementary education came back to Cañones in an unexpected way. The "community school" movement was growing in the United States as a reaction against the shift of control over the education of children from parents and communities to professional bureaucrats enforcing national standards, to national textbook publishing houses, and in general to homogenized national culture. The Cañones school fight contained elements that have aroused communities elsewhere, and attracted the attention of educational philosophers as well as politicians. This attraction makes sense if we label the old days of political but local (or at least regional) control the wave of the past, the national standards period the straightjacket present, and the community school movement the wave of the future. The waves of the past and the future have more in common with each other than either does with national straightjackets.

Julián Lovato, son of a Cañones family and raised in Española, is an educator involved with community schools. He has bachelor's and master's degrees in education from New Mexican institutions, and at the time of the school fight was teaching in Coyote. Lovato and his wife, a Mexican named Yolanda Carrasco, who also had a master's degree in education, came to Cañones in the summer of 1975 to tutor children in basic skills. They stayed for the school year 1975–76 to found La Academia Real in the middle of the placita, using contemporary theories of bilingual education and some instruction by adults in the community in their own culture. (In addition to visiting La Academia Real three or four times while it was in session and discussing it with many Cañoneros and its founder Julián Lovato, Kutsche interviewed Lorenzo Valdez, the second director, in July, 1980.)

That first year every Cañones child in grades one through eight was enrolled in the Academia, and the placita became a buzz of activity from the first cowbell at 8:30 in the morning until the end of class at 4:00 in the afternoon. The Lovatos moved a large mobile home to the spot where Marcelino Sandoval's house had stood, and built a classroom adjacent to it. These structures were the center of the Academia, but it spread to other buildings as well. Students were out of the buildings a good deal, and parents had frequent business in them, preparing lunch and bringing supplies. Funding came primarily from Title I, a federal program for children of migrant workers. This was a happy year for Cañones, full of optimism for adults, and full of bustle for the schoolchildren—sharp contrast to the courteous boredom of public elementary schools. Toward the end of the year, the Academia took about forty Cañoneros of all ages on a bus trip to Mexico, an exciting and memorable adventure.

The Lovatos left after one year, and a board of directors, consisting of Serafín Valdez, Orlinda Gallegos, and Aquilino Serrano, asked Serafín's nephew Lorenzo Valdez to direct it for the next year. Lorenzo, like Julián, comes from a Cañones family but was raised mostly in Española. He spent a few months each year in Cañones as a boy, however, and often accompanied his grandfather Belarmino Valdez on cofradía business. "I slept under the table while grandpa was talking with his hermanos," he says. He grew up greatly influenced by a number of old men—Belarmino, Saquello Salazar, Francisco Lovato, Ramón Jaramillo, and Pedro Velásquez, the last three of whom died in the mid-1960s. Most of these men were hermanos, and all of them were universally regarded with respect and affection as the embodiments of traditional values. Lorenzo was a VISTA volunteer in Española in 1976, working with another academia—the Academia de la Nueva Raza headed by Tomás Atencio of Dixon, which published *"El Oro del Barrio"* consisting of folklore from villages between Española and Taos. (Vicente Martínez, chairman of the Ghost Ranch land panel, was also active in this academia, and was Lorenzo's VISTA supervisor.)

The Academia Real board had no money to pay Lorenzo, who had no teacher's certificate and was not eligible for Title I pay, but was given free living quarters by Serafín, and his gas mileage by the Academia, and has his VISTA stipend for the first three months. When that ran out, "I was living by borrowing and begging." One certified teacher, an Anglo woman named Crystal Apple, received a salary from Title I and stayed through the year. Lorenzo found himself unable to stretch nothing per month far enough, and had to leave after seven months. Julián Lovato was able to finish out the year in his place.

Under Lorenzo Valdez, the Academia was very different from a traditional school, and close to other innovative community schools. Physically it was somewhat more spread out because the Lovato mobile home was gone, so the school used Delfinia Salazar's house in the lower placita, Juan Madrid's house close to Adelaida Lucero's just above the placita, and much of the outdoors between. The "open classroom" was both a necessity and a virtue.

Lorenzo's aim was to share with children what he had learned as a boy in Cañones, and to accomplish some of the same goals as the Dixon academia, even though the latter was not a school in a formal sense. "I wanted to start from where the community was at," he said. "So I asked what is it that gives everyone in Cañones the same itch, the same pinch in the shoe. This was the lawsuit in

1966 over the school. My measure of success was motivation of the kids to learn. I had them doing clay sculpture, pottery, photography, music, as well as other subjects."

A successful mathematics lesson was the attempt to even a lumpy earthen basketball court by surveying. The study of language became a game in which students brought Lorenzo words that he would help them search for in the dictionary, in the encyclopedia, and in other books if necessary. He translated hard words into Spanish and asked students to take them home and get their parents to explain how the word related to a Spanish-speaking life. The gift of a Polaroid camera by a friendly outsider led to pupils' pictures of Cañones and to discussions of the village, lessons in writing, and to chemistry. "I found about $50 from Title I funds for chemicals, taught them how silver reacts to light and so forth, and helped them make pinhole box cameras."

Two or three adults came to teach their special skills. Wenceslao Salazar helped out as much as his new insurance business permitted. Other adults held back, made timid by the definition of education as a specialized business only experts were competent to handle, but were beginning to overcome their diffidence by the time Lorenzo left. During these first two years the children of Cañones grew more enthusiastic about school, and so did the community in general.

From 1977 the Academia suffered from lack of certified teachers, lack of funds, and at times from disputes within the board. It started the 1979–80 year with a few students, but closed its doors in January, and all Cañones children are now in the public school in Coyote.

It seems fair to conclude that the Academia Real would have succeeded if it could have found a steady and reliable source of funds. The willingness of the whole village to contribute according to their individual talents (celebrated in chapters 7 and 8 as misericordia) came forward to some extent during the Academia's brief life, and seemed to be growing. What killed it was above all the lack of certified teachers who would spend a portion of their careers in Cañones, and the lack of administrative support. School district 53 took the attitude that a dollar of Title I funds to Cañones was a dollar not channeled through Gallina, and gave little or no assistance.

El Proyecto

In 1974 Cañones started its own economic development organization through contacts between Elipio García and representatives of the Save the Children Federation of Connecticut. The full name of this new entity is El Proyecto de Reconstrucción de la Comunidad de Cañones, and its purpose, according to bylaws filed with the state corporation commission in 1975, is "to ameliorate educational, agricultural, health and economic standards and social services for the community of Cañones." Wilfredo Vigil of Española, director of the Chicano Program of the Save the Children Federation, spelled out its goals and accomplishments, and added in an interview in July, 1980, that it tried to reinforce the older pre-1960 culture.

Our firsthand knowledge of El Proyecto is limited. In summer 1980, when Kutsche collected final information for this chapter, all of the present officers were away from Cañones, working or on other business, so he relied primarily on the interview with Wilfredo Vigil for data. While the facts reported here are mostly Vigil's, the interpretations are entirely Kutsche's.

Save the Children has been the prime funder of El Proyecto—initially about $17,000 per year, up to $20,000 and $25,000 per year while a community center building was under construction, in fiscal 1979–80 down to $8,000 as contributions to headquarters in Connecticut fell off. From 1976 to 1979 the federal CETA program funded jobs for five Cañoneros in El Proyecto, including two equipment operator trainees and an administrator. CETA assumes that private employers will pick up salaries after a start-up period; there is no such private employer in Cañones, so those jobs ended with the funding. In 1980 the New Mexico Arts Commission awarded a grant to El Proyecto to teach and market weaving; it had not gotten underway as this chapter was written.

The effect of El Proyecto on Cañones is visible and tangible. The new community center, still under construction on La Cuchilla close to the schoolhouse, contains a large meeting room equally appropriate for meetings and dances, plus a kitchen and several smaller meeting rooms and/or offices. A solar greenhouse is planned to stretch along its south face. The Proyecto bought a truck, a backhoe, and other equipment, and uses them for community projects. They are also available for rental to individuals. They have been used for improving acequias and digging graves, among other things.

Outside agencies, governmental and otherwise, seek a single agency in the village to deal with, and find it in El Proyecto. During the late 1970s it was responsible for meeting to discuss development ideas, with the exception of the Academia. Proyecto directors have hoped that the organization would be seen as the entire village in regard to community development planning.

What has happened is different. The directors and employees of El Proyecto have been predominantly, although not exclusively, members of the Assembly of God church, and the Catholics—especially the larger landholders—have not identified closely with it. (New board members were chosen in the fall of 1980, and El Proyecto may become more representative.) A subtler development is a change in work on behalf of the community from volunteer hand labor to paid machine labor. Grave digging will serve as a simple and clear illustration. The older custom (see chapter 6) was for a work party to dig graves by hand, and for the occasion to be an intimate expression of support for the surviving relatives and a reinforcement of the community's misericordia. The new custom is for one man to dig the grave with the Proyecto backhoe, and to fill the grave after the funeral. The labor saving is considerable, but the social loss, although unintentional, is also considerable.

Cañoneros who are critical of El Proyecto point to the difference in community work between the lawsuit in 1966 and Proyecto work in the 1970s. In the 1960s, they say, if the community needed (for instance) a trip to Santa Fe to consult with lawyers or state officials, those who could perform the service simply did it with no thought of reimbursement. Now all community work is paid. Those doing it look at the pay as coming from the government, and do not feel obligated to work very hard. Then, when the money runs out, as both CETA and Save the Children funds seem to be doing in 1980, community work just does not get done. The aim of the Proyecto founders to reinforce pre-1960 community values is certainly not being served. It is an interesting question whether El Proyecto is preparing Cañoneros for the expectations of a less personal and more commercial world, and whether it is doing so better or worse than jobs outside Cañones have always done. There is no question that it is an effective agent for change.

The Soil Conservation Service

In the late 1960s, two acequia systems began to improve their ditches. The Upper Cañones Community Ditch, with Saquello Salazar and later Wenceslao Salazar as mayor domos, from 1968 to 1980 built a log *presa* (diversion dam), carried water over arroyos with concrete and steel pipes, and also laid pipes at points of great seepage. The Polvadera Ditch, with Elipio García as mayor domo, from 1969 to 1976 built a new presa from the creek and another to collect the water of Los Ojitos, piped through a sandy cut, and made other improvements. The Cienaguita Ditch expects to make improvements in the near future.

The material result of these improvements is simply to get more water to fields with less sedimentation, less seepage, and less yearly maintenance. The social and administrative process by which these improvements are made offers a lesson in methods of development and their impact on villages.

The two key organizations are the ditch association in the village and the Soil Conservation Service, an agency of the U.S. Department of Agriculture. (The structure of this system was explained by Edward Romero, soil conservationist in SCS office in Española, interviewed July 2, 1980. He was field man for some of the work done in Cañones.) The association is always the active party, SCS the reactive. The process starts when an association approaches SCS with a request for assistance. SCS sets up a three-party meeting on the site of the acequia: SCS, ASCS (Agricultural Stabilization Conservation Service, also part of the Department of Agriculture), and the commissioners of the ditch. SCS insists that all of the ditch commissioners show up regardless of their work obligations elsewhere, as an indication of enthusiasm and commitment. As Edward Romero told us:

> We ask them, at that meeting, "What do you want to accomplish?" We then advise them whether the plan is technically and economically feasible, and make alternative suggestions. We don't try to argue them out of what they want to do, nor into what we want them to do. If the plan is not feasible, for whatever reason, we then offer feasible alternatives. We keep in mind that we are not consulting about federal land, so the aim is to help owners handle their own land to the best of their capabilities; we can't tell them what to do.

The meeting is conducted in Spanish or in English as the commissioners prefer; the whole SCS staff is bilingual.

The next step is a survey. The association must clear the underbrush, "otherwise we'd have to turn sight lines every few feet," and may be asked to lend help in the survey itself. This step is another test of the association's eagerness to have the job done.

The association must appoint an agent to work with SCS, who may or may not be the mayor domo. He must provide ASCS with a list of parciantes, their signatures, their social security numbers, and their total acreage. The signatures provide a third test, as refusal of a parciante is taken as a signal of problems in getting the work done.

SCS engineers then draw up blueprints, and the entire plan goes to the state engineer's office for approval for cost sharing by the state. Then SCS reviews the design with the commission.

An approved plan is cost-shared between ASCS (70 percent), the state (15 percent), and the acequia association (15 percent, which is often paid in labor). The advantage to the association of this arrangement is enormous. It accomplishes improvements that it could not have financed, and for which it lacked technical knowledge. SCS deliberately created the three tests of commitment mentioned above to protect its tiny staff (only three men in the Española office) against spending time and talent on projects which the association might not carry through.

Romero said that Cañones has always cooperated splendidly. Parciantes in Cañones since the work began in 1968 praise SCS highly, speak with delight about their improvements, and invest plenty of sweat. Saquello Salazar, a parciante on both ditches, labored on the Polvadera improvement up to a year or two before his death in 1975 at the age of seventy-four.

It is ironic that two agencies as different in the way they face Hispanic villages as SCS and the forest service are both in the Department of Agriculture. SCS believes, as Romero said in a 1980 letter, that "the small farmer and rancher is an endangered species and we hope to provide him or her with the assistance needed so that they may survive." The forest service prefers to deal with large cattle operations, which it regards as more economic than the subsistence scale of a village ranchero and the imprecise legal status of a Spanish or Mexican land grant. Local forest officials seem to feel that they have very little leeway in making policy, and are constrained at every turn by their own regulations.

Outside Changes

The picture of changes inside Cañones has been painted with broad strokes. Mention of changes outside Cañones must be even broader and more selective.

Educational philosophy and practice changed to include bilingual education programs in many parts of the state. (Wenceslao Salazar directed the program in Española before he returned home to live.) School district 53 now has bilingual education.

Sentiment about local control also changed, as we see from Leonard DeLayo's guest column in the Santa Fe *New Mexican* for June 17, 1975:

> . . . I do see a reversal of this trend toward the concentration of political power in Washington and Santa Fe in New Mexico's attitude toward public education.
>
> Recent actions by the legislature, the attorney general and the State Board of Education have strengthened the hands of parents, citizens and local school officials who wish to exercise their own judgment and initiative.

Depletion of energy supplies has both a direct and an indirect influence on villages like Cañones. One new development illustrates both. During the late 1970s, Peter van Dresser secured for the Ghost Ranch a federal grant to demonstrate the practicality of passive solar heating using the classic building materials of adobe and wood, insulated with pumice and sawdust, all of which are locally available, and glass, which is not. The resulting project trained a number of young Rio Arriba men as "solar technicians," including Leonardo Velásquez of Cañones. Interest in solar design is high in Cañones. The change in national thinking, of which solar energy is both a part and a symbol, emphasizes local decisions and local subsistence more than formerly. Federal policy stemming out of the War on Poverty appears to support the fight of localities to regain control, and to weaken somewhat the hold of the state over counties and villages.

Some events outside Cañones merely show how little has changed. Emilio Naranjo is no longer sheriff of Rio Arriba county, but the sheriffs are still Naranjistas. Emilio himself is now county manager and state senator, and runs a restaurant as well as real estate interests. The Raza Unida party, whose strength is in La Cooperación del Pueblo in Tierra Amarilla (an organization founded by Reies Tijerina's older brother Anselmo), has challenged the Naranjo forces but so far has not defeated them. Nor have criminal charges brought against Emilio by government agencies driven him out of office.

The scholarly world has paid more attention to Hispanic land grant villages, starting in the late 1960s. The Western Social Science Association, at the prompting of sociologist Clark Knowlton, formerly of Highlands University in Las Vegas, and now of the University of Utah, began to host an annual Mexican-American session. That session in turn, hosted one session each year devoted to historical research on Hispanic land grants. The Center for Land Grant Studies was formed out of this interest in 1976, and drew so big an audience at the 1980 meeting of WSSA in Albuquerque that it is considering hosting its own sessions in the future.

Elipio García gave a paper on community cohesion at the WSSA meeting in Lubbock in 1969, and Wenceslao Salazar organized and chaired a panel on villagers' views of the rest of the world in Albuquerque in 1980. The Center for Land Grant Studies is beginning to publish on numerous grants, including those in and near Cañones, and hopes to provide data that will encourage the drafting of remedial legislation, as well as aiding court challenges. The village advisory council of the center includes Elipio García, Serafín Valdez, and Sabiñano Lovato, and the annual business meeting of the Center was held in Cañones in September, 1978.

Islam is writing its mark on Rio Arriba, but to date no one knows how that mark will print, or how deep. A group of Moslems reputed to be financed by the Saudi Arabian royal family among others, has bought part of Alva Simpson's Rancho de Abiquiu, across the Chama River from the village of Abiquiu, and is erecting a mosque. The plan is apparently to establish a boarding school for the propagation of the faith in North America. The architectural impact of this new development may be the first to be felt, for the mosque is constructed almost totally without wood; arches and domes of adobes take the place of wooden lintels and vigas. Since it requires a semitrailer and a good deal of gasoline to bring down appropriate-sized trees from the sierra for those essential parts of traditional Hispanic houses, the arch may catch on as an inexpensive alternative. It is too early to tell.

Culture Change

Have the events of the past decade changed the way in which people in Cañones define their world and how they ought to behave in it? Emphatically. A better road, telephones, television, and education improve access between Cañones and the rest of the world, and tend to break down the sense of separation between the village and the outside. Outsiders coming to visit are less noteworthy than they were, although outsiders coming to build vacation homes are still regarded as a threat to the unity of the village, and selling property to them is considered disloyal.

Children speak English in ordinary conversation in the placita more than they did a decade ago. So far, they are still fluent in Spanish.

"The rest of the world" includes Hispanic cultural revitalization movements as well as Anglo communication devices, and it is likely that more Cañoneros can now write Spanish than previously. More are aware of the Chicano Movement, and some are affected by it in their political thinking. Several people from Cañones took part in the restoration of the chapel of Santa Rosa de Lima, the first Christian church along the middle Chama, which served the original settlement at Abiquiu. This partial reconstruction, directed by Gilbert Benito Córdova, native of Abiquiu and 1979 Ph.D. in education from the University of New Mexico, has become to an extent a symbol for people of Rio Arriba who are trying to cultivate their own cultural roots.

An inevitable consequence of better communication between Cañones and other places, then, is a perception of their own world as increasingly complex. It is a more hopeful perception than it was at the time of the school fight, because Cañones knows more of what Hispanos are doing elsewhere to gain autonomy, because it now influences local politics and has placed some of its own citizens in elective office (e.g., Dalio Gallegos and Modesto Vialpando have served on the district 53 board of education), and because it has a say in the implementation of programs funded from outside like HELP and Save the Children. In short, power is no longer regarded as a totally one-way flow downward. The existential postulate that fit a one-way flow was fatalism. What little there was of fatalism has almost disappeared, in favor of the view that one can influence one's own destiny.

Before discussing changes in values, it should be pointed out that even before we started our field work a great shift away from traditional Hispanic values had taken place, and that Cañones reached back to revive certain values because they helped the village overcome its divisions and unite itself for the school battle. The most important of these revived values are vergüenza, misericordia, and dignidad de la persona. The shift away from these three values since 1967 seems abrupt, but probably represents only resumption of a long-term trend.

Vergüenza

Facundo Valdez said almost all that needs to be said about what happens to vergüenza when the walls come down between a Hispanic village and the outside world (1979:105–6):

> When a whole community is threatened, as Cañones was by the order to send children to school over a bad road in 1966, then *vergüenza* is a strength. It defines the people who can be entrusted to organize the village to fight, to keep track of its money, without fear that these people will forget the rest of the village and go on to promote their own careers. . . .
>
> But . . . a rigid adherence to the value of *vergüenza* can keep Hispanos out of activities which are necessary to them as a whole group surviving today. . . . The more traditional rural Hispanos feel negatively about capitalist ventures and the type of behavior needed to operate entrepreneurial ventures . . . and they often advised their daughters not to prepare for professions at all. Yet Northern New Mexico needs good native lawyers, bankers, merchants, and politicians; and women are not content to remain confined in the house forever. . . .
>
> So long as villages are relatively autonomous and so long as most of the individual's life is carried on within the village, *vergüenza* guides the individual to proper behavior and helps hold the village together. But when Hispanic villagers have to cope with urban and especially non-Hispanic society, in the county, the state, or the region, then *vergüenza* impedes adjustment. *El hombre con vergüenza* is the ideal citizen of his village; he is not a skillful actor on a wider stage.

In this context, "*más antes éramos avergonzados*" (we used to be shy) narrows the sense of vergüenza so that one is almost saying "We used to be backward." Cañoneros make such statements more often than they used to.

Vergüenza has changed relatively little for a Cañones woman. A man, if he is self-conscious of his shifts of role from village to city, can change his behavior to fit the one and then the other just as state officials shift their values depending on whether they are on or off the job.

The pícaro has changed only by playing before a wider audience.

Respeto de la Casa

Within Cañones, respeto is as important as ever, for Cañones is still so small that everyone knows everyone else. When they are outside, there is plenty of opportunity for villagers to take advantage of the anonymity of the city and to be regarded as individuals rather than as representatives of their households and extended families. So long as Cañones remains small and with relatively stable land ownership, no important change in this value is likely.

Misericordia

The brief account of El Proyecto above sheds a sad light on both vergüenza and misericordia, for the more success Cañones enjoys in its fight for material gains like roads and jobs, the less need there is for either of these old-fashioned virtues. Elipio García's description of misericordia, quoted much earlier, is also the prophecy of its demise. At best, villagers do not need each other as much as when all were isolated and poor. At worst, new benefits from outside are used against each other, as when a Cañonero went to Rural Legal Services for a lawyer so he could sue his first cousin in a family squabble.

Machismo and Dignidad

Decreasing isolation decreases dignidad and increases the usefulness of machismo as a defense. A Cañonero outside the protection of northern New Mexican society is called "Mexican" or "Chicano," and is a member of a disadvantaged minority group. For many decades, the Hispano has been a man of stature, respect, eloquence, and wit (in Spanish) inside his own village, but a poor stumbling inarticulate unskilled laborer or petitioner in Santa Fe or Denver. In the all-important matter of address, he may be "*Don Luis, dueño de terreno*" (landholder) at home, but "Hey Looey, git off yer lazy ass 'n c'mon over here on the double" elsewhere. That dichotomy is not new, but the frequency of trips outside is new, and one needs to defend oneself with machismo more now than before.

But while it is true that dignidad is at the mercy of outsiders more than it used to be, national values are simultaneously changing from the melting pot toward cultural pluralism, and the Cañonero who was treated insultingly by his employer, as in the fictive quote above, may file a complaint or appeal to a political action group. The umbrella of protection for seeking dignity in various ways is shrinking locally but growing nationally.

The Minor Values

Generosity and hospitality are somewhat diminished in a cash economy. They were partly dependent upon misericorida, therefore upon the sharing of both abundance and scarcity. With so many people coming and going through the placita, a household that opened its doors equally to everybody could not care for its own, hence would lack vergüenza. Hospitality tended to be rather formal, with its "*Entre en la casa suya,*" and there is now less time for grand gestures. Cañones households in 1980 vary more than they used to in the degree of their hospitality. Generosity with produce is, so far as we know, as conspicuous as ever.

The emphasis on style, like the emphasis on verbal wit, remains strong. It seems safe to predict that, as gasoline grows scarcer, flamboyant horsemanship will rise once more in importance, and that Cañoneros will go to dances in Española less often but organize more dances in Cañones.

Intellectual curiosity is a new value that is just now appearing. Whereas curiosity about affairs outside northern New Mexico used to be thought irrelevant or slightly ill-mannered, the children and young adults now more often show a pleased interest in all sorts of topics that have no obvious connection to Cañones.

Drinking

The field team has no information that patterns of drinking have changed, nor that women's abhorrence of drinking has changed. The proportion of Catholics (who drink) to Pentecostals (who forbid themselves to drink) has not changed appreciably. (The reader is cautioned that change in the senior author over fourteen years may be more important to this topic than change in the community. Kutsche was a relatively young man resident in Cañones in 1967, participating in drinking sprees with unmarried men. At the age of fifty-four in 1981, paying only occasional short calls on families for business and sociability, he no longer knows what the young men do, and seldom discusses drinking with the elders.) A straw in the wind is that, at a Cañones dance in September, 1980, in honor of a Colorado College class, the door prize was a bottle of whiskey that the winner passed around inside the dance hall in view of the chaperones. No one got drunk from it, and virtually everyone took a sip. But the organizers thought it worth noting with delight that "there were no fights at this dance."

A New Challenge?

Could the village unite in 1980 as it did in 1967 to fight an external threat? Any answer is only a guess. Probably it could no longer unite 100 percent, because unity of thought has been too dispersed. But there is more education, more general knowledge, and slightly more money in Cañones now than formerly, and the village could organize in a more sophisticated way and draw on more outside resources. It would probably not even be wise any longer for hostile bureaucrats to ridicule scholars who were friendly to the village, for the body of historical and other data is piling up a convincing case to support the village claim of systematic and long-term oppression at the hands of government.

In Conclusion

We set out to write a brief but comprehensive account of Cañones, concentrating on a moment when its values and in some ways its very existence were challenged from the outside. We reached back with a summary of its history from first European settlement and before, and forward to the changes that it has undergone since the moment of crisis.

Cañones has never been static. It has survived and sometimes even flourished in its beautiful microbasin under three governments and, at times when Spain or Mexico could not protect it from Indian nomads, under almost no government. Improved roads, telephones, television, and education have neither drained its citizens into the cities (quite the opposite), nor have they destroyed its pride in its Hispanic life. It shows no signs of assimilating, no melting pot blurring of the edges of its separate identity. In fact, through such innovations as the appropriate technology movement and the land grant movements, it is working out new ways of making a peculiarly Hispanic adaptation to the land and the climate —solar heating, more efficient acequias, active defense of its claims to land, community education drawing on its own store of knowledge, and bootstrap political and economic efforts.

People complain vigorously about some aspects of change, and there is no doubt of loss of closeness between villagers. Even in the fall of 1966, a number of people said to Kutsche and Krusnik, "If only you had arrived a few years earlier, when Don Pedro Velásquez and Don Ramón Jaramillo were still alive. Then you'd have learned the real Cañones."

But the new technology and the new communication with the outside are used at least as much to tighten kin and friendship networks extending far beyond Cañones as they are to loosen personal relations within the village. And the village itself continues to provide refuge, security, and an unambiguous source of identification for those who remain and for those numerous descendants of Cañones who have returned. They go out or contract out their services to make a living; they come back to Cañones to live.

Alice Reich sums up the confidence of the field team about the viability of placitas like Cañones in a recent paper (1979:111–12):

> Their existence is not a sign of cultural conservatism, but of the tremendous continuing, even increasing importance of the village in the life of the Spanish American. Given the facts of history, and the present situation in New Mexico, given the number of towns and cities, the possibilities for employment and mobility and, in fact, the degree to which Spanish Americans have availed themselves of these possibilities, their villages are more than a holdover from the past; they are a specific and meaningful adaptation to the present.
>
> Spanish American culture was not made, once and for all, in the distant past. It is, as all culture is, continually produced. It is also, as all culture is, continually changing.

Cañones changes within the Hispanic tradition, not away from it. It takes the materials of its change from any sources that give promise of enhancing its survival, and uses them to weave freshly every day the fabric of the village. With even a modicum of understanding and support from the dominant Anglo legal and economic system, Cañones and villages like it will continue indefinitely to provide a physical home for their citizens, and a system of identity continuous with its Spanish and Mexican past that provides meaning for their future lives.

Glossary

adj = adjective
adv = adverb
dim = diminutive
imp = imperative
ind pro = indefinite pronoun
interj = interjection
interrog = interrogative
n = noun
pro = pronoun
rel pro = relative pronoun
v = verb
vulg = vulgar slang

abrazo [*n*]: embrace
abuelo(a) [*n*]: grandfather, grandmother [*dim* abuelito(a)] "Los abuelos" are adolescent males who play a boogeyman game before Christmas.
aceite [*n*]: oil
acequia [*n*]: irrigation ditch, or ditch system
adobe [*n*]: unfired brick
afuera [*adv*]: 1. away, 2. outside
ahijado(a) [*n*]: godchild
alabado [*n*]: hymn of praise
Aleluia [*n*]: member of the Pentecostal church (Asamblea de Dios)
amarillo(a) [*adj*]: yellow
americano(a) [*n*]: American. The term used by Hispanos for Anglos when speaking Spanish.
amor [*n*]: love

Anglo [*n*]: a non-Hispanic, chiefly a North American of British or European heritage. The term includes blacks.
apurado [*adj*]: hurried
aquí [*adv*]: here
Asamblea de Dios [*n*]: Assembly of God church
augusto [*adj*]: 1. august, 2. peaceful
avergonzado [*adj*]: 1. shy, 2. backward

baile [*n*]: dance
bautismo [*n*]: baptism
bendición [*n*]: blessing
bien [*adv*]: well
biscochito [*n*]: 1. a sweet pastry similar to a cookie, tart, or sweet English biscuit, 2. [*vulg*] the female genitals
blanco(a) [*n*]: a white person
bolillo [*n, vulg*]: an Anglo
brujería [*n*]: witchcraft
brujo(a) [*n*]: wizard, witch
Buenos días, le dé Dios: May God give you a good day
bunuelo [*n*]: sweet puffy fried bread
burrito [*n*]: rolled tortilla stuffed with chile, meat, beans, etc.
buslar [*v*]: New Mexico dialect for *burlar:* to mock

caballero [*n*]: 1. horseman, 2. gentleman
calavasa [*n*]: squash [*dim* calavasita]
campanilismo [*n*]: community spirit
campo santo [*n*]: Catholic cemetery (literally, holy field)
cantina [*n*]: bar or pub
cárcel [*n*]: jail
carpintero(a) [*n*]: carpenter
casa [*n*]: house [*dim* casita]
casorio [*n*]: 1. marriage, 2. wedding ceremony
chaquetero [*n*]: turncoat
Chicano(a) [*n*]: a member of the Mexican-American political movement, usually urban
ciénega [*n*]: marsh [*dim* cienaguita]
cofradía [*n*]: laymen's organization in the Roman Catholic church (literally, confraternity)
comal [*n*]: flat stone for cooking tortillas
comida [*n*]: 1. food, 2. a meal

comisión [*n*]: commission
comité [*n*]: committee
Como amenecío?: Good morning (literally, "How did you dawn?")
compadrazgo [*n*]: godparenthood
compadre, comadre [*n*]: person connected by any tie of godparenthood
contento(a) [*adj*]: contented
corriente [*adj*]: 1. plain, 2. easy, 3. ordinary, 4. acceptable
cosa [*n*]: thing
costumbre [*n*]: custom
coyote [*n*]: a person of Hispanic-Anglo birth
criado(a) [*n*]: 1. one to be raised, 2. servant
cual [*rel pron*]: which
cualquier [*pron*]: any
cuarto [*n, adj*]: 1. room, 2. a fourth
cuchillo [*n*]: knife
cuento [*n*]: story
cuerpo [*n*]: body
cultura [*n*]: culture
curanderismo [*n*]: the lore of curing
curandero(a) [*n*]: village medical practitioner
curioso(a) [*adj*]: strange

dedicación [*n*]: the ceremony of infant baptism in the Pentecostal church
dicho [*n*]: proverb
dificultad [*n*]: difficulty
difunto(a) [*n*]: the deceased
dignidad de la persona [*n*]: 1. grace, 2. worth, 3. psychic autonomy inherent in every human being
dinero [*n*]: money
Dios le bendiga: God bless you
don, doña: honorific titles given to the elderly (in Cañones, to one elderly male but to no female)
dueño(a) [*n*]: master, mistress
dueño de terreno [*n*]: landholder
duro(a) [*adj*]: hard

educado(a) [*adj*]: educated
embarazada [*adj*]: pregnant
enchilada [*n*]: flat or rolled tortilla with sauce and cheese topping

encinta [*adj*]: pregnant
enfermo(a) [*adj*]: 1. ill, 2. pregnant
enjarradoro(a) [*n*]: plasterer
entonces [*adv*]: then
era [*n*]: threshing floor
español(a) [*adj*]: Spanish (of Spain)
esperanda [*adj*]: pregnant
estaciones [*n*]: stations of the cross
estudiar [*v*]: to study
estufa [*n*]: cook stove

familia [*n*]: family
familiar [*adj*]: a relative of some kind
floresta [*n*]: 1. forest, 2. the National Forest Service
fogón [*n*]: 1. fireplace, 2. heating stove
frijol [*n*]: bean, always the pinto bean unless specified (frijol verde: green bean)

ganar [*v*]: to earn
gastar [*v*]: to spend
gaucho [*n*]: herdsman or Indian of the pampas
gavacho [*n, vulg*]: an Anglo
genízaro(a) [*n*]: Hispanicized Indian, defender of the frontier (from *janissary*)
gente [*n*]: 1. people, 2. family
gordo(a) [*adj*]: 1. fat, 2. pregnant
grávida [*adj*]: pregnant
gringo(a) [*n, vulg*]: an Anglo
grito [*n*]: shout

hermano(a) [*n*]: 1. brother, sister, 2. member of the cofradía
hijo(a) [*n*]: son, daughter
Hispano(a) [*n*]: a Mexican American of northern New Mexico (the term adopted by the authors)
historia [*n*]: history
hombre [*n*]: man
horno [*n*]: outdoor oven of adobe or stone

indio(a) [*n*]: Indian

jacal [*n*]: house made of vertical poles, usually plastered with soquete (colloquially, a miserable shack)
jefe político [*n*]: political boss
joven [*n*]: a male adolescent
joya [*n*]: open field
junta [*n*]: a business meeting

lengua [*n*]: language
leña [*n*]: firewood
luz [*n*]: light

machismo [*n*]: male preoccupation with sex and aggression
macho [*n, adj*]: 1. mule, 2. brave man, 3. aggressive, defensive, inadequate man
madre [*n*]: mother
madrina [*n*]: godmother
malcriado(a) [*n*]: an ill-bred person
marquesa [*n*]: marchioness
mayor domo [*n*]: person in charge of something (church, acequia duties, etc.)
mediano [*n*]: a male, from the age of eight until late adolescence
mejicano(a) [*n*]: Mexican, the term used by Hispanos to describe themselves when speaking Spanish
merced [*n*]: Spanish or Mexican land grant
mirar [*v*]: to look
misericordia [*n*]: compassion, empathy, "together in suffering"
mismo(a) [*adj*]: the same
molino [*n*]: mill
morada [*n*]: chapter house of the cofradía (literally, dwelling place)
muchacho(a) [*n*]: a boy or girl from the age of about eight, the term applied until the teens for males, until marriage for females
mujer [*n*]: woman
mujerón [*n*]: womanizer
mujerota [*adj*]: a woman who performs her obligations well
mula [*n*]: female mule

nada [*pro*]: nothing
nadie [*ind pro*]: no one
necesidad [*n*]: need

negro(a) [*n*]: a black person
niño(a) [*n*]: a child below the age of eight
nombre [*n*]: name
norte [*n*]: north
noviazgo [*n*]: courting
novio(a) [*n*]: sweetheart, fiancé(e), newlywed

ofender [*v*]: to offend
oficial [*n*]: official
ojalá! [*interj*]: God grant [in the sense of "If it were only possible!"]
ojitos [*n*]: springs

padre [*n*]: father
padrino [*n*]: godfather
parciante [*n*]: member of the acequia system
partera [*n*]: midwife
particular [*adj*]: 1. peculiar, 2. private, 3. individual
pasar [*v*]: 1. to pass, 2. to happen
pasearse [*v*]: to stroll about (colloquially, to waste time)
Pastores, Los [*n*]: The Christmas drama enacted in some northern New Mexico villages
patrón [*n*]: 1. employer, 2. aristocratic landowner who takes a paternal interest in his workers and exploits their labor
pegar [*v*]: to hit
peninsular [*n*]: native of the Iberian peninsula
peón [n]: 1. employee, 2. exploited laborer
perder [*v*]: to lose
permiso [*n*]: permit
picarismo [*n*]: 1. condition of being a picaro, 2. concerning picaresque behavior
pícaro [*n*]: 1. a man who celebrates the absurdity of the human condition for the entertainment of his fellows, 2. cheater, 3. deceiver
pierna [*n*]: leg
platicar [*v*]: 1. to talk, 2. to chat
plaza [*n*]: 1. central square, 2. settlement [*dim* placita]
plebe [*n*]: adolescents as a group
pluma [*n*]: feather (colloquially, 1. loose woman, 2. fart)
pobre [*adj*]: poor
poco(a) [*adj*]: a little

por qué? [*interrog*]: why?
preñada [*adj*]: pregnant
presa [*n*]: diversion dam for ditch system
primo(a) [*n*]: cousin
pronto(a) [*adj*]: soon
propio(a) [*adj*]: one's own
Protestante [*n*]: Protestant
pueblo [*n*]: village (any village, whatever the ethnic identity of its inhabitants)
puro(a) [*adj*]: 1. pure, 2. nothing but . . .

quebrar [*v*]: to break
quemar [*v*]: to burn
querer [*v*]: 1. to wish, 2. to desire

ranchero [*n*]: rancher
rancho [*n*]: ranch
remedio [*n*]: 1. remedy, 2. cure
respaldar [*v*]: to guarantee
respeto de la casa [*n*]: respect due to a household, family, lineage, both by outsiders and by those who live therein
río [*n*]: river
rito [*n*]: stream
romper [*v*]: to break
rosario [*n*]: rosary

sala de baile [*n*]: dance hall
salvación [*n*]: the "decision for Christ" made at about the age of twelve by a child in the Pentecostal church
santero [*n*]: sculptor or painter of santos
santo [*n*]: religious statue or painting
Santo Niño: the Holy Child
segundo(a) [*n, adj*]: second
señor, señora [*n*]: Mr., Mrs.
siguiente [*adv*]: following
simplicidad [*n*]: simplicity
sin vergüenza: 1. crooked, despicable, competitive (applied to the behavior of males), 2. shameless, immoral (applied to the behavior of females)
sobador(a) [*n*]: masseur, masseuse

sobrino(a) [*n*]: nephew, niece
soltero(a) [*n*]: an unmarried adult
soquete [*n*]: mud—the wet earth of which adobes are made, or the kind that mires cars on a wet road (not used for pottery clay)
soterrano [*n*]: underground storage building or room (cellar)
Spanish American [*n, adj*]: a rather old-fashioned term for Hispano, used chiefly by Anglos
suma [*n*]: sum

tamale [*n*]: corn husk stuffed with meat, etc.
tener [*v*]: to have
tienda [*n*]: store
tiendita [*n*]: little store
tiendita sin dinero: storage place for home produce, (literally, "little store without money")
tierra [*n*]: land
tinamaste [*n*]: iron tripod used to raise a comal from the fire
tío(a) [*n*]: uncle, aunt
tonto(a) [*adj*]: stupid
torcido(a) [*adj*]: morally crooked
tortilla [*n*]: unsweetened wheat or corn pancake
trabajar [*v*]: to work
trabajador(a) [*n*]: worker
traguito [*n*]: small drink
tranquilo(a) [*adj*]: quiet
travieso(a) [*adj*]: mischievous
triste [*adj*]: sad

vaca [*n*]: cow
valiente [*adj*]: brave
vara [*n*]: a linear measure of thirty-three inches
vega [*n*]: pasture
vela [*n*]: candle
velorio [*n*]: a wake in respect for the dead
venir [*v*]: to come
verdad [*n*]: truth
verdolaga [*n*]: purslane
vergüenza [*n*]: tender regard for the good opinion of one's fellow citizens

vez [*n*]: time
vicio [*n*]: vice
vida [*n*]: life
viejo(a) [*n*]: elderly man or woman [*dim* viejito(a)]
viga [*n*]: roof beam
Vuelva! [*imper*]: Return! Come back!

Bibliography

Adams, Eleanor B. and Angélico Chávez
1956 *The Missions of New Mexico, 1776* (Albuquerque: University of New Mexico Press).

Aguilera, Francisco Enrique
1978 *Santa Eulalia's People*, American Ethnological Society, Monograph 63 (St. Paul, Minn.: West Publishing Co.).

Borhegyi, Stephen F. de
1956 *El Santuario de Chimayó* (Santa Fe: Spanish Colonial Arts Society, Inc.).

Boyd, E.
1974 *Popular Arts of Spanish New Mexico* (Santa Fe: Museum of New Mexico Press).

Brown, Lorin W.
1978 *Hispano Folklife of New Mexico* (Albuquerque: University of New Mexico Press).

Digneo, Ellen Hartnett
1965–66 *Annual Progress Report, Western States Small Schools Project in New Mexico* (Santa Fe: State Department of Education).

Edmonson, Munro S.
1957 *Los Manitos.* Middle American Research Institute, Publication 25, (New Orleans: Tulane University).

Foster, George M.
1965 "Peasant Society and the Image of Limited Good," *American Anthropologist*, 67:293–315.

García, F. Chris, and Rudolph O. de la Garza

1977 *The Chicano Political Experience.* (North Scituate, Mass.: Duxbury Press).

Geertz, Clifford
1973 *The Interpretation of Cultures* (New York: Basic Books).

González, Nancie L.
1969 *The Spanish-Americans of New Mexico* (Albuquerque: University of New Mexico Press).

Hockett, Charles F.
1954 "Chinese Versus English: An Exploration of the Whorfian Theses," in *Language in Culture*, ed. Harry Hoijer, Memoir No. 79, American Anthropological Association.

Hoebel, E. Adamson
1958 *Man in the Primitive World*, 2nd ed. (New York: McGraw-Hill).

Jaramillo, Cleofas
1941 *Shadows of the Past* (Santa Fe: Seton Village Press).

Jenkins, Myra Ellen
1977 "Early Education in New Mexico," *The New Mexico School Review*, vol. 53, no. 1, pp. 2–13.

Jiménez Núñez, Alfredo
1974 *Los Hispanos de Nuevo México.* Publicaciones del Seminario de Antropología Americana, vol. 12 (Sevilla: Universidad de Sevilla).

Johnson, J. B.
1937 "The Allelujahs: A Religious Cult in Northern New Mexico," *Southwest Review*, 22:131–39.

Kluckhohn, Clyde
1951 "Values and Value-Orientations in the Theory of Action," in *Toward a General Theory of Action*, ed. T. Parsons and E. A. Shils (Cambridge, Mass: Harvard University Press) [Harper Torchbook 1962 edition used.]

Kluckhohn, Florence and Fred L. Strodtbeck
1961 *Variations in Value Orientations* (Evanston: Row Peterson).

Kroeber, Alfred Louis
1948 *Anthropology* (rev. ed.) (New York: Harcourt Brace & Co.).

Kutsche, Paul
1968 "The Anglo Side of Acculturation," in *Spanish-Speaking People in the United States*, pp. 178–95. Proceedings, annual meeting, American Ethnological Society (Seattle: University of Washington Press).
1976 "A New Mexico Test of Modernization Theory," *Papers in Anthropology* (Norman: University of Oklahoma), vol. 17, no. 2, pp. 138–49.

Kutsche, Paul (ed.)
1979 *The Survival of Spanish American Villages*, Colorado College Studies, No. 15 (Colorado Springs: Colorado College Research Committee).

Kutsche, Paul and Dennis Gallegos
1979 "Community Functions of the *Cofradía de Nuestro Padre Jesús Nazareno*," in *The Survival of Spanish American Villages*, ed. Paul Kutsche, Colorado College Studies, No. 15. (Colorado Springs: Colorado College Research Committee).

Kutsche, Paul, John R. Van Ness and Andrew T. Smith

1976 "A Unified Approach to the Anthropology of Hispanic Northern New Mexico: Historical Archaeology, Ethnohistory, and Ethnography," *Historical Archaeology*, 10, pp. 1–16.

Lecompte, Janet

1981 "The Independent Women of Hispanic New Mexico, 1821–1846," *Western Historical Quarterly*, 12:17–35.

Leeds, Anthony

1976 A review of *Anthropologists in Cities. American Anthropologist*, ed. George M. Foster and Robert V. Kemper, 78, pp. 448–49.

Leonard, Olen and Charles P. Loomis

1941 *Culture of Contemporary Rural Community: El Cerrito, New Mexico*, U.S. Bureau of Agriculture Economics, Rural Life Studies, No. 1 (Washington, D.C.).

Lewis, Oscar

1951 *Life in a Mexican Village: Tepoztlán Restudied* (Urbana: University of Illinois Press).

Lovato, Phil

1974 *Las Acequias del Norte*, Four Corners Regional Commission, New Mexico State Planning Office, Technical Report No. 1 (Taos: Kit Carson Memorial Foundation, Inc.).

Madsen, William

1964 *The Mexican-Americans of South Texas* (New York: Holt, Rinehart & Winston, Inc.).

Mead, Margaret (ed.)

1955 *Cultural Patterns and Technical Change* (New York: Mentor Books).

Menéndez Pidal, Ramón

1950 *The Spaniards in Their History* (New York: W. W. Norton & Co., Inc.).

Merriman, Roger Bigelow

1918 *Rise of the Spanish Empire* (New York: Macmillan, Inc.).

Minton, Charles E.

1973 *Juan of Santo Niño* (Santa Fe: Sunstone Press).

Nabokov, Peter

1969 *Tijerina and the Courthouse Raid* (Albuquerque: University of New Mexico Press).

National Education Association

1964 *Rio Arriba County, New Mexico: When Public Education Provides Patronage for a Political System*, National Education Association of the United States (Washington, D.C.).

Pack, Arthur Newton

1966 *We Called It Ghost Ranch* (Abiquiu, N.M.: Ghost Ranch Conference Center).

Paredes, Américo

1972 "The Anglo-American in Mexican Folklore," in *Literatura Chicana*, ed. A. C. Shular, R. Ybarra-Frausto and J. Sommers (Englewood Cliffs, N.J.: Prentice-Hall).

1977 "On Ethnographic Work Among Minority Groups," *New Scholar*, 6:1–32.

Peristiany, J. G. (ed.)
1966 *Honour and Shame* (Chicago: University of Chicago Press).
Redfield, Robert
1930 *Tepoztlán, A Mexican Village* (Chicago: University of Chicago Press).
1941 *The Folk Culture of Yucatán* (Chicago: University of Chicago Press).
1960 *The Little Community* (Chicago: University of Chicago Press).
Reich, Alice Higman
1977 "The Cultural Production of Ethnicity." (Ph.D. diss., University of Colorado).
1979 "Spanish American Village Culture: Barrier to Assimilation or Integrative Force?" in *The Survival of Spanish American Villages*, ed. Paul Kutsche, Colorado College Studies, No. 15. (Colorado Springs: Colorado College Research Committee).
Reynolds, C. Lynn
1974 "Decision Making and Culture Change: The Status of Spanish-American Small Farms in Northern New Mexico." (Ph.D. diss., Southern Methodist University).
Rubel, Arthur J.
1966 *Across the Tracks* (Austin: University of Texas Press).
Salazar, J. Richard
1976 "Santa Rosa de Lima de Abiquiu," *New Mexico Architecture* 18 (5):13–19.
Simmons, Marc
1974 *Witchcraft in the Southwest* (Flagstaff: Northland Press).
1979 *People of the Sun* (Albuquerque: University of New Mexico Press).
State Department of Education of New Mexico
1965 *Standards for New Mexico Schools* (Santa Fe).
Swadesh, Frances León
1972 "The Social and Philosophical Context of Creativity in Hispanic New Mexico," *Rocky Mountain Social Science Journal*, 9:11–18.
1974 *Los Primeros Pobladores* (Notre Dame: University of Notre Dame Press).
1979 "Structure of Hispanic-Indian Relations in New Mexico," in *The Survival of Spanish American Villages*, ed. Paul Kutsche, Colorado College Study No. 15 (Colorado Springs: Colorado College Research Committee).
U.S. Bureau of the Census
1973 *Persons of Spanish Origin*, Department of Commerce, Subject Report Series, PC 2–1C (Washington, D.C.).
1975 *Historical Statistics of the United States, Part I*, Department of Commerce (Washington, D. C.).
U.S. Department of Agriculture
1936 *Reconnaissance Survey of Human Dependency on Resources in the Rio Grande Watershed.* Regional Bulletin 33, Conservation Economics Series 6 (Washington, D. C.).
1967 *Water Supply Outlook for Western United States*, Soil Conservation Service (Washington, D. C.).

Valdez, Facundo
1979 "*Vergüenza*," The Survival of Spanish American Villages, ed. Paul Kutsche, Colorado College Study No. 15 (Colorado Springs: Colorado College Research Committee).

van Dresser, Peter
1972 *A Landscape for Humans* (Albuquerque: Biotechnic Press).

Van Ness, John R.
1969 "The Prehistory of the Chama River Drainage, New Mexico" (M.A. thesis, University of Pennsylvania).
1976 "Spanish-American *vs.* Anglo-American Land Tenure and the Study of Economic Change in New Mexico," *Social Science Journal* 13:45–52.
1979a "Hispanos in Northern New Mexico: The Development of Corporate Community and Multicommunity" (Ph.D. diss., University of Pennsylvania).
1979b "Hispanic Village Organization in Northern New Mexico: Corporate Community Structure in Historial and Comparative Perspective," *The Survival of Spanish American Villages*, ed. Paul Kutsche, Colorado College Studies, No. 15 (Colorado Springs: Colorado College Research Committee).
1980 "Introduction," in *Spanish and Mexican Land Grants in New Mexico and Colorado*, ed. Christine M. and John R. Van Ness (Manhattan, Kansas: Sunflower University Press).

Walter, Paul A. F., Jr.
1938 "A Study of Isolation and Social Change in Three Spanish Speaking Villages of New Mexico" (Ph.D. diss., Stanford).

Weber, Kenneth R.
1979 "Rural Hispanic Village Viability from an Economic and Historic Perspective," in *The Survival of Spanish American Villages*, ed. Paul Kutsche, Colorado College Studies, No. 15 (Colorado Springs: Colorado College Research Committee).

Weigle, Marta
1976a *Brothers of Light, Brothers of Blood* (Albuquerque: University of New Mexico Press).
1976b *A Penitente Bibliography* (Albuquerque: University of New Mexico Press).

Wiley, Thomas M.
1973 *Forty Years in Politics and Education* (Albuquerque: Calvin Horn).

Wolf, Eric
1966 *Peasants* (Englewood Cliffs, N. J.: Prentice-Hall).

Woodward, Dorothy
1935 "The Penitentes of New Mexico" (Ph.D. diss., Yale University).

Index